Jesus
and the Judaism of
His Time

For Esther

Jesus
and the Judaism of
His Time

Irving M. Zeitlin

Polity Press

British Library Cataloguing in Publication Data

Zeitlin, Irving M.
    Jesus and the Judaism of His Time.
    1. Jesus Christ–Jewish interpretations
    2. Judaism
    I. Title
    232   BT590.J8

ISBN 0–7456–0448–X

Library of Congress Cataloging in Publication Data

Zeitlin, Irving M
Jesus and the Judaism of His Time
Includes index.
    1. Jesus Christ—Jewish interpretations.   2. Jesus
Christ—Biography.   3. Christian biography—Palestine.
I. Title.
BM620.Z45   1988   232.9   87–35519

ISBN 0-7456-0448-X

Typeset in 10 on 12pt Ehrhardt
by Alan Sutton Publishing Limited
Printed in the USA

Contents

Preface

Where did Jesus of Nazareth stand in relation to the Judaism of his time? This is the key question that needs to be addressed if we wish to understand the Jesus of history. This question presupposes an adequate grasp of the nature of Judaism in the first century. Who were the Pharisees, Sadducees, Essenes and Zealots? What were the fundamental religio-ethical precepts common to them all, and what is it that distinguished one 'party' from another? It is only against such a background that we can begin to catch a few reliable glimpses of the way Jesus understood himself, and the way he was understood by his disciples, critics and adversaries.

If there is a single general concept that can effectively guide our analysis, it is the concept of *charisma*. The outstanding German sociologist Max Weber was among the first to apply the concept of charisma systematically in his comparative-historical studies of the world religions. Charisma, meaning literally 'gift of grace', is a form of authority based upon the extraordinary personal qualities of an individual who, thanks to those qualities, is able to call forth an absolutely personal devotion to his leadership. Typically, a charismatic leader is self appointed and is followed by those who feel themselves to be in a state of distress; they follow the leader because they believe him to be extraordinarily qualified. Charisma is conditional in that the leader must authenticate his special gifts through miracles, revelations or other 'superhuman' feats. Success in such feats is essential for the maintenance of his authority; failure leads to ruin. In Weber's words:

> The holder of charisma seizes the task that is adequate for him and demands obedience and a following by virtue of his mission. His success determines whether he finds them. His charismatic claim breaks down if his mission is not recognized by those to whom he feels he has been sent. If they recognize him, he is their master – so long as he knows how to maintain recognition through 'proving' himself. But he does not derive his 'right' from their will, in the manner of an election. Rather the reverse holds: it is the *duty* of those to whom

he addresses his mission to recognize him as their charismatically qualified leader.[1]

'Pure' charisma is, by its very nature, the opposite of all 'institutional' social structures, and independent of them:

> In order to do justice to their mission, the holders of charisma, the master as well as his disciples and followers, must stand outside the ties of this world, outside of routine occupations, as well as outside the routine obligations of family life.[2]

It is fairly obvious that Weber arrived at this conception of charisma through reflection on the role of the historical Jesus. Indeed, Weber cites the Gospels:

> Charismatic rule is not managed according to general norms, either traditional or rational, but, in principle, according to concrete revelations and inspirations, and in this sense, charismatic authority is 'irrational' [or non-rational]. It is 'revolutionary' in the sense of not being bound to the existing order: 'It is written – but I say unto you . . .!'[3]

An essential element of charismatic leadership, then, is the challenge it presents to traditional authority.

Was Jesus a charismatic leader in Weber's sense? If so, what was the source of his charisma – that is, what was it about him that struck his contemporaries as extraordinary? Does charisma imply 'popularity'? The concept of charisma does seem to carry such an implication and Jesus definitely appears to have drawn crowds; but he was also unpopular. Indeed, not only his influential contemporaries, but the common people as well, found some of his words to be offensive. If charisma implies a conflict with traditional authority, then how did Jesus fit into the religious traditions of the Judaism of his time? It appears that he was at odds with certain 'traditions of the elders'. Was it his intention, however, to break radically with the laws of Moses and to supplant them *in toto*? Or is the truth rather that Jesus diverged from specific norms in a striking, significant and unique manner? And what was the nature of Jesus' self-understanding with regard to his mission? If he felt himself called to fulfil the Messianic role, why was there so much confusion as to who he was? We are told, after all, that his own family did not believe in him, that his disciples abandoned him, that Peter denied him and that Paul, at first, was among the harshest persecutors of Jesus' followers. Furthermore, is it possible that Jesus was himself not certain who he was? What other meaning can we give to his question, 'Who do men say that I am?'. Finally, why was he executed by the Romans as a political rebel? These and other central questions require a knowledge of the setting in which Jesus worked – a knowledge, in particular, of the fundamental unifying principles of first century Judaism, as well as the varieties of religious experience within it.

Acknowledgements

The author and publishers are grateful for permission to quote from the following:

W.D. Davies, *The Setting of the Sermon on the Mount* (Cambridge University Press, 1964); Hans-Herbert Stoldt, *History and Criticism of the Marcan Hypothesis*, translated and edited by D.L. Niewyk (Mercer University Press, 1980); H.J. Schoeps, *Paul: The Theology of the Apostle in the Light of Jewish Religious History* (Lutterworth Press, 1961); William Riley Wilson, *The Execution of Jesus* (Charles Scribner's Sons, 1970).

Part I

Judaism in the Time of Jesus

1

The Unifying Principles

Josephus, the famous Jewish historian, is one of our major sources of information for the Jewish traditions of the first century. He was born in Jerusalem in the first year of the reign of Caligula (AD 37/38). His father, Matthias, descended from a distinguished priestly family, ensured that Josephus would receive a careful religious education and a thorough knowledge of the Torah, or law. At the age of 16 he went through the schools of the Pharisees, Sadducees and Essenes, one after the other. Still searching for a deeper religious understanding he withdrew to the wilderness to join a hermit named Bannus. After spending three years with him, Josephus returned to Jerusalem and in his nineteenth year, joined the Pharisees.[1]

Josephus states that when the Jewish war broke out against the Romans (AD 66), he had at first opposed it (*Life* 4). This is quite possible as the Jewish aristocracy in general took part in the war only under coercion. Once the initial blows had been struck, however, he joined the uprising and even became one of its leaders, acquiring the important post of commander in chief of Galilee (*Life* 7). His career as commander ended with the fall of the fortress Jotapata in AD 67 and his capture by the Romans (*War* 3:344). Led before Vespasian, Josephus predicted the Roman general's ascent to the imperial throne, and was therefore treated from the beginning with consideration and respect. Two years later, in AD 69, Vespasian was in fact proclaimed emperor by the legions in Egypt and Judea, thus fulfilling Josephus' prophecy. Vespasian remembered his special prisoner and granted him his freedom as a mark of gratitude (*War* 4:622). Following his proclamation as emperor, Vespasian, accompanied by Josephus, proceeded to Alexandria where he turned over his command of the war to Titus. Josephus then returned to Palestine in Titus' entourage and was forced, under the Roman general's orders and with considerable danger to his life, to call on the Jews to surrender. With the fall of Jerusalem to the Romans, Titus, in gratitude, urged Josephus to 'take what he wanted'; Josephus merely appropriated some sacred books and pleaded for the freedom of his brother and other prisoners who were his friends. He was able to persuade the Roman commander to take down three men who had already been crucified, one of whom recovered (*Life* 75).

At the close of the war Josephus accompanied Titus to Rome where, benefiting from his favoured status, he carried on with his studies and writing. Vespasian provided him with a dwelling in a house in which he himself had once lived, granting him both Roman citizenship and an annual pension (*Life* 76). It was in these favourable circumstances that Josephus composed his voluminous works. The first of these, *The Jewish War*, is a history covering the period from Antiochus Epiphanus and the Maccabean uprising (175–164 BC) through the conquest of Jerusalem and the war's aftermath, including the liquidation of the last remaining insurgents. Vespasian, Titus and other Romans who had participated in the war attested that Josephus had recounted the events correctly and faithfully. Agrippa II, the exiled Jewish king, agreed with their assessment.

The Jewish Antiquities, Josephus' other famous work, reviews the history of the Jewish people from earliest times to the outbreak of the war with the Romans in AD 66. It is in this work that Josephus has a few words to say both about Jesus (*Antiq.* 18:63–4) and his brother James (*Antiq.* 20:200). This famous passage about Jesus, referred to as the *Testimonium Flavianum*, appears to have been tampered with by a later hand. It will be discussed in detail in chapter 10. In addition to *The Jewish War* and *The Jewish Antiquities*, Josephus composed *The Life* and *Against Apion*, a polemic defending the Jewish faith against pagan critics. *The Life* is not a full autobiography, as it deals almost exclusively with Josephus' activities as a commanding officer in Galilee in AD 66/67.

When Josephus' several works are compared, there are discrepancies to be found in his recounting of certain events. In *The Jewish War*, for example, Josephus represents himself as having been the military commander of Galilee from the outset; in *The Life* the young priest of 29 is sent together with two other priests on a mission to dissuade the insurgents and to endeavour to maintain the peace. Later in this work, however, Josephus does mention that he held supreme command. A distinguished Josephus scholar, H. St John Thackeray, has described Josephus as an egoist, a 'self interested time-server and flatterer of his Roman patrons'; he was no Thucidides who recorded the 'tragedy of his nation with strict and sober impartiality'.[2] Thackeray maintained that 'Josephus was commissioned by the comquerors to write the official history of the war for propagandist purposes. It was a manifesto, intended as a warning to the East of the futility of further opposition and to allay the after-war thirst for revenge, which ultimately found vent in the fierce outbreaks [of Jewish revolt] under Trajan and

Hadrian'.[3] For all of his criticisms, however, Thackeray acknowledges, in the end, that 'the narrative of our author [i.e., *The Jewish War*] in its main outlines must be accepted as trustworthy'.[4]

Other Josephus' specialists agree that

> as a historian, Josephus aimed at accuracy . . . He knew the importance of evidence in support of a statement, as his list of [Roman] decrees shows (*Antiq.* 14:185ff.) . . . He is the main authority for the Roman period of Jewish history up to AD 70, and a very creditable one. Without Josephus' works, we should be very doubtful about the siege of Jerusalem, and our knowledge of the rise of the Herods would have to be pieced together from coins and incidental references . . . To appreciate the value of Josephus' works, we have to imagine ourselves without them'.[5]

In *Against Apion* Josephus provides us with a full and systematic exposition of the nature of the Jewish faith in the first century. Thackeray has called this work a 'fine apology' for Judaism.[6] But as F. J. Foakes Jackson has observed, 'one reason why Josephus is of so much interest to us in this respect is because we have so little *contemporary* authority for the Judaism of the first century of the Christian era, the [other] Jewish writers on the subject mostly belonging to a later age'.[7] In sum, although Josephus in *Against Apion* is explaining Judaism to pagans, there is no good reason to doubt the accuracy of his explanation. For it is confirmed, as we shall see, by two other major sources, the New Testament and the Mishnah. We need to remind ourselves that the New Testament is at least in part a Jewish book, in that large portions of it were written by Jewish writers who, despite their new Christian faith, present a picture of the central core of first century Judaism which is entirely compatible with that of Josephus. Besides Josephus and the New Testament, a third source needs to be taken into account, namely the Mishnah,[8] composed *c*.AD 200. Although the Mishnah and the other parts of the Talmud were composed much later than the period under consideration, they do contain references to first century teachers, events, beliefs and practices. Used with care, therefore, this source can also be illuminating for our purposes.

From *Against Apion* we gain a rather clear picture of the Law, the temple, the sabbath and other central institutions of Judaism. Apion was a grammarian who wrote, among other things, an Egyptian history containing harsh invective against the Jews. Among all the pagan opponents of the Jews, this Apion stood out for the depth of his hatred and the lengths to which he went in fabricating falsehoods concerning the Jewish faith. He was therefore treated with a special bitterness and contempt by Josephus who refuted each of his false accusations. All in all, Josephus' polemic gives us a good insight into the fundamentals of first century Judaism, a summary of which follows.

The Jews have always prided themselves on the education of their children; and they believe that the most essential task in life is to observe the laws and pious practices which they have inherited (*Ag. Ap*. I: 58–63). This has been true not only in Palestine but in the Diaspora as well. Apion himself attested to this by taking the Jews to task for not worshipping the same gods as the Alexandrians. He was surprised 'at the allegiance to their original religious laws of a people who came to Alexandria from another country' (II:65–7). In accusing the Jews of sedition for not erecting statues to the Roman emperors, Apion likewise confirmed that the Jews residing in Egypt made no images whatsoever. As for the Palestinian Jews, the calamities to which their Holy City was subjected are well known; yet when the successive conquerors occupied the temple, they found nothing but that which was prescribed by the Torah. Anyone who has ever seen our temple, wrote Josephus,

> is aware of the general design of the building, and the inviolable barriers which preserved its sanctity. It had four surrounding courts, each with its statutory restrictions. The outer court was open to all, foreigners included; women during their impurity were alone refused admission. To the second court all Jews were admitted and, when uncontaminated by any defilement, their wives; to the third, male Jews, if clean and purified; to the fourth the priests robed in their priestly vestments. The sanctuary was entered only by the high priests, clad in the raiment peculiar to themselves. So careful is the provision for all the details of the service, that the priests' entry is timed to certain hours. Their duty was to enter in the morning, when the temple was opened, and to offer the customary sacrifices, and again at midday, until the temple was closed . . . No vessel whatever might be carried into the temple [cf. Mark 11:16], the only objects in which were an altar, a table, a censer, and a lampstand, all mentioned in the Law [i.e., the Torah]. There was nothing more; no unmentionable mysteries took place, no repast was served within the building . . . there are four priestly tribes [cf. Exra 2:36; Neh. 7:39], each comprising upwards of five thousand members, [and] these officiate by rotation for a fixed period of days; when the term of one party ends, others come to offer the sacrifices in their place, and assembling at midday in the temple, take over from the outgoing ministers the keys of the building and all its vessels, duly numbered. Nothing of the nature of food or drink is brought within the temple; objects of this kind may not even be offered on the altar, save those which are prepared for the sacrifices. (*Ag. Ap*. II:103–9)

In tracing the Jewish law to Moses, Josephus observes that whereas some peoples had entrusted the supreme political power to monarchies, others to oligarchies and still others to the masses, Moses eschewed all these forms of polity and gave his construction the form of a 'theocracy',[9] placing all sovereignty and authority in the hands of God. To God he persuaded all to look, as the author of all blessings, both those which are common to all mankind, and those which they had won for themselves by prayer in the crises of their history. He [Moses] convinced them that no single action, no secret thought, could be hid from Him. He represented Him as one, uncreated [i.e., not born as were the Greek and other pagan gods] and immutable to all eternity; in beauty surpassing all mortal thought, made known to us by His power, although the nature of His real being passes knowledge. (*Ag. Ap.* II:164–7)

Josephus observes that the wisest of Greeks may have borrowed their conceptions of God from the principles laid down by Moses, a theory that had been propounded earlier by Aristobulus (second century BC) and adopted afterwards by Philo and later writers. Josephus cites Pythagoras, Anaxagoras, Plato, the Stoics and other philosophers, all of whom appear to have held similar views concerning the nature of God. Nevertheless, there is an important difference between even the wisest of the Greek philosophers and the principles imparted by Moses. Whereas the philosophers addressed themselves to the select few, ignoring the masses who retained their own notions, Moses,

by making practice square with precept, not only convinced his own contemporaries, but so firmly implanted this belief concerning God in their descendants to all future generations that it cannot be moved. The cause of his success was that the very nature of his legislation made it far more useful than any other; for he did not make religion a department of virtue, but the various virtues – I mean justice, temperance, fortitude, and mutual harmony in all things between the members of the community – departments of religion. *Religion governs all our actions and occupations and speech; none of these things did our lawgiver leave unexamined or indeterminate.* (*Ag. Ap.* II:169–71, italics added)

Furthermore, Moses so combined precept and practice that it was not only unprecedented in his own time, it had yet to be followed by the non-Jewish peoples of Josephus' time. Moses had taken great care to ensure that there be practical training in morals for all, and that the letter of the law be followed in daily life.

Starting from the very beginning with the food of which we partake from infancy and the private life [or diet] of the home, he left nothing, however insignificant, to the discretion and caprice of the individual. What meats a man should abstain from, and what he may enjoy; with what persons he should associate; what period should be devoted respectively to strenuous labour and to rest – for all this our leader made the Law the standard and rule, that we might live under it as under a father and master, and be guilty of no sin through wilfulness or ignorance.

For ignorance he left no pretext. He appointed the Law to be the most excellent and necessary form of instruction, ordaining not that it should be heard once for all or twice or on several occasions, but that every week men should desert their other occupations and assemble to listen to the Law and to obtain a thorough and accurate knowledge of it . . . (*Ag. Ap.* II:173–5).[10]

The 'Law' in Josephus' time included, at the very least, the Torah [Pentateuch], the Prophets and the Psalms and, most likely, other components of the Hebrew Scriptures as well. Josephus wants to underscore that in contrast to other cultures in which individuals hardly know their laws, often discovering them only after they have been transgressed, all Jews know their Law. They have *internalized* the Law because it has been systematically and unceasingly inculcated from early childhood. 'Internalization of the Law' is no exaggeration, for 'should anyone of our nation be questioned about the laws, he would repeat them all more readily than his own name. The result, then, of our thorough grounding in the laws from the first dawn of intelligence is that we have them, as it were, engraven on our souls. A transgressor is a rarity; evasion of punishment by excuses an impossibility' (*Ag. Ap.* II:178).

It is a fact, Josephus maintained, that the unity of religious belief in Judaism is a unique phenomenon. His point is not that there was no diversity in Judaism, for he himself had had first-hand experience with the religious 'parties' of his time. His point is rather that the diversity necessarily remained within the boundaries of the unified world-view of ethical monotheism. 'Among us alone', wrote Josephus,

will be heard no contradictory statements about God, such as are common among other nations, not only on the lips of ordinary individuals under the impulse of some passing mood, but even boldly propounded by philosophers; some putting forward crushing arguments against the very existence of God [sceptics such as Pyrrhon and his disciple Timon], others depriving Him of His providential care for mankind [e.g., the Epicureans]. Among us alone will be seen no difference in the conduct of our lives. With us all act alike, all profess the same doctrine about God, one which is in harmony with our Law and affirms that all things are under His eye. Even our women folk and dependents would tell you that piety must be the motive of all our occupations in life. (*Ag. Ap.* II:179–81)

In Judaism there is the fundamental conviction that the Law was instituted in accordance with the will of God. The theocratic constitution cannot be improved, Josephus avers, for 'Could there be a finer or more equitable polity than one which sets God at the head of the universe, which assigns the administration of its highest affairs to the whole body of priests, and entrusts to the supreme high-priest the direction of the other priests?' (*Ag. Ap.* II: 184).

The first and most fundamental principle of the theocracy is that the universe is in God's hands and that 'He is the beginning, the middle, and the end of all things' (II:190). There is but one temple for the one God and all of one's prayers are for the welfare of the entire community, not merely for ourselves; 'for we are born for fellowship, and he who sets its claims above his private interests is especially acceptable to God' (II: 193–7). As for the marriage laws of Judaism, the 'Law recognizes no sexual connections, except the natural union of man and wife . . . The husband must have union with his wife alone; it is impious to assault the wife of another. For anyone guilty of this crime the penalty of death is inexorable, whether he violates a virgin betrothed to another or seduces a married woman' (II:201). The Law enjoins that *all* the offspring should be brought up, and that they should learn to read about the words and deeds of their forefathers, and imitate them in their goodness. Honouring one's parents ranks second only to honouring God. Moreover, the laws of Moses also demand the equitable treatment of aliens. 'It will be seen that he [Moses] took the best of all possible measures at once to secure our own customs from corruption, and to throw them open ungrudgingly to any who elect to share them. To all who desire to come and live under the same laws with us, he [Moses] gives a gracious welcome, holding that it is not family ties alone which constitute relationship, but agreement in the principles of conduct [cf. Ex. 20:10; 22:21, etc.] . . .' (II:209–10).

The Law, says Josephus, orders us to show consideration 'even to declared enemies'. It forbids us 'to burn up their country or to cut down their fruit trees, and prohibits even the spoiling of fallen combatants or outrage to prisoners of war, especially women.' Instruction in gentleness and humanity extends even to the beasts, which if they take refuge in our houses we are forbidden to kill; and even in enemy country the beasts employed in labour are to be spared. For severe offences against the Law the penalty is death: for adultery (Lev. 20: 10), for violating an unmarried woman (Deut. 22:23), for outrage upon a male (Lev. 20:13). Lesser punishments are imposed for fraud in weights and measures, for deceit in trade and for purloining another man's property.

So there are penalties for violations of the Law, but there is also a supreme reward for piety: the reward of a future life. Here Josephus presents a characteristically Pharisaic belief. 'Each individual,' he writes,

> relying on the witness of his own conscience and the lawgiver's prophecy, confirmed by the sure testimony of God, is firmly persuaded that to those who observe the laws and, if they must needs die for them, willingly meet death,

God has granted a renewed existence and in the revolution of the ages the gift of a better life. I should have hesitated to write thus, had not the facts made all men aware that many of our countrymen have on numerous occasions ere now preferred to brave all manner of suffering rather than to utter a single word against the Law. (*Ag. Ap.* II:218–19; cf. *Ag. Ap.* I:43; II:233; *War* 2:152ff.)

In the face of the uninformed and malicious attacks by Apion upon the Jewish conception of God, Josephus could not resist contrasting it with the views of the Greek and other pagan cultures. Their gods are numerous and engendered in all manner of ways. They reside in definite localities like animal species, some under ground (Hades, Persephone), others in the sea (Poseidon, Amphitrite, Proteus). The god to whom the Greeks have allotted heaven is a tyrant

> with the result that his wife and brother and daughter, whom he begot from his own head, conspire against him, to arrest and imprison him, just as he himself had treated his own father ... Furthermore, ... the father himself, after seducing women and rendering them pregnant, leaves them to be imprisoned or drowned in the sea; and is so completely at the mercy of Destiny that he cannot either rescue his own offspring or restrain his tears at their death. Justly do these tales merit the severe censure which they receive from their intellectual leaders. (II:239ff)

Josephus concludes his encomium on the Jewish Law by observing that it has stood the test of time and has been widely imitated. Not only have the greatest Greek philosophers been inspired by Moses' teachings, so have the masses who show a keen desire to adopt Jewish religious observances; for

> there is not one city, Greek or barbarian, nor a single nation, to which our custom of abstaining from work on the seventh day has not spread, and where the fasts and the lighting of lamps and many prohibitions in the matter of food are not observed ... The greatest miracle of all is that our Law holds out no seductive bait of sensual pleasure, but has exercised this influence through its own inherent merits; and, as God permeates the universe, so the Law has found its way among all mankind. (II:282ff)

In *Against Apion* Josephus' tribute to the Law stresses the unity of Judaism's world outlook; in his other writings, however, he gives due attention to the diversity within that unity. It is to that remarkable diversity that we now turn.

2

Varieties of Jewish Religious Experience

The Pharisees

The Pharisees, Josephus informs us, concerned themselves with the strict observance of the Torah in all its details. They 'are considered the most accurate interpreters of the laws' (*War* 2:162). They pride themselves on their adherence to ancestral custom and the Law of the fathers (*Antiq.* 17:41). They 'simplify their standard of living and make no concession to luxury' (*Antiq.* 18:12). Their ideal was to live in accordance with the Torah, but not necessarily with the *letter* of the Law as it is found in the Pentateuch. Their ideal was rather to live in conformity with the Law as interpreted by their forefathers from the time of Ezra and Nehemiah, and the return of the Jews from the Babylonian exile. The Pharisees were therefore the representatives of the course followed by Judaism as it continually adapted itself to the changing socio-historical circumstances of the post-Exilic epoch. Their 'party' was an important and highly influential movement within the body of Palestinian Jewry in the first century.

The relationship of the Pharisees with the Sadducees was one of considerable tension, in which the religio-political animosity between them could often rise to a high pitch. 'Sharp economic and social differences added to the political controversies. The Sadducees, representatives of the priest and lay aristocracy, had every reason to resist customs and beliefs evolved by the masses under the leadership of middle class and "plebeian" intellectuals [i.e., the Pharisees]'.[1] Once the Pharisaic party came into being, most of the distinguished Torah scholars emerged from its ranks. If there were any Sadducee scribes we have no knowledge of them, for they have left no mark on history. Whenever either Josephus or the New Testament mentions the party allegiance of Torah scholars, they are all regularly described as Pharisees (*Antiq.* 15:3; *Life* 191; Acts 5:34).

In the Pharisee outlook 'Torah' meant not only the Scriptures (written Torah) but 'oral Torah' as well, with equal zeal for both. 'The Pharisees', wrote Josephus had passed on to the people certain regulations handed down by former generations [Greek: from the tradition of the fathers] and not recorded in the Laws of Moses, for which reason they were rejected by the Sadducean group, who hold that only those regulations should be considered valid which were written down, and that those which had been handed down by former generations need not be observed. (*Antiq.* 13:297)

Josephus' view coincides in this respect with that of the New Testament, where Jesus' disciples are accused of transgressing the 'tradition of the elders' (Matt. 15:2; Mark 7:3).[2] This 'tradition of the fathers' or 'oral law', elaborated by the Torah scholars over a period of centuries, became, by the time of Jesus, no less binding than the written Torah. The oral or traditional law was eventually called '*Halakhah*' (Heb. 'The Way') in the earliest strata of the Mishnah: 'The sword comes upon the world because of the delaying of justice and the perverting of justice; and because of them that teach the Law not according to the *Halakhah*' (Mish. Aboth 5:8; cf. 3:12).

Another distinguishing feature of Pharisaic doctrine was their belief in *resurrection* – that souls have the power to survive death: 'Eternal imprisonment is the lot of evil souls' (*Antiq.* 18:14); but the souls of the righteous 'are allotted the most holy place in heaven, whence, in the revolution of the ages, they return to find in chaste bodies a new habitation' (*War* 3:373ff). 'Because of these views they [the Pharisees] are . . . extremely influential among the townsfolk; and all prayers and sacred rites of divine worship are performed according to their exposition' (*Antiq.* 18:15). The Sadducees, in contrast, 'hold that the soul perishes along with the body' (*Antiq.* 18:16). They acknowledge no observance of any kind that is not written down in the Scriptures; and though they dispute with the Pharisees and resist their ways, the Sadducees yield to them in the end. Whenever 'they assume some office, though they submit unwillingly and perforce, yet submit they do to the formulas of the Pharisees, since *otherwise the masses would not tolerate them*' (*Antiq.* 18:17, italics added). Jesus, it is clear, espoused the Pharisaic doctrine of resurrection (Matt. 22:23ff; Mark 12:18; Luke 20:27); and where the belief in resurrection is concerned, the book of Acts is in agreement with Josephus' characterization of the Pharisees and Sadducees.

The doctrine of resurrection is first attested as a basic feature of Judaism in the book of Daniel: 'And many of those who sleep in the dust of the earth shall awake, some to everlasting life, and some to shame and everlasting contempt' (12:2). With the triumph of Pharisaism, however, the doctrine became evident in all subsequent Jewish literature, including the New Testament. The belief in resurrection acquired fundamental importance since salvation depended on it. So fundamental was the belief that the Mishnah states: 'these are they who have no share in the world to come

[Heb. *Olam Haba*]: he that says that there is no resurrection of the dead '(Mish. Sanh. 10:1). This certainly helps us to understand why the Pharisees were popular and the Sadducees were not; the latter undermined the people's hope for salvation. 'By denying resurrection and immortality in general, the Sadducees rejected simultaneously the entire Messianic hope . . .'.[3] The Pharisees are said also to have believed in the existence of angels and spirits, while the Sadducees denied them (Acts 23:8). In this respect too, the Pharisees represented the outlook of the later Rabbinic ages.

Josephus also ascribes to the Pharisees and Sadducees significant differences with regard to divine providence and human free will. The Pharisees attribute everything to destiny and God; 'they hold that to act rightly or otherwise rests, indeed, for the most part with man, but that in each action destiny cooperates' (*War* 2:163). 'Though they postulate that everything is brought about by Providence, still they do not deprive the human will of the pursuit of what is in man's power, since it was God's good pleasure that there should be a fusion between human will and Providence' (*Antiq.* 18:13). They 'say that certain events are the work of Providence, but not all; as to other events, it depends upon ourselves whether they shall take place or not' (*Antiq.* 13:172).

The Sadducees, in contrast, deny Providence altogether, 'and remove God beyond, not merely the commission, but the very sight of evil. They maintain that man has the free choice of good and evil, and that it rests with each man's will whether he follows the one or the other' (*War* 2:164–5). Rejecting totally the determining role of Providence or destiny, the Sadducees hold 'that there is no such thing and that . . . all things lie within our own power, so that we ourselves are responsible for our well-being, while we suffer misfortune through our own thoughtlessness' (*Antiq.* 13:173). (This aspect of the Sadducean outlook strikes one as the ideological rationale of a privileged group, wishing not only to maintain its prosperity, but also needing to believe that it deserves the advantages it has.)

Some readers of Josephus who have noted his attribution of 'philosophies', a Greek concept, to the Jewish parties of his time, have wondered whether he authentically described their respective beliefs. Their suspicion is strengthened by the parallels Josephus explicitly drew between the Pharisees and the Stoics and between the Essenes, who taught that destiny is absolute, and the Pythagoreans (*Life* 12; *Antiq.* 15:371). Upon reflection, however, it becomes clear that Josephus is simply taking account of his Hellenized audience. If, therefore, the Greek garb is removed, the content itself is clearly Jewish. Josephus is simply formulating in his own terms an outlook that can be traced to the Scriptures where God is, of course, omnipotent, intervenes in history and influences human actions, good and bad. At the same time, however, human conduct does have some influence on God's actions. The essence of the covenantal idea, after all, is that the human being has been taught the difference between right and wrong, and that he possesses sufficient autonomy of will to choose between them. He is therefore morally responsible for his actions. He incurs guilt and punishment when he does wrong, and he gains merit and reward for his goodness. This is a genuinely biblical view. The same logic holds for later Judaism where the moral independence of the human being remains a fundamental presupposition underlying the zeal for the Torah and the hope for the future. Thus the Pharisees promulgated a line of thought that was authentically Jewish. They adhered with equal determination to both principles: to divine omnipotence and to human freedom and responsibility. Essentially this was also the view of Jesus, who taught that the Kingdom of Heaven will break in when God intends it to; but God will act in response to a higher human righteousness. In the second century we hear the same principle enunciated by the famous Rabbi Akiba: 'all is foreseen, but freedom of choice is given' (Mish. Aboth 3:16). This strongly suggests that in this respect too, the Pharisees represented not a sectarian viewpoint, but the dominant outlook of Judaism.

When it came to politics the Pharisaic attitude was likewise genuinely Jewish, in that political questions were approached not from a secular but from a religious standpoint. In these terms we need to qualify the term 'party' as applied to the Pharisees, since strictly speaking they were not a political party at all. Their aims were religious not political. So long as the Torah, the twofold Law, was rigorously observed, they could live with any government – and here too we may observe that this appears to have been Jesus' attitude when he said, 'Render unto Caesar the things that are Caesar's, and to God the things that are God's' (Mark 12:17). Only when the secular government interfered with the observance of the Torah did the Pharisees unite to oppose it, thus acquiring temporarily the characteristics of a political party, countering power with power. This first occurred with the *Hasidim*, the precursors of the Pharisees, during the oppression of Antiochus Epiphanes and the Maccabean revolt to which it gave rise. It occurred again when the Pharisaic rulings were opposed from a Sadducean standpoint, by the Hasmonean princes, John Hyrcanus and Alexander Jannaeus. But if the Pharisees were in opposition under these princes, they later held a leading position in the government of Queen Alexandra who left all religious matters in their hands. Politics as such was a matter of indifference to them.

The Pharisees were neither a 'party' nor a 'sect', but rather a socio-religious movement. And we should note that within the boundaries of the Pharisaic movement one can discern at least two different religious approaches to a given political situation. The different approaches became especially evident when Palestine was ruled by a pagan power or by a Jewish government friendly to it. The key question concerning foreign domination, direct or indirect, was whether it was with the will of Divine Providence. Those who answered it affirmatively believed that the domination of the Jews by the Romans was desired by God, who gave them power over his people to punish them for their transgressions. It followed that it was necessary to submit willingly to the divine chastisement, so long as the observance of the Torah was not thereby obstructed. This seems to be the standpoint from which the Pharisees Pollion and Sameas counselled their fellow countrymen to accept the rule of Herod (*Antiq.* 14:174; 15:3). If, on the other hand, foreign domination was regarded as contrary to the will of God, then it was an outrage which had to be purged. The Holy Land had only one king, God alone; and Israel should therefore acknowledge no ruler other than the one anointed by God from the house of David. Accordingly it was also a Pharisee, Zadok, who together with Judas the Galilean founded the revolutionary party, the Zealots, in AD 6 (*Antiq.* 18:4). From the point of view of such Pharisees it could not have been anything but unlawful, i.e., contrary to the Torah, to pay tribute to the pagan authorities. Hence, we can appreciate the complexity of the question put to Jesus (Matt. 22:17ff; Mark 12: 14ff; Luke 20:22ff). One wing of the Pharisaic movement, then, exercised some influence on the revolutionary trend which gained ground among the Jews in the first century. It is therefore quite evident that prior to AD 70 'Pharisaism', so-called, far from being a monolith, was a rather complex and heterogeneous religious movement.

The term 'Pharisees' is derived from the Hebrew *Perushim*, of which the Greek *Pharisaioi* is a transliteration. The Hebrew word means, literally, 'the separated ones' or 'those who separated themselves'. Separated from whom and under what circumstances? Later, when we explore the origins of the Pharisaic movement, we shall see that the term 'pharisee' has nothing to do with separation from the Gentiles; nor from the alleged uncleanness of the mass of the people. There is no sign in the New Testament nor in any other contemporary source of any such separation from the masses as such. Most likely, '*Perushim*' was an epithet hurled at the Hasidim in the Hasmonean period when they separated themselves from the Aaronite, Sadducee, priestly aristocracy. That it was their Sadducean opponents who gave the *Hasidim* the name of 'separatists' is strongly suggested by the evidence of the Mishnah where the term appears in only three passages, and in one of them issues from the mouth of a Sadducee (Mish. Yad. 4:6–8; Mish. Hag. 2:7; Mish. Sot. 3:4).

Some scholars have alleged that the Pharisees were a 'sect' in the narrowest sense, and that they represented no one but themselves. But if any Jewish party in Palestine became *the* popular movement of the masses, it certainly was the Pharisees. There is no evidence to support the view that the

Pharisees had set themselves apart from the rest of the people, or from the humbler social levels of society. Nor is there any Pharisaic opposition to the *am ha-aretz* (literally 'people of the land') for their lack of learning or education. The uneducated man as opposed to the scholar is known as *hediot* in Hebrew, and as *idioteis* in Greek. As we shall see in a later context, those who most often fell short of the requirements of the strict observance of the twofold law were not the so-called common people, but rather the privileged and well-to-do. The notion that the 'people of the land' were somehow less devout or less observant of the Law than the townspeople is nowhere attested either in the Gospels or in any other component of the New Testament. Jesus never set foot in the large cities of Galilee; he preached in the synagogues of the villages. In the New Testament the Pharisees express no contempt for the humble people, nor do they accuse Jesus himself, though he was the son of a carpenter (Gr. *tekton*), of being either unclean or unlearned.

Nevertheless, as a religious party or, better yet, 'brotherhood' whose spiritual orientation was quite rigorous and demanding, the Pharisees considered themselves *haverim*, 'brothers of the covenant,' who regarded as the true community of Israel only those who strictly observed the twofold Torah. There is evidence in the Mishnah (Mish. Hag. 2:7; Mish. Dem. 2:31; Mish. Toh. 7:4 to) suggest that the Pharisees kept themselves apart only from such people as fell short of the Pharisaic standards of purity. In the Gospels, similarly, we find the Pharisees criticizing Jesus for keeping company with 'tax collectors and sinners' and with disciples who fail to wash their hands before eating (Mark 2:14–17; Matt. 9:9–13; Luke 5:27–32).

The Pharisaic Revolution

Pharisaism existed in principle if not in fact from the time of Ezra and Nehemiah, when Judaism was organized so as to ensure the daily fulfilment and obedience to the ordinances of the Torah. Its first appearance as a 'party', however, cannot be traced farther back than to the time of the Maccabean revolt. The first book of Maccabees informs us that the *Hasidim* (Heb.), the Pious, *oi Asidaioi* (Gr.) participated in this struggle at least in its earliest phases (I. Macc. 2:42; 7:12ff). Although they fought at the side of Judah the Maccabee to defend the faith of their fathers, they were not identical with the Maccabean party.

The distinctive features of Pharisaism, as we have seen, are the twofold Law – the written and the oral – and the idea of eternal life through resurrection. These features of the Pharisaic movement were innovations so discontinuous with the Jewish past that they amounted to a socio-religious revolution. Ellis Rivkin, basing himself on the first book of Maccabees

14:25–48, has produced a highly plausible reconstruction of the events that gave rise to the Pharisaic movement. 'A Great Synagogue', he writes,

> of the priests, the people, the rulers of the nation, and the elders of the country proclaimed that Simon the son of Mattathias of the family of Joarib was to be the leader and High Priest of the Jews forever, until a true prophet arose. For this proclamation there is absolutely no Pentateuchal warrant. The Pentateuch is clear and explicit that Phinehas the son of Eleazar the son of Aaron is to have for himself and his seed after him a covenant of an everlasting priesthood (Num. 25:13).[4]

The promise is further confirmed in the book of Joshua (22:13–34), in I Chronicles (6:1–15, 49–53) and in Ezra (7:1–5). The act of the Great Synagogue was a radical departure from the past inasmuch as the family of Joarib the Hasmonean, though a priestly family, was not a high-priestly family. Neither Jonathan, who already held the office of high-priest, nor Simon, who was now installed in that office, had any legitimacy according to the Pentateuch. The Hasmoneans were not the direct descendants of the Aaron, Eleazar, Phinehas, Zadok line. Thus it appears that the circumstances that gave rise to the Maccabean revolt also provided an opportunity for a very significant socio-religious change.

The Maccabean revolt was largely provoked by the high-priests who, by their outrageous behaviour, had thoroughly discredited themselves in the eyes of the pious masses. This occurred when Jason purchased for himself the high-priesthood from Antiochus, the Hellenistic-Syrian King, and then had Onias III, the rightful incumbent, exiled. This flagrant violation of Pentateuchal law, far from having been foisted upon Jason by the foreign power, came about at his own initiative. An even greater outrage followed when Menelaus bought the high-priesthood and, ousting Jason, went on to encourage sacrifices on the temple altar of swine's flesh to Zeus. The breach with the devout masses was now complete, and the door was thus opened for a new leadership consisting of the highly respected scribes, and Torah scholars and teachers.

It was the actions and teachings of these new leaders that earned them the epithet 'Pharisees' ('separatists') from their opponents; and it was these opponents who came to be called 'Sadducees' (i.e., 'Zadokites') because of their insistence that the high-priest's office was the exclusive prerogative of the Aaron, Eleazar, Phinehas, Zadok line. And, as Rivkin observes,

> the only time this right was challenged by Jews utterly loyal to God and his revelation, and not Hellenists at all, was when Jonathan took over the High-Priesthood and when a Great Synagogue – publicly proclaimed this transfer of power sacrosanct. The rejection of this act by the Zadokites–

Sadducees set them in opposition to those who had legitimized this transfer of power on the basis of an authority *not* written down in the law of Moses. These must have been the champions of the laws not written down . . .

Whoever sanctioned the legality of the transfer must have been a class whose authority was acknowledged by both the Hasmoneans and the people at large as legitimate. It had to be a class that affirmed the right of the Great Synagogue to do what it did, even though it had no Pentateuchal warrant. This class could not have been the Zadokites–Sadducees. The only other class attested to by Josephus as functioning at this time, which was also a class continuously clashing with the Sadducees, were the Pharisees. According to Josephus, the Pharisees, along with the Sadducees and the Essenes, were functioning in the time of Jonathan – the first Hasmonean to serve as High-Priest and, hence, the first to have provoked the opposition of the Zadokites–Sadducees. Josephus mentions the Pharisees and the Sadducees for the first time in his writings at that very moment when the issue of who should be the High-Priest, once the hostilities came to an end, emerged.[5]

The so called 'Pharisees', then, were already in Maccabean times the religious and intellectual leaders of the community, enjoying the support of the people. The Mishnah, I Maccabees and Josephus all presuppose this 'Pharisaic revolution', for all three sources take for granted the twofold Law – that the oral Law was no less revealed to Moses on Sinai than the written Law. All three sources likewise share the view that the scribes, scholars and Torah teachers were the 'carriers' of what the New Testament calls the 'tradition of the elders'.

Both the Mishnah and the New Testament attest to another innovation of the scholars, one which might be called 'prooftexting'. The Pentateuch and the other biblical books had no need for prooftexting, since the contents of each book, it was believed, had been revealed to the writer by God himself. Throughout the Mishnah, in contrast, one finds the Hebrew formula, *shene' emar*, 'as it is stated in the Scripture'. It was this innovative method of prooftexting which enabled the scholarly community to challenge the Zadokites and to establish their own authority.[6] They accomplished this precisely by remaining faithful to the proposition that the Pentateuch was the very word of God. They acknowledged that God had chosen Aaron and his descendants for the eternal priesthood, but they also noted that God had chosen a non-priest, Joshua, to succeed Moses as Israel's leader. When Moses dies, it is Joshua to whom God speaks; it is Joshua who leads the tribal confederacy in its conquest of Canaan. But nowhere in the book of Joshua does God speak directly to Eleazar or Phinehas. Similarly in other books of the Bible, God makes his will known to judges and prophets, but never directly to an Aaronide. Thus the 'scholar class', that came to be called 'Pharisees', could cite scripture to demonstrate that God's authority had been transmitted from Moses to Joshua and from Joshua to the non-Aaronide prophets.[7] This understanding of the transmission of authority is succinctly summarized in the opening paragraph of Mishnah Aboth (The Ethics of the Fathers):

> Moses received the Law (Torah) from Sinai and committed it to Joshua, and Joshua to the elders [Josh. 24:31], and the elders to the prophets; and the prophets committed it to the men of the Great Synagogue. (Mish. Aboth 1:1)[8]

Moreover, the Pharisees could also draw upon the historical books of the Bible to show that a non-Aaronide like Elijah, for example, had authority to offer up sacrifices on a 'high place' (Heb. *bamah*). And inasmuch as the scriptural prophets had also learned God's will directly, the Pharisees could legitimately claim that the words and deeds of the prophets had the status of unwritten laws. Finally, in their effort to adapt the Mosaic legislation to changing circumstances, they could note the many variations, discrepancies and ambiguities in the Pentateuch and therefore insist on the necessity of alternative interpretations.

As for the Pharisaic idea of immortality, though it is nowhere expressly stated in the Scriptures, one finds many hints there of life after death. Thus Enoch is simply taken by God (Gen. 5:24); the witch of Endor draws Samuel's spirit out of the earth (I Sam. 28:8–19); Elijah revives a child (I Kings 17:17–24) and he himself is swept into heaven on the wings of a chariot (2 Kings 2:9–12); Ezekiel envisions the coming alive of very dry bones (Ezek. 37:1–4); and Job anticipates that when his flesh is no more, he shall see God.

It was during the crisis that led to the Maccabean revolt, therefore, that the Pharisee movement established itself as the religious leadership of the nation. The opportunity was provided by the collapse of the high-priestly leadership, which had thoroughly discredited itself by its blatant Hellenization of the temple cult. This opportunity enabled the devout scholars of the nation, fully conversant with the Holy Scriptures, to find ample warrant there for the revolutionary change they were determined to bring about in order to preserve the traditional faith in the one and only God. The organizational means they employed in this socio-religious revolution was the *Synagoge Megale* (Gr.), the Great Synagogue (Heb. *haknesset hagedolah*). It was this great assembly of scholars, priests, elders and pious people that elevated Simon to the high-priesthood, and canonized the books of the Prophets and the Hagiographa, thus constituting those writings together with the Pentateuch as the Holy Scriptures (Heb. *Tanach*), the so-called Old Testament. It is also quite likely that the synagogue (Heb. *bet haknesset*) became a more firmly established institution soon after the Hasmonean revolt. The term *knesset* is never used in the Scriptures where the 'words for an assembly are *edah, kahal* and *kehilla,* . . . Hence the very usage *knesset hagedolah* and *bet haknesset* testifies to non-biblical institutions'.[9] Rivkin posits the Great Synagogue as having been a constituent assembly of sorts, and the synagogue as a place where the Pharisees met not only to study and pray, but to plan and promote their religio-political efforts as well. Perhaps that is why Josephus felt justified in calling the Pharisees a *haeresis,* a religio-philosophical school and 'party'. In these terms the synagogues served as revolutionary committees; they were the assemblies of the Pharisees and their followers, an organizational network employed for the attainment of their goals, 'as they supported, with arms and prayers, the uprising of the Hasmoneans'.[10]

In a later period, however, under Hyrcanus I and his son Aristobulus, the Pharisees appear as opponents of the Hasmoneans, their opposition flaring into open revolt under Alexander Jannaeus. For six years Jannaeus, with his mercenaries, waged war against his own people led by the Pharisees (*Antiq.* 13:376). Jannaeus evidently had provoked the revolt by usurping the high-priesthood, for which the people believed he was unfit (*Antiq.* 13:372). Although thousands of his countrymen were slain by Jannaeus, he never fully succeeded in defeating his Pharisaic adversaries, for they had the mass of the people on their side. The conflict ended only with Queen Alexandra who, for the sake of peace with the people and also because she personally favoured the Pharisees, handed over power to them. The entire conduct of religious affairs was now wholly in their hands, 'and whatever regulations, introduced by the Pharisees in accordance with the tradition of their fathers, had been abolished by her father-in-law Hyrcanus, these she again restored. And so, while she held the title of sovereign, the Pharisees had the [religious] power' (*Antiq.* 13:408–9). The Pharisees were the religious authorities in all subsequent regimes as well, maintaining their spiritual leadership amid all the changes in government, under the Romans and the Herodians. All 'prayers and sacred rites of divine worship are performed according to their [the Pharisees'] exposition' (*Antiq.* 18:15). The Pharisees had the greatest influence on the ordinary people and the 'support of the masses' (*Antiq.* 13:298). So influential were they that the Sadducees yielded to them in religious matters, 'since otherwise the masses would not tolerate them' (*Antiq.* 18:17).

The New Testament is in full accord with Josephus' view that the hallmark of the Pharisees was the twofold Law, the 'tradition of the elders' (Matt. 15:1–9; Mark 7:1–13; Phil. 3:5–6; Gal. 1:13–14). Matthew, in particular, provides us with a considerable amount of additional information concerning the Pharisees of the first century. They 'traversed sea and land to make a single proselyte' (23:15); they 'tithed mint and dill and cummin'

(23:23); they insisted that eating-utensils be properly cleaned, and that the law concerning cleanness and uncleanness be observed (23:25–6); they attached great importance to the punctilious observation of the Law (23:27–8); they wore phylacteries and fringes (*tsitsioth*) (23:5); they sought honour (23:6–7), gave alms (6:2–4), fasted (6:16–18) and prayed publicly (6:5–6). And although the author of Matthew regards these actions of the Pharisees with contempt, they are not actions from which the Pharisees would have wished to dissociate themselves. Matthew himself insists that all of 'these you ought to have done [but] without neglecting the others' (23:23); that the Pharisees 'have their reward' (6:2, 5,16); and that the scribes and Pharisees are righteous – though an even greater righteousness than theirs is demanded (5:20). If, therefore, we temporarily suspend judgment concerning the *motives* of the Scribes–Pharisees, which the Gospels impugn, then we can see that, judging by the other sources, namely Josephus and the Mishnah, the Gospels describe the words and deeds of the Pharisees rather accurately. In Matthew's words, 'The scribes and Pharisees sit on Moses' seat; so practise and observe whatever they tell you (23:2–3). This statement of Matthew's recognizes the legitimacy of the Pharisees' claim to ultimate religious authority. For we can be sure that if their claim had possessed no legitimacy, he would have exposed it as fraudulent.

The Sadducees

If the Pharisees were the party of the people, the Sadducees were the representatives of the aristocracy. This seems to be their most salient characteristic, as repeatedly stressed by Josephus: the Sadducees have 'the confidence of the wealthy alone but no following among the populace, while the Pharisees have the support of the masses' (*Antiq.* 13:298). 'There are but few men to whom this [the Sadducee] doctrine has been made known, but these are men of the highest standing' (*Antiq.* 18:17). The Sadducees were the wealthy lay and sacerdotal aristocracy that had ruled the Jewish state from the early Hellenistic and even the Persian period. Josephus and the New Testament concur in viewing the high priestly families as adherents of the Sadducean party (Acts 5:17; *Antiq.* 20:199). The contrast, then, between the Sadducees and the Pharisees is one of a temporal and clerical aristocracy *vis à vis* an essentially lay group, which derived its authority and social honour from learning and piety.

However, the priests and the Pharisees were not necessarily hostile to each other. Indeed, it was possible to be both priest and Pharisee, as was the case with Josephus. The Pharisees opposed themselves not to the priests as such, but only to the chief priests and the urban patricians, those who by virtue of their wealth and office held influential positions in civil life and refused to accept the basic Pharisaic principles of the twofold Law. We have seen that the Sadducees derived their Hebrew name *Tsedukim* (Gr. *Saddou-kaioi*) from the priest Zadok whose descendants had held the high priestly office in Jerusalem since the time of Solomon. After the return from the Babylonian exile, although other clans (for example, Ithamar) gained authority to fill priestly offices (I Chron. 24), the Zadokites held a near monopoly of the high-priesthood in the period of the second temple.

In contrast to the Pharisees, the Sadducees, as we have already noted, acknowledged only the written Torah as binding, and rejected the entire body of traditional interpretation 'handed down by former generations and not recorded in the laws of Moses' (*Antiq.* 13:297–8). They rejected the whole of the *paradosis ton presbyteron*, the tradition of the elders and their ordinances developed over centuries by the Pharisaic Torah scholars in their supplementing of the written Law. Josephus describes the Sadducees as 'more heartless than any of the other Jews . . . when they sit in judgment' (*Antiq.* 20:199). This may well have been the result of the Sadducees' strict adherence to the letter of the Law. Just as their rejection of the Pharisaic belief in bodily resurrection may also have been prompted by a strict and literal reading of the scriptural texts. For with the exception of the book of Daniel, as we earlier noted, the Hebrew Scriptures have only vague intimations of the resurrection of the body, and life after death. Similarly foreign to the Scriptures is the belief in angels and demons, which, under Pharisaic influence, became characteristic of later Judaism. The Sadducees were thus faithful to the earliest outlook of the Holy Scriptures.

To understand how the Sadducees became more of a party in the political sense, we need to recall that already in the Persian, but especially in the Hellenistic period, the priestly upper classes were in charge of political affairs. The high-priest served as head of state, and he together with other leading priests directed the *Gerousia*, the high council which eventually became the *Synedrion* (Sanhedrin). In time, political interests so profoundly affected their lives that such interests often took precedence over those of religion. This tendency became especially pronounced in the Hellenistic period, when worldly, political success largely depended on one's attitude towards the Hellenistic rulers and culture. Thus, even the leading priests of Jerusalem, as we have seen, had made such far-reaching concessions to the pagan culture, and had so alienated themselves from the pious masses, that they provoked the Maccabean uprising and the Pharisaic revolution. Follow-ing the Maccabean victory, though the extreme Hellenizers were either expelled or silenced, the priestly aristocracy remained worldly minded and comparatively lax in matters of religion. It was precisely the Pharisaic revolution that heightened the tensions and conflicts with the ruling priestly and patrician aristocracy; for the latter continued to resist being bound by the tradition of the elders, which they viewed as an encroachment on their hereditary privileges and authority. Given their conservative and autocratic tendencies and their secular interests, it is not surprising that they resisted the Pharisees' imposition of the Oral Law wherever possible. As many of the leaders of the aristocratic party claimed descent from the ancient priestly clan of Zadokites, they and their followers remained known as the Sadducees. Notwithstanding the clear hegemony of the Pharisees' spiritual authority, the Sadducean aristocracy effectively retained its political power, a consequence, in part, of the Pharisees' indifference to politics *per se*. Thus in the Herodian–Roman period, with which we are primarily concerned, several of the high-priestly families belonged to the Sadducean party (Acts 5:17; *Antiq.* 20:199). But the price they had to pay for their political dominance was to submit, albeit unwillingly, to the religious formulas of the Pharisees which were accepted by the masses (*Antiq.* 18:17).

With the destruction of the Jewish state in AD 70, the Sadducees vanished once and for all from the historical stage. Political leadership having been their main role, it became superfluous when the autonomy of the Jewish state came to an end. The Pharisaic movement, in contrast, or more accurately one powerful school or section of the movement, was not only unaffected by the destruction of the political state, but knew how to exploit the new situation to establish itself as the exclusive religious leadership of the Jewish people

In the time of Jesus, the daily religious life of Palestinian Judaism was characterized by a considerable accumulation of purity laws and other commandments and obligations. An extreme emphasis on such ordinances could lead some adherents of the Pharisaic movement to a petty formalism, and to an ostentatious rather than an authentic piety. Doubtless this is the experiential basis for the sayings Matthew and Luke attribute to Jesus, sayings in which he excoriates perceived excesses, abuses and hypocrisy (Matt. 23:24; 23:25; Luke 11:19; Matt. 23:27–8; Luke 11:11). It goes without saying, however, that just as there were those motivated primarily by strict social conformity, there were others – the majority most certainly – who possessed a sincere, inner spirituality. If we assume sincerity, as we must, on the part of both Jesus and the majority in the Pharisaic movement, then the essential question still remains: what was the nature of the doctrinal and other differences between them? It is clear that Jesus, as a devoutly religious Palestinian Jew of the first century, shared with the Pharisees several fundamentals of their outlook. But it is equally clear that he differed with some of them in several conspicuous respects. Before we begin to address this question, however, we need to consider two more religious groups which have a definite bearing on the central question.

The Essenes

Josephus describes the Essenes alongside the Pharisees and Sadducees as a third Jewish *haeresis*. This difficult Greek term has been translated by most scholars as 'sect' or 'party'. We have seen, however, that the Pharisees were no sect, but the leaders of a mass movement. The term 'party' also has only limited application to the Pharisees, since their primary interests and aims were religious, not political. As applied to the Sadducees, however, the term 'party' does seem quite appropriate, inasmuch as they were the ideological representatives of the aristocracy. The Essenes, however, were neither a party nor a movement, but a quite different social and religious phenomenon.

The Essenes were more in the nature of a monastic order. Josephus typically refers to them as *Esseinoi*, but also as *Essaioi*. For Philo, the Jewish philosopher of Alexandria, they are always the latter, *Essaioi*. Though it is commonly held that the term is of Semitic origin, there is little agreement as to its meaning. Following the discovery of the Dead Sea Scrolls and the light they have shed on the Qumran community, a rather convincing etymology has been advanced by the distinguished specialist Geza Vermes, who derives *Essaioi* from the Hebrew word *Isi*, meaning 'healers'. This is also suggested by Josephus' underscoring of the Essenes' interest in ancient writings concerned with 'the welfare of soul and body; with the help of these [writings], and with a view to the treatment of diseases, they make investigations into medicinal roots and the properties of stones' (*War* 2:136).

Josephus states that the number of Essenes in Palestine in his time amounted to more than 4,000 (*Antiq.* 18:21), and that they could be found in every *town*. It would be an error, then, to suppose that all the Essenes had secluded themselves in the desert near the Dead Sea – although that settlement does appear to have been the largest. Wherever they found themselves, similar principles of community organization were implanted. At the head were superiors whom the rank and file members unconditionally obeyed. Those who desired to enter the order were presented with a small hatchet, an apron and a white robe, and were required to undergo a year of probation before being admitted to the ritual ablutions; and it was only after two additional probationary years that the initiate was allowed to take the distinctive oath, thereby entering fully into the order and joining the other members at the common table.[11] Only adult men were accepted as members, though the community did take in children to educate them in the principles of the order (*War* 2:120). Violations of the community's principles were judged by a court consisting of at least 100 members. Severe transgressions were punished with explusion from the community.

The striking and distinguishing feature of the Essene order was its absolutely common ownership of property:

Riches they despise, and their community of goods is truly admirable; you will not find one among them distinguished by greater opulence than another. They have a law that new members on admission to the sect shall confiscate their property to the order, with the result that you will nowhere see either abject poverty or inordinate wealth; the individual's possessions join the common stock and all, like brothers, enjoy a single patrimony (*War* 2:122–3).

There is no buying or selling among themselves, but each gives what he has to any in need and receives from him in exchange something useful to himself; they are, moreover, freely permitted to take anything from any of their brothers without making any return (*War* 2:127).

They elect officers to attend to the interests of the community, the special services of each officer being determined by the whole body (*War* 2:123).

They neither bring wives into the community nor do they own slaves, since they believe that the latter practice contributes to injustice and that the former opens the way to a source of dissension. Instead, they live by themselves and perform menial tasks for one another (*Antiq.* 18:22).

There was a branch of the Essenes, however, that permitted marriage (*War* 2:160–1). Philo similarly states

that no individual possesses any private property, neither a house, nor slave, nor field, nor flocks, nor anything that procures abundant wealth. But they place all things together and enjoy the common profits of them all.

The wages which they earn through different trades are handed over to . . . the steward [*tamias*] elected by them. He receives them [the wages] and at once buys what is necessary and provides ample food and whatever else human life requires.

Not only their food, but also their clothing is held in common. For the winter, thick cloaks are available, and for summer, light tunics so that each may use them according to his pleasure. For whatever one possesses is held to belong to all; and whatever they all possess, as belonging to each one.[12]

There is only one money chest for all, and common disbursements and common garments and common food at common meals. For the sharing of roof, life and table is nowhere found so firmly established in actual practice . . . For all the wages they earn in a day's work they keep not as their own, but they rather put it into the common stock and allow the benefit of their labours to be shared by those who wish to make use of it. The sick are not neglected on account of their inability to earn, since they can assuredly meet expenses out of the plentiful reserves.[13]

All this applied not only to the settlement in the vicinity of the Dead Sea, but to Essene communities wherever they found themselves. Travelling members of the order always found a hospitable reception in every town, where a special officer was available to attend to the needs of the visiting brethren. 'Consequently, they carry nothing whatever with them on their journeys, except arms as a protection against brigands' (War 2: 124–5).

Strictly regulated, the daily routine of the Essenes began with prayer, after which they went off to work. At the fifth hour they reassembled and, girding their loins with linen cloths, bathed their bodies in cold water. After this purification they proceeded to the refectory where the priest recited grace and where they silently ate their morning meal followed by a further grace. They returned to their labours until evening and then partook of the evening meal, again with prayers before and afterwards.

Highly disciplined, they did nothing without orders from their superiors except acts of charity – rendering assistance to fellow members. They were modest, frugal and ascetic, and their allotments of food and drink were no larger than was essential for life. They controlled their tempers and refrained from self-righteous behaviour. Their word was sufficient, having more force than an oath; and they avoided swearing, 'regarding it as worse than perjury, for they say that one who is not believed without an appeal to God stands condemned already' (War 2:135). However, the oaths they took upon admission to the order form an exception. Indeed, before being admitted to the common table, the initiate was made to swear, in Josephus' words, 'tremendous oaths':

> first that he will practice piety towards the Deity, next that he will observe justice towards men; that he will wrong none whether of his own mind or under another's orders; that he will forever hate the unjust and fight the battle of the just; that he will forever keep faith with all men, especially with the powers that be, since no ruler attains his office save by the will of God; that, should he himself bear rule, he will never abuse his authority nor, either in dress or by other outward marks of superiority, outshine his subjects; to be forever a lover of truth and to expose liars; to keep his hands from stealing and his soul pure from unholy gain; to conceal nothing from the members of the order and to report none of their secrets to others, even though tortured to death. He swears, moreover, to transmit their rules exactly as he himself received them; to abstain from robbery; and in like manner to preserve the books of the order and the names of the angels. Such are the oaths by which they secure their proselytes. (War 2: 139–42)

The ascetic way of life of the Essenes included bathing in cold water not only before each meal but after the calls of nature (War 2:149), and following contact with a non-member (War 2:150). They were stricter than all Jews in abstaining from work on the sabbath. Not only do they prepare their food on the day before, to avoid kindling a fire on that one, but they do not venture to remove any vessel or even go to stool' (*War* 2:147). In exercising their natural functions on other days, they largely followed the strict rules of hygiene and cleanliness laid down in Deuteronomy 23:12–14. They 'dig a trench a foot deep with a matlock – such is the nature of the hatchet which they present to the neophyte – and wrapping their mantle about them, . . . sit above it. Then they replace the excavated soil in the trench. For this purpose they select the more retired spots. And though the discharge of the excrements is a natural function, they make it a rule to wash themselves after it, as if defiled' (*War* 2:148–9).

In their religious doctrine the Essenes believed that everything was in the hands of God and that the soul was immortal. Although they sent votive offerings to the temple, they performed their own sacrifices, employing a different ritual of purification. For this reason they were barred from the precincts of the temple. After God, they held most in awe the name of their lawgiver, Moses. There were among them members who professed 'to foretell the future, being versed from their early years in holy books, various forms of purification and apothegms of prophets: and seldom, if ever, do they err in their predictions' (*War* 2:159).

The Essenes and the Qumran Community

The Essenes had their own distinctive books, numerous examples of which appear to have been found at Qumran. Are the Essenes of Josephus and the Qumran community of the Dead Sea Scrolls one and the same group? In reply to this question Geza Vermes, a leading authority on the scrolls, has this to say:

> Although a minority of scholars, whilst acknowledging a degree of relationship between the two movements, refuse to admit that they are the same, the wide consensus of opinion favours an identification of the people of Qumran with the Essene sect.
>
> The main arguments in support of the [Qumran]–Essene identity are: (1) short of discovering another more appropriate site, the sectarian establishment of Khirbet Qumran would appear to be the principal Essene settlement located by Pliny between Jericho and Engedi. (2) Chronologically, the Essenes flourished, according to Josephus, between the rule of Jonathan and the first Jewish war (*Antiq.* 13:171; *War* 2:152; 2:567). The occupation of the Qumran site is dated by archaeologists to approximately the same period. (3) The organization of the common life described in the two sets of sources, as well as their rites, doctrines and customs, show so many and such striking similarities, that the hypothesis equating Qumran sectaries with Essenes appears to be endowed with the highest degree of probability.[14]

Just as the historical origins of the Pharisees and Sadducees may be traced to the crisis that caused the Maccabean revolt, so may the origins of the Essene–Qumran movement. Originally the Essenes, like the Pharisees, were among the Hasidim who at first gave their support to the Maccabean uprising. At the point, however, at which Jonathan accepted the office of high-priest (153/2 BC), one group of *Hasidim* broke away from the others – those who eventually became known as the 'Pharisees'. The breakaways were led by the Teacher of Righteousness (Heb. *Moreh Tsedek*), the founder and organizer of the Qumran/Essene movement. A priest of high Zadokite lineage, the Teacher of Righteousness could reconcile neither himself nor his followers to the installation of a non-Zadokite in the supreme clerical office. Jonathan became the 'wicked priest' in their eyes and thereafter the Teacher of Righteousness and his followers avoided the temple and created their own sacrificial cult.

The aims and aspirations of the Essene/Qumran group were expressed in these words:

> [The master shall teach the sai]nts to live [according to] the Book of the Community rule, that they may seek God with a whole heart and soul and do what is good and right before Him as He commanded by the hand of Moses and all His servants the prophets . . .
>
> They shall separate from the congregation of the men of falsehood and shall unite, with respect to the Law and possessions, under the authority of the sons of Zadok the priests who keep the convenant, and the multitude of the men of the Community who hold fast to the Covenant. Every decision concerning doctrine, property and justice shall be determined by them.
>
> They shall practice truth and humility in common, and justice and uprightness and charity and modesty in all their ways. No man shall walk in the stubbornness of his heart so that he strays after his heart and eyes and evil inclination, but he shall circumcise in the community the foreskin of evil inclination, and of stiffness of neck that he may lay a foundation of truth for Israel, for the Community of the everlasting Covenant. They shall atone for all those in Aaron who have freely pledged themselves to holiness, and for those in Israel who have freely pledged themselves to the House of Truth, and for those who join them to live in community.[15]

The Essenes, then, emerged as a distinct group when they vehemently opposed the removal of the high priesthood from the Zadokite lineage in the time of Jonathan. This distinguished them from the rest of the *Hasidim–Pharisees* who approved the expropriation of the Zadokites. Thus differing with the Pharisees on the issue of the high-priest's office, and with the Sadducees on the twofold law, the Teacher of Righteousness and his adherents had no recourse but to create a community of their own, most likely Qumran.[16]

Zealots and Sicarii

What was Jesus' relationship to the Zealots? Some New Testament specialists have advanced the claim that Jesus was closely associated with them, so closely in fact that this would account for his execution at the hands of the Romans. (This claim and the response it has provoked will be critically scrutinized in Part III of the present study.) The question of Jesus' relationship to the Zealot movement is crucial for a clarification of his self-understanding; and no less crucial for a clarification of how he was perceived by the individuals and groups with whom he came in contact. This being the case, a good grasp of the nature of the Zealot movement is essential.

Josephus, who again in this regard is our main source, states that this school of thought was established by Judas the Galilean. His followers agreed in all 'respects with the opinions of the Pharisees, except that they have a passion for liberty that is almost unconquerable, since they are convinced that God alone is their leader and master. They think little of submitting to death in unusual forms and permitting vengeance to fall on kinsmen and friends if only they may avoid calling any man master' (*Antiq.* 18:23). The occasion for the proclamation of Judas' *credo* was the census of Quirinius (AD 6/7) which Judas and his followers looked upon as an evil policy designed to reduce the people to slavery. This was an unacceptable condition for a nation whose lord was God alone. So Judas and his fellow Zealots (Heb. *kannaim*) called upon the Jews to rebel against Rome.

Scholars are largely in agreement that Josephus' description of the Zealots is not free of bias. It seems clear that he held them responsible for having precipitated the destruction of the Judean state in AD 70. From Josephus' standpoint they were irresponsible 'hotheads' who, with their sustained violence against Roman authority and the insurrection of AD 66, had provoked the catastrophe. Josephus describes those engaged in violent opposition to Rome as 'brigands' (*lestai*) (*War* 2:228), 'rebels' (*stasiastai*) (*War* 2:431, 441) and 'revolutionaries' (*neoterizontes*) (*War* 1:4); and somewhat more respectfully as 'the Jewish revolutionary party' (*War* 1:4).

Judas the Galilean's family played a prominent role among these freedom fighters. His father Ezekias had opposed Herod's tyranny; and his sons Simon and Jacob were crucified for anti-Roman activities under Tiberius Julius Alexander. It was Judas' descendant Menahem who seized the fortress of Masada at the beginning of the revolt of AD 66 (*War* 2:433–4), and who remained the leader of the revolution in Jerusalem until his murder by Eleazar ben Simon's rival group (*War* 2:445–9). And it was Menahem's nephew Eleazar ben Jair who led the last stand of the freedom fighters at Masada (*War* 2:410–end). During the period AD 6–66, what Josephus describes as the 'fourth philosophy' (the first three being the Pharisees,

Sadducees and Essenes), the Zealot movement, gained more and more adherents, which has led scholars, from the time of Hermann Samuel Reimarus in the eighteenth century, to associate Jesus with this movement.

Judas' religiously motivated hostility to Roman domination was probably the common property of all the revolutionary groups, though they certainly were not always united. The 'fourth philosophy's' first distinguishing mark was the desire for freedom (*eleutheria*). The legend on the coins minted during the war of AD 66–70 reads *heruth tsion*, 'freedom of Zion,'[17] On other coins *ligeulath Zion*, 'the redemption of Zion', was proclaimed. Judas and his disciples had set out to establish the Kingdom of God on earth; as God alone was their acknowledged Lord, none of Judas' followers or successors called any man master (*despoteis*). They were prepared to put their opponents to death and submit to death themselves, rather than acknowledge human lordship. Josephus brands these ideas as 'folly' (*Antiq.* 18:23) and blames them for the ills that befell the nation (*Antiq.* 18:9).

The Zealot movement appears to have drawn its inspiration from the Hasmoneans (i.e., the Maccabees) and from Phinehas, the grandson of Aaron. When Israel in the wilderness had sinned by worshipping Baal of Peor, and when an Israelite and his Midianite woman flouted Moses' commands, it was Phinehas who in his zeal for the Lord slew them both, thus turning away God's wrath from the people of Israel (Num. 25: 1–15). Like Phinehas, the Hasmoneans were zealous for God's law by ridding the land and the temple of apostates (I Macc. 2: 19–28). The Zealots drew on such traditions. Josephus, however, accuses them of lawlessness for putting to death, without the Sanhedrin's confirmation, actual or potential collaborators with Rome (*War* 4:138–46). The Zealots fought 'in guerrilla fashion' (*War* 3:170; 6:357), and their actions provoked savage reprisals on innocent people. During their last stand in Jerusalem, the Zealots and their followers elected a high-priest by lot, fortified the temple, abolished the customary sacrifice on behalf of Caesar, and used the oil and wine stored in the temple for their own support.

There is still another term which Josephus employs to designate those associated with the Zealot movement. He states that a 'new species of banditti was springing up in Jerusalem, the so called *sicarii* [i.e., 'assassins', from the Latin word *sica*, meaning a curved dagger], who committed murders in broad daylight in the heart of the city. The festivals were their special seasons, when they would mingle with the crowd, carrying short daggers concealed under their clothing with which they stabbed their enemies' (*War* 2:254). It is highly probable that the Roman authorities used the term *sicarii* to describe all those who employed force and violence against them and their Jewish collaborators. The Zealots were also called 'Galileans'. Judas, the organizer of the freedom movement, bears, both in the book of Acts (5.37) and in Josephus, the sobriquet 'the Galilean'. The stubborn resistance in Galilee against Herod, and the insurrection after his death, show that this province was early on a centre of revolutionary opposition to the foreign power and its clients. It was quite natural, then, for rebels throughout the land to be called 'Galileans'.

Regarding the Greek word *zelotes* as employed by Josephus, Martin Hengel has observed that in the Septuagint the Hebrew words *El Kannai* ('zealous God') are translated as *Theos Zelotes*. The word *zelotes* in the general Greek literature has a moral connotation which is retained in the Septuagint, the Hellenistic Jewish translation of the Hebrew Bible. This word, however, has a distinctive meaning in the Jewish culture of the time, for which there is no Greek equivalent, namely, devout and zealous in the religious sense.[18] Thus it became the name of a 'party' that was zealous for God.

In the New Testament we find that among the disciples of Jesus Luke mentions 'Simon who was called the Zealot' (6:15), employing the Greek term. In Mark and Matthew, however, the Aramaic equivalent remains intact (Mark 3:18; Matt. 10:3). There we find *o kananaios*, a transliteration of the Aramaic *kanana* (Heb. *kannai*). We may justifiably infer, then, that in the time of Jesus there existed a definite group within the Jewish community bearing the name of 'Zealot'. Josephus' 'brigands', 'rebels', and '*sicarii*' are simply epithets, given his bias, for the politico-religious movement called the 'Zealots' (Heb. *ha kannaim*). And we have already seen how this term has deep roots in the Jewish tradition going back to the time of Phinehas who was zealous for God and his Torah.

The Zealots as a social and religious movement were committed to the fundamental principle that God was the sole ruler of the Holy Land, and that the Jews had only one master. It followed that they could never reconcile themselves to foreign domination. Freedom was their overriding concern. The adage, 'God helps those who help themselves', accurately describes the outlook of the Zealots, who believed that the people cannot expect God to aid them in the attainment of freedom if they will not endeavour to help themselves. The Zealots, then, may be seen as a splinter group within the broad Pharisaic movement, which contained other significant divisions such as the schools of Hillel and Shammai.

The exclusive kingship of God (Yahweh) had already been firmly established in the Hebrew Scriptures. The designation of God as 'King' appears there no fewer than 50 times. 'King', in the Scriptures, is understood in the universal sense – King of all the nations, of the entire world as its Creator and Master and, of course, of Israel his people. Hence, for Judas the Galilean and his followers there could be no compromise between the profane, heathen kingdom of Caesar (the Romans), and the Kingdom of God. Because the Emperor laid claim to a divine status, obedience to him was a violation of the first of God's commandments, and no less than idolatry.[19] For the Zealots the point was to translate the first commandment into a political reality in the Holy Land. The redemption of Israel is a cooperative venture between man and God. The ideal of freedom and redemption (Heb. *geulah*) was well grounded by this time, deeply rooted in that great foundational event in the history of the people, the Exodus from Egypt, and in the new life that had been breathed into the ideal by the glorious Maccabees.

The movement founded by Judas the Galilean was therefore motivated by ancient religious traditions. For the Zealots, he who paid tribute to Caesar was 'as a Gentile and a tax-collector'. These words, attributed to Jesus by Matthew (18:17) suggest Zealotic influence. In order therefore to grasp the motives of the Zealots authentically, we must not describe them in such anachronistic secular terms as 'fanatics devoted to political freedom and love for the fatherland'; 'patriots'; 'fighters for national independence'; 'national and social revolutionaries'. All of these terms are misleading if we fail to grasp the purely religious motivation of Judas and his adherents, who saw themselves interpreting God's laws and certain traditions in their own way. Just as the Pharisees sought to adapt the Torah to the changing exigencies of life, seeing themselves as obeying the spirit, not the letter of the Law; and just as the Essenes resolved to seclude themselves from the world's apparent godlessness, the Zealots represented a third way: they attempted by force and violence – often against reason and the interests of the people, and without regard for the real relationships of power – to obey God's commandment by bringing into being his sole and exclusive kingship in the Holy Land.[20] Israel was for the Zealots first and foremost a religious community, and only secondarily a 'nation'. They despised the collaborators with Rome 'and in every way treated them as enemies, plundering their property, rounding up their cattle, and setting fire to their habitations; protesting that such persons were no other than aliens, who so ignobly sacrificed the hard won liberty of the Jews and admitted their preference for the Roman yoke' (*War* 7:255). That the primary motivation of the Zealots was religious and not national in the pragmatic-political sense is fully acknowledged by Josephus (*War* 4:263: 5:4, 345, 526; 6:364). After the destruction of the temple and after all of Judea was subdued by the Romans, Josephus relates that several hundred of the *sicarii* fled to Egypt where they continued to promote their revolutionary schemes within the Jewish community. Meeting with opposition from certain Jews of rank, they murdered them and agitated among the people to rise up against the Romans. The elders and leaders of the community soon recognized that if the *sicarii* continued their activities they would provoke the Roman authorities and bring ruin upon the entire Jewish community. Accordingly the elders called upon the general assembly of the community to round up the *sicarii* and turn them over to the Romans for the sake of maintaining the peace with them. In the balance of the narration of these events, Josephus, despite his powerful antipathy towards the Zealots, cannot deny the profoundly religious well-spring of their actions:

> Realizing the gravity of the danger, the people complied with this advice, and rushed furiously upon the *sicarii* to seize them. Six hundred of them were caught on the spot; and all who had escaped into Egypt and the Egyptian Thebes were ere long arrested and brought back. Nor was there a person who was not amazed at the endurance and – call it which you will – desperation or strength of purpose displayed by these victims. For under every form of torture and laceration of body, devised for the sole object of making them acknowledge Caesar as lord, not one submitted nor was brought to the verge of utterance; but all kept their resolve, triumphant over constraint, meeting the tortures and the fire with bodies that seemed insensible of pain and souls that well nigh exulted in it. But most of all were the spectators struck by the children of tender age, not one of whom could be prevailed upon to call Caesar lord. So far did the strength of courage rise superior to the weakness of their frames. (*War* 7:410–19)

In sum, what Josephus refers to as the 'fourth philosophy' was a movement founded by Judas the Galilean long before the outbreak of the Jewish war. The adherents of this movement were called *kannaim* ('Zealots') by their own people and *sicarii* by the Romans and their collaborators. The immediate circumstance that brought the movement into being was the census imposed by Quirinius in AD 6/7. This census enforced the payment of tribute (i.e., taxes) to Caesar, which the *kannaim* looked upon as an act against God. The Zealots were the most militant wing of the Pharisees, distinguishing themselves from the general Pharisaic movement with their unconditional demand that the Holy Land be ruled under the sole and exclusive kingship of God. No one but God was to be called Master or Lord. Thus they stood in uncompromising opposition to the heathen kingship that was forcibly imposed on the land and the people. The Zealot outlook was grounded in the Scriptures and in the expectation of redemption; their conception of freedom was thoroughly religious and eschatological, not secular and political. Their rebellion against the heathen overlord was to be the prelude to the God-ordained and God-assisted redemption of Israel. Redemption would not come solely as a God-given gift; for it depended directly on the actions of self-help taken by the righteous and devout. To bring about the exclusive rule of God, a genuine theocracy, armed resistance was sanctioned, just as it had been with the Maccabees. This radical eschatological message became the *credo* of a substantial popular movement.

By the time of the outbreak of the Jewish revolt against Rome in AD 66, the most radical of these Zealots had evidently caused a split within the nation – one was either for or against them, no middle ground having been acceptable.

If Jesus was born *c* 6 BC, and if the immediate impetus for the formation of the Zealot movement was Quirinius' census of AD 6/7, then we can say that as Jesus was growing up in Galilee he was almost certainly exposed to the ideas of Judas the Galilean. Indeed, a holy zeal for God, in various forms, was an essential characteristic of Jewish piety in Jesus' time. In Paul's speech before the people, as reported in the book of Acts, he stated: 'I am a Jew, born at Tarsus in Cilicia, but brought up in this city [i.e., Jerusalem] at the feet of Gamaliel [a leading Pharisee], educated according to the strict manner of the law of our fathers, being *zealous for God* as you all are this day' (Acts 22:3). One can see obvious zeal in Paul's actions prior to his 'conversion' (Acts 22:4) and in Jesus' 'cleansing of the temple' (Mark 11:15ff and parallels). Zeal for the things of God, for intensifying devotion to the Torah (Matt. 5:17ff) inspired the vast majority of Palestinian Jewry from the time of the Maccabees, most notably the *Hasidim*, the Pharisees and the Essenes. And, doubtless, the original Jewish–Christian congregation, under the leadership of James the brother of Jesus, was similarly inspired.

Holy zeal was rooted in Israel's belief in its uniquely elect status. Zeal for the holiness and redemption of Israel demanded a total devotion to God's will, a readiness to suffer and even to sacrifice one's life. What distinguished the Zealots from all others, however, was their conviction that against the heathen oppressor and the Jewish collaborators the use of force was a solemn duty. For them, so long as Israel tolerated the heathen yoke, God remained angry, and the Kingdom of Heaven was delayed. Hence, active efforts to remove the yoke would also hasten the coming of the great change.[21]

In the period between the death of Herod (4 BC) and the destruction of Jerusalem (AD 70), the Jewish freedom movement founded by Judas the Galilean and Zadok the Pharisee, suffered a large number of casualties. They fell both in open battle and at the hand of the Roman executioner. However they may have been viewed by the ruling Sadducean circles, the vast majority of the people looked upon the freedom fighters as genuine martyrs. The outbreak of the Jewish war and its continuation for four years would scarcely have been possible in the absence of a sympathetic attitude towards the Zealots on the part of the people. The growing number of martyrs indicates that in the eyes of many this was a time of testing. Only through the certainty of the eschatological significance of their martyrdom could the untold number of victims in the struggle retain their morale and their sanity: they were paving the way for the imminent Kingdom of God.[22]

For those inspired by the religious vision of the Zealots, the God-ordained redemption ushering in the new epoch would not be delivered to Israel as a gift, as a divine miracle alone. Redemption could only come through an actual holy war against the godless worldly power. In this holy war the Zealots gave little or no attention to the real power relations between Judea and Rome, since they saw themselves as fulfilling God's will – striking the opening blow that ultimately would lead to the destruction of Roman might. The expectation prevailed that there were several possible ways in which this would be accomplished: with God's direct intervention; through his legions of angels; through self-destruction, or through an attack by peoples from the East; through some or all of these in combination and, most likely, under the leadership of an extraordinary human individual whom the people called 'the Messiah' (Heb. *ha-mashiah*, 'the anointed one'). The Zealots had thus anticipated that the overthrow of Rome would be accomplished by armed struggle under the leadership of the Messiah and with the supernatural assistance of God. A purely passive waiting for God's intervention was thus rejected by the Zealots.

There was, of course, a 'national' dimension to the Zealot movement, an Israel-centeredness that also characterized the earliest Jewish-Christian congregation (Matt. 19:28; Luke 22:28; 24:21). There can be no doubt, as we shall see, that both among the disciples and the crowds that Jesus attracted, there were those who looked upon him as the one who would 'restore the kingdom of Israel' (Acts 1:6).

In his *Antiquities* (18:4), Josephus informs us that in organizing the rebellion against Quirinius' census, Judas the Galilean enlisted the aid of a Pharisee named Zadok. Josephus also states, that the 'fourth philosophy' of Judas the Galilean 'agrees in all other respects with the opinions of the Pharisees, except that they have a passion for liberty that is almost unconquerable' (*Antiq.* 18:23). Zadok's cooperation with Judas together with this statement by Josephus suggests that there existed a radical wing of the Pharisees which accepted the Zealot doctrine. Could this have been the school of Shammai, or a substantial section of it? Martin Hengel has remarked that the great, pioneering Jewish historian Heinrich Graetz was probably right in maintaining that the school of Shammai tended to show some receptivity to the doctrine of Judas. Hengel convincingly suggests that it is in their respective attitudes towards Zealotism that the key to the later developments of the two major schools – Hillel and Shammai – should be sought. While the Shammai group appears to have had the preponderant influence prior to the catastrophe of AD 70, they lost it afterwards, the spiritual leadership of the people passing decisively to the Hillelites. And in the same vein G.F. Moore also observed that 'the Shammaites were the more numerous, as well as the more aggressive, and it was perhaps only after the fall of Jersualem that the Hillelites gained the ascendancy'.[23] So it is a reasonable hypothesis that Judas' followers first appeared as a radical, Pharisaic splinter group, but very soon established themselves as an independent party, but retaining close and amicable relations with the Shammaite wing of the Pharisaic movement.[24]

There was also, in all likelihood, a social dimension to the Zealot movement which should not be overlooked. Josephus informs us that 'Distributing themselves in companies throughout the country, they [the Zealots] looted the houses of the wealthy, murdered their owners, and set the villages on fire' (War 2:265). This appears to have been an attack by the rural poor against the wealthy landlords, some of whom may have been collaborators with the Romans. In the countryside the military tactics of the freedom fighters resembled those of the young David and of the Maccabees in the early stages of their struggle. From caves and other secluded areas in the eastern mountains of Judea they launched surprise attacks on small Roman units, travelling Roman officials and against the estates of rich landlords. To the plain people, however, they showed as much kindness and gave us much aid as they could. The social dimension is further evident in the first acts of the rebels when they captured the upper city in c. August AD 66. The rebels, wrote Josephus,

> burst in and set fire to the house of Ananias the high-priest and to the palaces of Agrippa and Berenice; they next carried their combustibles to the public archives, eager to destroy the moneylender's bonds and to prevent the recovery of debts, in order to win over a host of grateful debtors and to cause a rising of the poor against the rich, sure of impunity . . . After consuming the sinews of the city in flames, they advanced against their foes; whereupon the notables and chief priests made their escape, some hiding in the underground passages, while others fled with the royal troops to the palace situated higher up, and instantly shut the gates . . . (War 2:426ff)

It was the 'leading men' who wished to capitulate to the Romans (War 4:414), and it was the poor and indebted masses who gave steadfast support to the rebels. Thus, notwithstanding its fundamentally religious character, the Jewish rebellion bore the aspect of a social revolution and civil war. Like the Essenes and the early Jewish Christians, the Zealots also looked upon 'the poor' as especially deserving of attention and honour (Luke 6:20; 4:18; 7:22; Matt. 5:3; 11:5; Rom. 15:26; Gal. 2:10).

The Zealots, then, sought to hasten the coming of the Messianic era by means of an armed struggle against the Roman imperial rulers. They strove to establish God's kingdom on earth by means of force. This was one variety of the Messianic idea. In a later context we shall explore the relevance of the Zealot ideology for an understanding of Jesus' mission. Did he see himself fulfilling a Messianic role, and if so, what, precisely, was the nature of that role? How did the disciples perceive Jesus in the several stages of their relationship with him? Finally, there is the question of the crowds' perception of Jesus, and how they understood his words and actions. Clearly, these questions require an adequate grasp of the Messianic idea in Jesus' time.

3

The Messianic Idea in Israel

At the heart of the Messianic idea is the hope and expectation of a better future.[1] This was a basic element of the Jewish religious consciousness at least from the time of the Scriptural prophets. The expectation received a renewed impetus with the Maccabean uprising and continued to undergo transformation thereafter. The earliest prophetic visions were oriented to this world and concerned with the future of the nation. It was the hope of the pre-exilic prophets that the community would cleanse itself morally so that it might enjoy the divine reward of peace and respect among the nations. As in the vision of Isaiah, Israel would then be ruled by a just, wise and powerful king from the house of David, and peace and happiness would prevail. Whereas in the biblical period hopes for salvation centred on the destiny of the nation, the post-biblical, second-temple era shows a concern for individual salvation, the earliest of its manifestations being the belief in resurrection.

This new idea, expressed explicitly in the visions of the book of Daniel (c. 167–165 BC), emerged out of the same crisis that provoked the Maccabean revolt and gave rise to the Pharisaic movement. In the age of trouble and misfortune (Heb. *et tsarah*, Dan. 12:1) which had befallen Israel following the wicked policy of Antiochus Epiphanus, Daniel foresees a coming deliverance. God himself will judge the kingdoms of this world. He 'will set up a kingdom which shall never be destroyed, nor shall its sovereignty be left to another people. It shall break in pieces all these kingdoms and bring them to an end, and it shall stand forever' (2:44). 'And the kingdom and the dominion and the greatness of the kingdoms under the whole heaven shall be given to the people of the saints of the Most High; their kingdom shall be an everlasting kingdom, and all dominions shall serve and obey them' (7:9–27). As we have already noted, the truly novel element in this vision of deliverance is the promise that

> many of those who sleep in the dust of the earth shall awake, some to everlasting life, and some to shame and everlasting contempt. (12:2)

It is not clear whether Daniel envisioned a Messianic king standing at the head of the saints of the Most High. In any event, he makes no mention of such an individual. And although Daniel sees that 'with the clouds of heaven there came one like a "son of man" [*kebar enash*]' (7:13), this is not an individual Messiah, since the author clearly states that what appears in the form of a man is the *people* of the saints of the Most High (7.18, 22, 27). (This explicitness, however, has not prevented the Danielic figure from being identified with the individual Messiah.) Just as the empires of the world are symbolized by beasts ascending from the sea, so the kingdom of the saints is represented by a human form travelling with the clouds. The essence of Daniel's Messianic hope is therefore the universal dominion of the devout and righteous. This will be brought about not by God's judgment alone, as might appear from chapter 7, for it is the kingdom of saints that will 'break in pieces all these kingdoms and bring them to an end' (2:44). This suggests that the ungodly will be destroyed by the force of arms, though, of course, in accordance with God's will.

After Daniel, judging from other inter-testamental sources such as the apocryphal and apocalyptic books, the Messianic idea assumed a new form. The era just prior to the Messianic age is to be a time of ordeal and confusion. Friend will be against friend, son against father, daughter against mother. Nations will rise against nations, and there will be fire, famine and earthquakes besides (Baruch 70:2–8; 4 Ezra 6:24; 9:1–12; 13:29–31).[2] This is also stated in the New Testament which, as we have already remarked, may be regarded as a reliable source of information for the religious ideas of Judaism in the first century (see Matt. 24:7–12, 21; Mark 13:19; Luke 21:23; I Cor. 7:26; Tim. 3:1).

The age of the ordeal draws to a close with the reappearance of the prophet Elijah who returns to prepare the way for the Messiah. This role was attributed to Elijah on the basis of Malachi and is assumed in Ben Sirach (Ecclesiasticus) (43:10–11). The New Testament contains frequent allusions to Elijah's coming, including speculation as to whether John the Baptist was Elijah come back to life (Matt. 11:14; 16:14; 17:10; Mark 9:11; 6:15; 8:28; Luke 9:8, 19; John 1:21). It is Elijah's mission, according to Malachi (4:5), to establish peace on earth:

Behold I will send you Elijah the prophet before the coming of the great and terrible day of the Lord. And he shall turn the heart of the fathers to the children, and the heart of the children to their fathers . . .

After Elijah has prepared the way, the Messiah himself will appear. In pre-Christian Judaism this figure is an extraordinary but fully human being descended from the house of David. An earthly king and ruler, the Messiah is nevertheless endowed by God with special gifts and powers. That the Messiah is conceived as entirely human, in accordance with the constraints of ethical monotheism, is particularly clear in the apocryphal Psalms of Solomon. There he appears as a learned human being, free from sin, and endowed by the holy spirit with power, wisdom and righteousness (ch. 17). The same conception is found in the Sibylline Oracles (3:49). It is true, however, that in the apocalypse 4 Ezra and in the Parables of Enoch the Messiah is endowed with supernatural qualities (12:32; 13:26; 14:9; 14:52). This indicates that in certain circles at least, apocalyptic fantasy created a supramundane Messiah whose extraordinary qualities soon lifted him out of the bounds of common humanity.

In the Parables of Enoch one finds similar speculation in which the particular phrase 'son of man' is linked with the Messiah (1 Enoch 46:1–6; 48:2–7; 62:5–9, 14; 63:11; 69:26–29; 70:1; 71:17). Here the phrase 'son of man' is an application of Daniel's image (7:13) to a heavenly Messianic or quasi-Messianic figure. As the chosen instrument of God he is called 'the Elect', – chosen, hidden and preserved from the beginning by the Most High. Enoch, guided by an angel through the heavenly regions, sees 'the Elect' and 'his dwelling place near the Lord of the Spirits' and 'all the righteous and elect shone before him as fiery lights' (39:6–7). In other passages (46:1; 46:3; 49:2–4) the Messiah soon acquires such superhuman qualities that some scholars assume a Christian influence here, an influence which cannot be entirely ruled out since it cannot be demonstrated that this work is definitely pre-Christian. Other scholars have convincingly observed that 'such ideas are fully comprehensible from Old Testament premises. Statements such as that in Micah 5:1, that the origins of the Messiah are from ages past, from the beginning of days, may easily be taken in the sense of pre-existence from eternity. And Daniel 7:13–14 needs only to be understood to refer to the person of the Messiah, and his travels in the clouds as a descent from heaven, and the doctrine of the pre-existence reveals itself.'[3]

With the appearance of the Messiah the hostile transgressing powers will come together for a final assault against him. This expectation, most clearly expressed in the Sibylline Oracles (3:663), in 4 Ezra (13:33ff) and in Enoch 90:16, can also be traced to the Hebrew Scriptures, notably Psalm 2:

> The kings of the earth set themselves, and the rulers take counsel together, against the Lord and his anointed, saying, 'Let us burst their bonds asunder and cast their cords from us' . . . I will tell you of the decree of the Lord: He said to me, 'You are my son, today I have begotten you. Ask of me, and I will make the nations your heritage, and the ends of the earth your possession. You shall break them with a rod of iron, and dash them in pieces like a potter's vessel.'

The Messianic king, in accordance with God's design, will destroy the hostile powers, gather in the exiles, renew Jerusalem and establish the kingdom of glory in the Holy Land (Sibyl. 3:704–6, 717, 756–9; Ps. Solomon 17:1, 38, 51). In the Messianic era *all* nations will acknowledge the God of Israel, as was already prophesied in the Hebrew Scriptures (Isa. 2:2ff; Mic. 4:1ff; 7:16ff; Jer. 3:17; 16:19ff; Zeph. 2:11; 3:9; Zech. 8:20ff; Isa. 55:5; 56:1ff); and the Messiah 'shall stand as an ensign to the peoples; him shall the nations seek, and his dwellings shall be glorious' (Isa. 11:10).

From the time of the eighth-century prophets, universalism was an essential element of the messianic era. In the pre-Messianic age, however, it was first the task of Israel alone to repent and atone, to cleanse itself morally, and to reach the highest rung of human righteousness. For this reason and for others, as we shall see, it is not at all unlikely that Jesus would have said, 'Go nowhere among the Gentiles, and enter no town of the Samaritans, but go rather to the lost sheep of the house of Israel' (Matt. 10:5).

The last judgment was to be preceded by a general resurrection. In the interval between death and resurrection, however, there would be a separation of the just from the unjust, an initial state of blessedness for the former and torment for the latter. This expectation is found in the apocryphal literature (I Enoch 22:4; 4 Ezra 7:75–107), in Josephus and in the Mishnah. By the first century it was a basic tenet of Pharisaic doctrine: 'eternal imprisonment is the lot of evil souls, while the good souls receive an easy passage to a new life' (*Antiq.* 18:14). Souls that have remained 'spotless and obedient, are allotted the most holy place in heaven' (*War* 3:374). And the Mishnah states that 'all Israelites have a share in the world to come' (Mish. Sanh. 10:1), except for sinners, who will be excluded (10:1–4). The last judgment will distinguish between those destined for eternal bliss and those for damnation. The wicked will be cast into the fire of *Gehinnon* (2 Baruch 44:15; 51:1–2, 4; 6; and 4 Ezra 7:36–8, 84). Though some sources regarded this damnation as eternal, others hold the view that the pains of *Gehinnom* ('hell') will be only temporary and that it will cease to exist in the world to come. The Hebrew word *Gehinnon*, New Testament Greek *Gehenna* (Matt. 5:22, 29ff; 10:28; 18:9; 23:15, 33; Mark 9:43, 45, 47; Luke 12:5) means literally 'Valley of Hinnom', a valley near Jerusalem where two Judean kings, under Assyrian domination, sacrificed to Moloch (2 Kings 21:4–5). Jeremiah therefore prophesied that that very same place would be the site of doom, of a terrible massacre of the Israelites (Jer. 7:31ff; 19:5ff). In Enoch (26–7) there is the anticipation that all the wicked will be gathered together in this valley for judgment to be executed upon them. Although the name *Gehinnom* is not specifically stated there, the place is described as the valley between Zion and the Mount of Olives – that is, a real valley near Jerusalem. By New Testament times *Gehinnom* came to symbolize a place of punishment in the netherworld into which the godless will be cast; and eventually the New Testament *Gehenna* was equated with the Greek Hades, and 'hell'.

In the New Testament we also hear of 'Satan', who in later times becomes associated with *Gehenna*. The Hebrew word *satan* means simply an 'adversary' (1 Sam. 29:4; 2 Sam. 19:22; 1 Kings 5:4; 11:14, 23, 25; Num. 22:22, 32; Ps. 109: 6). This original sense of the word is still found in Jesus' rebuke of Peter in Matthew 16:23. It is used as a proper name four times in the Hebrew Scriptures (Job 1:6, 12; 2:1; Zech. 3:1; 1 Chron. 21:1). It is in the Book of Job that we find for the first time a definite mention of 'Satan' as an 'adversary' of Job. And though he instigates the testing of Job, there is an emphatic stress on Satan's subordinate position and the absence of all but delegated power. Notwithstanding the often alleged Persian influence on the concept, there is no dualism here, for Satan bears no resemblance to the Persian *Ahriman*, the spirit of evil. In the New Testament he is spoken of as a 'spirit' in Ephesians 2:2, as a prince or ruler of the 'demons' in Matthew 12:24–26, and as having 'angels' subject to him in Matthew 25:41 and Revelations 12:7, 9. The power attributed to him in these passages is wholly spiritual, exercising a direct and evil influence as the leader of a host of evil spirits who do his bidding, and for whom the 'eternal fire is prepared' (Matt. 25:41). In another passage Matthew identifies these spirits with the 'demons' who had power to possess the souls of men (12:24–6). Beelzebul, or the 'prince of demons', is also called the 'prince of the world' in John (12:31; 14:30; 16:11) and even the 'god of this world' in 2 Corinthians (4:4). The Greek *ho diabolos* ('the devil'), already current in the LXX (Septuagint) as a translation of the Hebrew *ha-satan*, implies 'setting at odds by slander', attempting to break the bonds of communion between God and humanity. The slander of man to God is illustrated by the Book of Job; but in the New Testament the satanic method also includes the temptation and possession of human beings.

Messianism and False Prophets

In the period under consideration the Messianic idea in Israel gave rise to the phenomenon of false prophets. Significantly, it is in the same general context as his discussion of the *sicarii* (see ch. 2) that Josephus calls attention to this phenomenon, describing the false prophets as 'another body of villains, with purer hands but more impious intentions, who no less than the assassins ruined the peace of the city'. Josephus goes on to tell us that they were imposters and deceivers who, under the pretence of being divinely inspired, fostered revolution by persuading the multitude to gather in the wilderness and prepare for deliverance. Against them, the Roman authorities, alarmed by what appeared to be the initial stage of an insurrection, dispatched a large body of both cavalry and heavily armed infantry 'and put a larger number to the sword' (*War* 2:258–60).

Another tragic incident was provoked by an Egyptian false prophet. Gathering to himself a following of thousands,[4] he led them from the wilderness to the Mount of Olives. From there he had planned to force his way into Jerusalem and, after overwhelming the Roman garrison, to establish himself and his followers in power there. Felix the procurator, anticipating the Egyptian's moves, brought out against him the Roman heavy infantry, and the leader of the revolt escaped with only a few of his men. Most of his force were either killed or taken prisoner (*War* 2: 261–4). Still another, but earlier imposter named Theudas, had persuaded a multitude

> to take up their possessions and to follow him to the Jordan River. He stated that he was a prophet and that at his command the river would be parted and would provide them an easy passage. With this talk he deceived many. Fadus, however, . . . sent against him a squadron of cavalry. These fell upon them unexpectedly, slew many of them and took many prisoners. Theudas himself was captured, whereupon they cut off his head and brought it to Jerusalem. These, then, are the events that befell the Jews during the time that Cuspius Fadus was procurator. (*Antiq.* 20:97–9)

This event is also mentioned in the book of Acts (5:36), where the leading Pharisee Gamaliel, recalling the experiences of Theudas and Judas the Galilean, admonishes the fellow members of the Council to leave Peter and the other apostles unmolested. Gamaliel is represented as uncertain of the apostles' claims, for he says: 'Keep away from these men and let them alone; for if this plan or undertaking is of men, it will fail; but if it is of God, you will not be able to overthrow them. You might even be found opposing God!' (5:38–9). Although there are chronological discrepancies between Josephus and Acts,[5] it is almost certain that the Theudas mentioned in both sources refers to the same individual. The name is relatively uncommon, and the Theudas cited by Gamaliel must have caused a disturbance of considerable proportions if his illustration was to have any effectiveness. Hence, the disturbance could not be ignored by Josephus either.

What emerges from this brief discussion of false prophets and false Messiahs is first, that in the period under consideration, Messianic expectations were so high among the people that several pretenders managed successfully to attract to themselves large numbers of followers; and, secondly, that the Roman authorities treated all such gatherings of crowds under the leadership of popular individuals as the preliminary stage of a violent insurrection. Accordingly, they reacted swiftly and ruthlessly to suppress all such demonstrations and disturbances. We may also make a few inferences about the circumstances that prompted Gamaliel's remarks. What we learn from chapter 5 of Acts is that the high-priest and other members of the Sadducean party were the most vehement opponents of the early Jewish–Christian congregation in Jerusalem. The apostles appear to be sufficiently popular after the execution of Jesus to warrant caution on the part of the temple captain and his officers. They brought Peter and the others before the Council 'but without violence, for they were afraid of being stoned by the people' (Acts. 5:26). The Pharisees on the Council, represented, presumably, by the highly respected Gamaliel – 'held in honour by all the people' – were not only more tolerant in their attitude towards these earliest Jewish-Christians, they were undecided, as yet, about the status of the apostles' claims. Although Gamaliel appears to have associated Peter and the others with the Zealot movement, he and his Pharisaic colleagues were still waiting to see whether the apostles' undertaking was of God or merely of man. These observations will become especially relevant in Part III, when I consider the chain of circumstances that led to Jesus' execution.

Having reviewed the nature of Judaism in the first century, the varieties within it as well as its underlying unity, we may now proceed with our attempt to situate the man Jesus in that context.

Part II

Jesus of Nazareth: Charismatic Religious Virtuoso

4

Jesus the Pious Palestinian Jew

As we reflect on the 'philosophical schools' constituting the Judaism of Jesus' time, we can see that if he fits into any of them, it is certainly not easily. We have no ready made term with which to embrace the complexity and versatility of the man Jesus. A term that comes close, however, is Max Weber's 'religious virtuoso'. 'The important empirical fact', writes Weber,

> that men are *differently qualified* in a religious way stands at the beginning of the history of religion . . . The sacred values that have been most cherished, the ecstatic and visionary capacities of shamans, sorcerers, and pneumatics of all sorts, could not be attained by everyone. The possession of such faculties is a 'charisma', which, to be sure, might be awakened in some but not in all. It follows from this that all intensive religiosity has a tendency toward a sort of *status stratification*, in accordance with differences in the charismatic qualifications. 'Heroic' or 'virtuoso' religiosity is opposed to mass religiosity. By 'mass' we understand those who are religiously 'unmusical'; we do not, of course, mean those who occupy an inferior position in the secular status order.[1]

'Charismatic religious virtuoso' implies genius. Let us grant that there are 'religious geninuses' just as there are geniuses in music, art, literature, science and other human endeavours. Let us further acknowledge 'revelation', if only in the secular sense of inspiration. Surely, all the great founders of the world religions had experienced 'revelations' in that sense. They were extraordinarily creative individuals, each of them inspired by a unique personal experience, which most often occurred in solitude. Without the analysis of the individual mind, therefore, we cannot take one step in the understanding of the origins of religious ideas. To apprehend the peculiar genius of a religious virtuoso we need to grasp his words, acts and feelings authentically, that is, as he had intended them. But a caution is in order with regard to the concept of religious genius. For even the most extraordinary of such individuals lived and worked within the currents of history and the constraints of his culture. The ideas he gave to the world were necessarily rooted in an inherited tradition.

His genius was not a matter of creating something out of whole cloth, but rather of diverging from certain traditions in a striking, significant and novel manner. To see how this proposition applies to the historical Jesus, we need first to analyse his rootedness in the Judaism of his time.

Jesus (*Yeshu*)[2] was, of course, a Jew, not a Christian. This obvious and fundamental fact is lost sight of all too often. He was circumcised as a Jew, lived as a Jew and prayed as a Jew; he performed the Jewish rites and he preached in Aramaic to his fellow Jews in the synagogues of Palestine. All of this is related frankly and unabashedly in the Gospels. Jesus was deeply rooted in the early first-century Jewish world. Rudolf Bultmann, a scholar who is extremely sceptical of the possibility of catching any reliable glimpses of the historical Jesus in the Gospels, nevertheless acknowledges that 'however much his preaching in its radicality is directed against Jewish legalism, still its content is nothing else than true Old Testament Jewish faith in God radicalized in the direction of the great prophets' preaching'.[3]

Implicit in this fundamental fact is another, namely, that Jesus was a fully human being and understood as such by the early church: 'Even at the end of the first and the beginning of the second century AD, the basic offence against a proper understanding of Jesus was described as follows: his coming in the flesh is denied; Jesus is not confessed[4] . . . In short, in the community's confession about Jesus, his humanity was beyond dispute. Thus our starting point with Jesus the human being is not a concession that has to be wrested laboriously from the New Testament. Jesus the true human being is the clear foundation of the New Testament.'[5] And Bultmann, again, writes:

> The church proclaimed him as prophet and teacher and beyond that as the coming Son of Man, but not as a 'divine man' of the Hellenistic world, who was a numinous figure. Not before the growth of legend on Hellenistic soil was the figure of Jesus assimilated to that of the 'divine man.' The Old Testament–Jewish world knew neither 'Heroes' in the Greek sense nor *homines religiosi* in the Hellenistic sense.[6]

T. W. Manson advances the following grounds for the view that Jesus was not only a religious Jew, but one thoroughly conversant with the language and schools of Judaism:

> (a)   As his quotations from the Old Testament show, his knowledge of the Hebrew Scriptures was both extensive and profound.[7] Anyone who had the acquaintance with the language of the Scripture shown by these quotations would have little difficulty with the language of the scholars. (b)   He is addressed as *didaskalos* (= Rabbi) not only by his own disciples (Mark 4:38; 9:38, etc.) or by members of the public (Mark 9:17) but by the learned themselves (Mark 12:14, 32). This suggests that they recognized him as a

competent scholar who could meet them on their own ground. (c) In the early part of the ministry he is reported as teaching in the synagogue. We are certainly told that his teaching differed from that of the Scribes; but the possibility of taking up an attitude different from or hostile to that of the Scribes implies an acquaintance with their methods. Moreover, if, as seems probable, the teaching in the synagogue consisted in expounding and applying the synagogue lessons for the day and formed part of the regular order of service, it seems unlikely that anyone would be called on to carry out this duty who was not considered to have some qualification for the task. (d) We have a story of Jesus at age 12 sitting among the Teachers (Rabbis) in Jerusalem.[8] If there is any reliance to be placed on this story – and there is nothing improbable about it – we must ask what happened in the intervening 18 years before the beginning of the ministry.[9] Is it not likely that much of this time was spent in the continuation of just such studies as these? . . . (e) The fact that Jesus was brought up in a humble household and to manual labour does not tell against his being a scholar in the Jewish sense. Many of the most distinguished ornaments [sic] of Rabbinical scholarship were men of humble origin who supported themselves and their families by manual labour while prosecuting their studies in the schools of the Law.[10]

There is, then, good reason to suppose that Jesus knew and employed the language of the Scribes and Pharisees. To the unlearned people, however, Jesus spoke Aramaic, the only language in which many of them could converse. In Mark 5:41, for example, he says '*Talitha cumi*', ('Talitha, rise!'), which seem to be his actual words.

In a short, thoughtful essay relevant to our subject, Manson critically analyses the words attributed to Jesus in Matthew 10:5ff: 'Go nowhere among the Gentiles, and enter no town of the Samaritans, but go rather to the lost sheep of the house of Israel'. The likelihood that these words express Jesus' own attitude derives support from Galatians 2, one of the earliest New Testament references to non-Jews. There Paul attests to the fact that it was only after considerable resistance by the 'Pillars' of the Jerusalem Congregation that his mission to the Gentiles was approved. There was at first disagreement over the question whether pagans converted to Jewish-Christianity had to be circumcised and subject to the other laws of the Torah as well. The Council of Jerusalem (Acts 15) laid down firm guidelines for a mission to the Gentiles, but there continued to be strong opposition from Jewish-Christians who maintained that ' . . . unless you are circumcised according to the custom of Moses', and 'keep the Law of Moses', there can be no salvation. So Manson accepts it as a fact that Jesus' activities were largely confined to Jewish soil in Palestine – though there were some apparent exceptions as in the accounts of the Syro-Phoenician woman (Mark 7:24–30) and of the centurion at Capernaum who had been especially kind to Jews (Luke 7:1–10). Manson cites the work of Albrecht Alt who had made a geographical survey of the places in Galilee in which Jesus is said to have carried on his ministry. It was Alt's conclusion that Jesus did not cross national boundaries to seek out non-Israelites – a conclusion similar to that of Joachim Jeremias in his *Jesus' Promise to the Nations*. 'The command to avoid Gentiles and Samaritans', writes Manson, 'is coupled with the command to go to the Israelites. This latter order was clearly meant to be obeyed, and was in fact obeyed, literally; and we must assume that the former was meant, and obeyed literally too.'[11]

Manson observes that the story about the Syro-Phoenician woman (Mark 7:24–31; Matt. 15:21–8) presents a difficult problem. For there it appears that Jesus was unwilling to respond to a case of human need and distress. Furthermore, Jesus replies to her plea for help in harsh nationalistic terms: 'Let the children [i.e., Israel] first be fed, for it is not right to take the children's bread and throw it to the dogs' (Mark 7:27). Manson's convincing comment on this episode is that Jesus' healing was based on the faith of Israel, and there was no reason to believe that this woman had any such faith. It was only after she answered, 'Yes, Lord; yet even the dogs under the table eat the children's crumbs', that Jesus agreed to help her anyway. Thus Manson concludes that Jesus saw his immediate task as one of delivering his message to Israel, '. . . in the faith that it would transform the life of his own people, and that a transformed Israel would transform the world'.[12]

In Mark 12:18ff, the Sadducees put to Jesus a provocative question concerning the doctrine of resurrection. Jesus' effective reply shows that on this matter he shared the outlook of the Pharisees. A Scribe, overhearing the exchange and seeing that Jesus answered well, asks: 'Which commandment is first of all?' Jesus' reply could hardly be more Jewish: 'The first is, "Hear, O Israel: The Lord our God, the Lord is one; and you shall love the Lord your God with all your heart, and with all your soul, and with all your mind, and with all your strength". The second is this, 'You shall love your neighbor as yourself". There is no other commandment greater than these' (Mark 12:28ff).

Now, T. W. Manson uses this exchange between Jesus and the Scribe to make the claim that although similar questions were raised by the rabbinical schools from time to time, the answers given were mere *Haggadah*, 'material for edification', 'not binding as rules of faith or conduct'. Hence, according to Manson, the importance assigned by the rabbis 'to this or that commandment was entirely relative'. For Jesus, in contrast, says Manson, the priority he assigns to the two great commandments is absolute. 'For Jesus these two [commandments] stand in a class by themselves. There is no other commandment that can come before them to claim man's obedience. They enjoy priority, not logical or relative, but *absolute*.'[13] Then, in a footnote intended to discredit Matthew's account of the same episode, Manson proposed that the absolute priority of the two great commandments has been softened down to an assertion of merely logical priority in Matthew. 'There is not another commandment greater than these' (Mark 12:31) gives place to 'on these two commandments hang the whole law and the prophets' (Matt. 22:40). By this change the whole mass of the Torah and tradition which has just been shown out at the front door is quietly brought in again at the back. This is just another indication that *where the Law is in question Matthew is simply not to be trusted*.'[14]

We need to make several observations about these claims, the first being that, according to Mark, the Scribe agreed entirely with Jesus, saying, 'You are right, Teacher ...' (Mark 12:32). That is to say, that this Scribe–Pharisee, who is not portrayed as in any way unusual, assigned precisely the same importance to these commandments as did Jesus. Second, the so-called 'softening down' that Manson imagines he discerns in Matthew is non-existent. Indeed, Matthew's statement is, if anything, a stronger one, for he hinges the whole of the Law and the prophets on these two commandments. Third, although the Marcan version assigns priority to these two commandments, there is nothing in it, either explicit or implicit, to indicate that the other commandments are unimportant or to be ignored. Thus when Manson says that the whole 'mass of the Torah' has been shown out the front door by Mark, this appears to be a transparently tendentious interpretation, unsupported by the textual evidence.

In a further effort at an invidious distinction between Jesus' view and that of the Jewish sages of his time, Manson recounts the well-known story involving Hillel, Jesus' older contemporary. A non-Jew, rebuffed by Shammai, once approached Hillel offering to become a proselyte on the condition that the whole Torah could be taught to him in a few words. Whereas Shammai had regarded the offer as an impertinence, the more patient Hillel took up the challenge and said: 'What is hateful to thee do not to anyone else; this is the whole Torah and the rest is commentary; go and study.' Manson then comments: 'For Hillel the commentary is every whit as essential as the Golden Rule. For Jesus the two commandments are in themselves sufficient, without any supplement whatever ... '[15] One must observe, however, that Manson is straining too hard to drive a wedge between Jesus and Hillel. For if, as Manson alleges, the two commandments were sufficient in themselves as 'a complete guide to anyone who wishes to live', why did Jesus provide substantial commentary in the form of sermons and parables, and even polemics against his critics?

Finally, Manson makes the claim that Matthew 5:17ff[16] is incompatible with Mark 10:5–9, and that 'it is not difficult to determine which of the two genuinely represents the mind of Jesus.'[17] In this way Manson attempts to discredit Matthew and an integral part of the Sermon on the Mount. But surely it is totally implausible that Jesus, a devout Jew in all the respects we have shown, would have advocated the abolition of the Torah. And, as we shall see, although Jesus had an attitude towards divorce different from that of some of his contemporaries (Mark 10:5–9), this is a far cry from repudiating the Law as a whole. That Jesus was willing to throw out all the commandments but two is a fundamentally preposterous notion. Jesus the pious Jew fastidiously observed the Law; he celebrated Passover (Mark 14:12ff), taught in the temple (Mark 14), and wore *tsitsit* (Mark 6:56), the fringe or tassels attached to the four corners of a robe in fulfilment of the commandment in Numbers 15:37–41 and Deuteronomy 22:12. In addition, Jesus showed due regard for the temple by paying the half shekel tax (Matt. 17:27); and he acknowledged that 'the scribes and Pharisees sit on Moses' seat; so practise and observe whatever they tell you' (Matt. 23:2–3).

Is Matthew Untrustworthy Where the Law is Concerned?

At this point it is necessary to address this key question, which has obvious methodological implications for our study of Jesus' outlook. According to the First Evangelist Jesus said:

> Think not that I have come to abolish the law and the prophets. I have come not to abolish them but to fulfil them. For truly, I say to you, till heaven and earth pass away, not an iota, not a dot, will pass from the law until all is accomplished. Whoever then relaxes one of the least of these commandments and teaches men so, shall be called least in the kingdom of heaven; but he who does them and teaches them shall be called great in the kingdom of heaven. For I tell you, unless your righteousness exceeds that of the scribes and Pharisees, you will never enter the kingdom of heaven (Matt. 5:17–20).

It is this well known passage which some scholars have called into question. It is 'too Jewish', in their opinion, and does not authentically reflect Jesus' own attitude towards the Law. Then how did it come about that Matthew placed these words in Jesus' mouth and what prompted him to do so? Scholars suspicious of Matthew's attribution of these words to Jesus answer this question by proposing that Matthew was not actually the first and earliest evangelist. They claim that Mark was the earliest; Matthew, they say, wrote his Gospel later, using Mark, in part, as his basic source and adding materials from another source – a hypothetical 'sayings-source', which the advocates of Marcan priority call 'Q', from the first letter of the German word *Quelle*, meaning 'source'. Matthew, so the argument goes, having written later than Mark, was reacting against certain antinomian tendencies in the early church (or against Jewish accusations of antinomianism), which he sought to counteract by inserting (inventing?) that passage in 5:17–20.

According to these scholars, then, Matthew's statement, far from having been Jesus' own, was rather a manifestation of a 're-Judaizing' tendency in the early church.

However, proponents of the 're-Judaizing' thesis have had to contend with the fact that the author of Luke, most probably a non-Jewish Christian, has much in common with Matthew. On the assumption of Marcan priority, 90 per cent of the subject-matter of Mark is reproduced in Matthew in language very similar, while Luke reproduces more than half of Mark. In addition to their Marcan material both Matthew and Luke share other matter in common, some of it expressed in nearly identical Greek words and the remainder in different Greek words. There are three possible explanations for this non-Marcan material common to Matthew and Luke:

1 Matthew used Luke.
2 Luke used Matthew.
3 Both Matthew and Luke employed a common source, the so called 'Q'.

The first explanation has found virtually no support; and the second is upheld by only a few scholars. Most supporters of Marcan priority have adopted the third explanation – that Matthew and Luke employed a common source other than Mark. This has become known as the 'Q hypothesis'. It needs to be stressed that the existence of such a source is entirely hypothetical, since no epigraphic evidence for 'Q' has ever been produced; and no two reconstructions of 'Q' have agreed entirely. The 'Q hypothesis' is thus very far from having been proved. Indeed, the entire theory of Marcan priority is now being vigorously challenged by a growing number of New Testament specialists. The latter, though still a minority, have presented stout arguments in favour of a return to the hypothesis that was dominant until about 150 years ago – the so called 'Owen-Griesbach' hypothesis.

The first three Gospels are so closely related in content that it is possible to lay out their respective texts in parallel columns to give an overall view of their similarities. This was first done in 1774–6 by Johann Jacob Griesbach, who coined the term 'synopsis' (i.e. 'seen together') for this technique. The works of the first three Evangelists are therefore referred to as the 'Synoptic' Gospels. Griesbach, on the basis of a painstaking analysis, defended the priority of Matthew, showing that his Gospel properly belongs exactly where it has been placed in the canon. Somewhat earlier, Henry Owen had reached quite similar conclusions in his *Observations on the Four Gospels* (London:, 1764). Defenders of the Owen–Griesbach or 'Two-Gospel' hypothesis maintain that it is Mark who employed and conflated Matthew and Luke, and that this is a more economical way to explain relationships among the three Synoptics than by starting with Mark and speculating how it was expanded into two longer Gospels. The advantage of the 'Two-Gospel hypothesis' is that it traces the basic Gospel tradition of the church to two actual Gospels, Matthew and Luke, rather than to totally hypothetical documents such as 'Q' and ur-Marcus, an older, original form of Mark no longer extant. The expression 'Two-Gospel hypothesis' is also favoured by these scholars because, in W. R. Farmer's words, it is an 'effective way of discharging the highly charged question of priority. "Priority of Matthew" conjures up for some the spectre of "Papal Primacy", and for others, the disquieting image of a rather "too-Jewish Jesus".'[18]

The Marcan hypothesis, which emerged some 150 years ago and still enjoys a dominant position among New Testament specialists today, has failed in at least one important respect. For it has left a fundamental question unanswered: 'Where is the literary evidence for Q?'[19] However, a similar failure may be discerned in the 'Two-Gospel hypothesis', since it has provided no satisfactory answer to the question: 'Where did Matthew and Luke get their material?'[20] A dissatisfaction with both these positions has led to a third standpoint, which argues the independence of Matthew and Mark. John Rist has called attention to the fact that ancient church traditions attributed no literary interdependence to the First and Second Evangelists. He also challenges what he regards as a misleading axiom of New Testament scholarship, 'that at most oral tradition could account for differences, but not similarities'. 'This axiom', writes Rist,

> depends on a fundamental misconception of the material available in the years between AD 35 and 65. For the 'tradition' in this period is still dependent on the living disciples. Oral tradition among groups that are separate from these disciples depends on their versions of events, and is constantly subject to checking and correction by these eyewitnesses. If one tells the same story, particularly if one is concerned to repeat original or the gist of original words, as accurately as possible, one is liable [i.e., likely] indeed to present similarities. It is absurd to suppose that such a tradition could only account for the differences in the synoptics.[21]

There is no good reason for ruling out oral tradition, aided by notes perhaps, as the basis of the similarities in the first three evangelists. This would account for the 'situation in the early patristic period when Mark and Matthew were independent documents, the surviving witnesses of a thirty year long and largely oral tradition. And we may, if we wish, accept those writers who make Matthew earlier, but only provided we do not argue from priority in time (however minimal) to literary paternity.'[22] For all practical scholarly purposes we need feel no anxiety in dispensing with the hypothetical but highly elusive 'Q' document; and we may console ourselves for the loss of 'Q', Rist convincingly argues, by noting that with the independence of Matthew and Mark 'the credibility of at least some of the tradition is strengthened by its being represented to us by two rather than by one identifiable primary document'.[23]

In sum, the proponents of Marcan priority have provided no solid grounds for impugning the credibility of Matthew where the law is concerned. Moreover, the truth is that in order to do justice to the quest for the historical Jesus we need all three Synpotics and the Fourth Gospel as well. As compared with the Synoptics, the Fourth Gospel not only exhibits a very different language in the discourses of Jesus, but also presents a chronologically and topographically divergent representation of his activities. Researchers in the nineteenth century therefore postulated this alternative: either the Synoptics or John. As a result of their rejection of the scholarly use of John for research into the life of Jesus, the Synoptic authors soon acquired the dominant position in the study of the sources. In the twentieth century, however, New Testament specialists have increasingly recognized that John cannot be ignored and that his Gospel is indispensable for insight into certain events in Jesus' life.

To return more directly to the question of Matthew's trustworthiness, it is significant that Luke, who was probably a Gentile Christian (see Col. 4:11, compared with verse 14), highlights without hesitation all the essential dimensions of Jesus' Jewishness. He informs us that Jesus was circumcised at the end of eight days (2:21), that he was brought up to Jerusalem for purification according to the law of Moses, and presented to the Lord – that is, sacrifices were offered in the temple on his behalf (2:22ff. And when his family had performed there 'everything according to the law of the Lord, they returned into Galilee, to their own city Nazareth' (2:39). Jesus' 'parents went to Jerusalem every year at the feast of Passover. And when he was twelve years old, they went up according to custom; and when the feast was ended, as they were returning, the boy Jesus stayed behind in Jerusalem'. This was the occasion on which Jesus' parents, discovering that they had left the boy behind, returned to Jersualem to find him 'sitting among the teachers, listening to them and asking them questions; and all who heard him were amazed at his understanding and his answers' (2:41ff).

When Jesus began his ministry at the age of 30, he taught in the synagogues of Galilee. In Nazareth, 'where he had been brought up', 'he went to the synagogue, as his custom was, on the sabbath day' and read from the prophet Isaiah (3:23–4:19). He preached in the synagogues of Judea as well (4:44). After curing a leper, Jesus urged the man to show himself to the priest and 'make an offering for your cleansing, as Moses commanded' (5:14). Jesus also went into the hills to pray 'and all night he continued in prayer to God' (6:12). In Capernaum, the Jewish elders besought Jesus to heal the centurion's slave, saying, 'He is worthy to have you do this for him, for he loves our nation, and he built us our synagogue'. And Jesus consented.

When Jesus, heading for Jerusalem, wished to pause in a village of the Samaritans, they would not receive him 'because his face was set toward Jerusalem' (9:51ff). In reply to an individual in the crowd who asked Jesus to intervene on his behalf and to bid his brother to divide an inheritance with him, Jesus replies: 'Take heed and beware of all covetousness . . .' (12:15) – thus confirming his respect not only for the 'great commandments', but for a lesser one as well (Ex. 20: 17). And although the words Luke attributes to Jesus concerning the Law are not identical to Matthew's, they nevertheless express the same attitude. For Luke has Jesus say that '*it is easier for heaven and earth to pass away, than for one dot of the law to become void*' (16:17). And in the parable about Lazarus and the rich man who finds himself in Gehenna pleading with Abraham, Luke places these concluding words in Abraham's mouth, which presumably represented Jesus' own outlook: 'If they do not hear Moses and the prophets, neither will they be convinced if someone should rise from the dead' (16:31). On the way to Jerusalem he meets ten lepers and, as previously with the single leper, instructs them to go and show themselves to the priests (17:11ff). In Jerusalem, after he drove out 'those who sold', he taught daily in the temple (19:47; 20:1; 21:37). As the feast of the Unleavened Bread approached, he sent Peter and John to prepare 'the Passover [lamb] for us, that we may eat it' (22.1ff). And it is noteworthy that Luke sees fit to tell us that after the crucifixion of Jesus the women who prepared spices and ointments rested on the sabbath 'according to the commandments' (23:56). When Jesus appears to his disciples and followers in a vision, it is highly significant that Luke takes Jesus' piety so much for granted that he has him bless the bread before breaking it (24:30). No less significant is Luke's taking for granted the piety of the disciples; for he concludes his Gospel by relating that '. . . they returned to Jerusalem with great joy, and were continually in the temple blessing God' (24:53).

So there is evidence aplenty that whatever else Jesus may have been in the eyes of the Evangelists, he was also a pious Jew who respected and observed the laws of Moses – though he undeniably differed with some of his contemporaries on the question of how specific laws should be interpreted and applied. Before we address Jesus' distinctive attitude, however, we should explore that of his brother James for the light it might shed on Jesus' own outlook.

James the Brother of Jesus

It appears that Jesus' brothers were not his disciples during his lifetime (Mark 3:21, 31; 6:3 and parallels; John 7:5, 10).

This phenomenon, so relevant for an understanding of how Jesus was perceived by those close to him, is one to which we must return in a later context. For the present, however, we may simply observe that Jesus' mother and brothers identified themselves with the Jerusalem Jewish-Christian congregation only after the belief in the resurrection took hold (Acts 1:14). Along with the disciples these relatives enjoyed exceptional prominence in the congregation. The brothers, accompanied by their wives, went on evangelical and inspection tours in other Jewish-Christian communities (I Cor. 9:5). In the book of Acts we hear in several places of a 'James' who occupies a prominent position in the congregation. If we had to rely on Acts alone we could never be sure to which James the text refers; for it is only from Galatians that we learn that this is James the brother of Jesus. By putting together Paul's letters and the book of Acts we learn that though James (Heb. *Yaacob*) joined the congregation after his vision of the resurrection, he soon attained the leading position alongside Peter (Cephas) and John (son of Zebedee). In Galatians 1:18 Paul still looks upon Peter as the most influential individual in the Jerusalem congregation. In Gal. 2:9 James takes precedence over Peter and John in the list of *Stuloi* ('pillars'); and in 2:12 Peter 'drew back and separated himself' before 'certain men' sent by James. The book of Acts eventually describes James as *the* head of the Jerusalem congregation and of its elders (Acts 15:13; 21:18). The grounds for James' authority appear to be that in addition to his own outstanding personal qualities, he was Jesus' brother according to the flesh. The decisive factor, however, which accounts for the honour accorded James, was not merely the matter of blood kinship. After the resurrection Jesus himself is said to have appeared to James (1 Cor. 15:7). Doubtless it was this appearance that James interpreted as his 'call'. In the eyes of the other members of the congregation this placed James on an equal footing with the other primary witnesses of the resurrection; and his name was delivered to Paul and, through him, to all the Pauline congregations as news 'of first importance' (1 Cor. 15:3ff.). In later Christianity the titles given to James emphasize not his kinship with Jesus but rather his ascetic way of life and his devotion to the Law (Torah); he is called *ho dikaios* ('the righteous one').

Josephus also mentions James. 'The younger Ananus', he wrote,

who had been appointed to the high priesthood, was rash in his temper and unusually daring. He followed the school of the Sadducees, who are indeed more heartless than any of the other Jews, as I have already explained [*Antiq.* 13:294], when they sit in judgment. Possessed by such a character, Ananus thought that he had a favourable opportunity because Festus [the former procurator] was dead and Albinus [the new procurator] was still on the way. And so he convened the judges of the Sanhedrin and brought before them a man named James [*Iakobos*], the brother of Jesus who was called the Christ, and certain others. He accused them of having transgressed the law and delivered them to be stoned. Those of the inhabitants of the city who were considered the most fair minded and *who were strict in observance of the law [i.e., the Pharisees] were offended at this*. They therefore secretly sent to King Agrippa urging him, for Ananus had not even been correct in his first step, to order him to desist from any further such actions. Certain of them even went to meet Albinus, who was on his way from Alexandria, and informed him that Ananus had no authority to convene the Sanhedrin without his consent. Convinced by these words, Albinus angrily wrote to Ananus threatening to take vengence upon him. King Agrippa, because of Ananus' action, deposed him from the high priesthood ... (*Antiq.* 20:200ff; italics added)

This passage may be regarded as complementary with those in Acts and in Paul's letters. We learn from Josephus that in some circles in Jerusalem Jesus was called the Messiah; that this circle and their leader, James, were prominent enough to come to the historian's attention; that the convening of the Sanhedrin and the execution of James by a Sadducean high-priest was regarded as an outrage that led to his dismissal; that James had a reputation among the Pharisees for holiness and strict observance of the Law (cf. Acts 21:20). The fact that James attracted the hostility of the high-priesthood, but not of the Pharisees and the people as a whole, will become relevant later in our consideration of the circumstances that led to Jesus' execution.

Acts 15:13–20 relates the decision of the famous Apostolic Council of *c.* AD 48–50, which is given in the name of James who introduces it with the strong phrase *ego krino*, 'I decide' or 'resolve'. The policy enunciated by James is that it should be made less difficult for pagans to become Christians by absolving them from the full Jewish observance of the Law. Nevertheless, converts were enjoined to abstain from:

1   Food prepared for or offered in idolatrous worship.
2   Illicit and promiscuous sex.
3   Meat of animals not appropriately slaughtered.
4   Drinking blood, which implies abstention from raw meat as well.

Evidently a letter containing these injunctions was sent to the various Jewish-Christian communities in the Diaspora. What was it that persuaded James, who up to that point had resisted all concessions, to allow two standards, one for born Jews and another for born pagans? The answer, apparently, is Peter's vision, which also speaks loudly with regard to Jesus' attitude towards the dietary laws. Peter, we are told, went up on the housetop to pray:

And he became hungry and desired something to eat; but while they were preparing it, he fell into a trance and saw the heaven opened, and something descending, like a great sheet, let down by four corners upon the earth. In it

were all kinds of animals and reptiles and birds of the air. And there came a
voice to him, 'Rise, Peter; kill and eat.' But Peter said, 'No, Lord; for I have
never eaten anything that is common or unclean.' And the voice came to him
again a second time, 'What God has cleansed, you must not call common.'
(Acts 10:9ff)

Now, if Peter had never eaten anything common or unclean, surely it would
be too much to believe that his Master, Jesus, would have 'declared all foods
clean', as Mark alleges (7:19b). Clearly it was the exigency of the circumstances that prompted Peter's vision: the strict Jewish dietary laws had made
it exceedingly difficult to win over pagan converts. Preoccupied with this
problem, he unconsciously sought a solution and found it in his trance. In
any event, James, apparently accepting what Peter had regarded as a
revelation, approved a different standard for the pagan converts. It appears,
however, that for Paul even this concession by Peter and James did not go far
enough. Reports had reached Palestine that Paul preached the abandonment
of circumcision; but James, unable to reconcile himself to this, sent
emissaries to Antioch demanding that the Gentiles believing in Jesus should
be circumcised, and that they should observe the rest of the Mosaic laws and
customary practices.

The view summarized here of James the brother of Jesus strongly suggests
that he and Peter, who knew Jesus personally, were closer to him in outlook
than was Paul who, most likely, had never known Jesus personally. Some
New Testament specialists, however, have challenged this interpretation.
Thus David R. Catchpole writes that

> the appeal to subsequent [Jewish] Christian viewpoints must not concentrate
> on James and the Jerusalem church to such an extent that the positions of Paul
> and also of the Stephen group are neglected. Arguments for continuity must
> take into account the circumstantial pressures and theological climate.
> Whereas the position of James coincides with tendencies in Judaism, that of
> Stephen and Paul does not, and some starting-points for the divergence from
> Torah-centricity in e.g., Acts 6:13 and Rom. 14:14 must be found. Such can
> only be located in the teaching of Jesus, and together with the fact of Paul's
> earlier implacable opposition as a Pharisee to Christianity [i.e., to the
> Jewish–Christian group in Jerusalem], must indicate that Jesus was not a
> Pharisee. But in this case, the divergence of the Jerusalem church from Jesus is
> in no way a problem: the Acts–Galatian problem shows the circumstantial
> pressure to which that church was subjected . . .[24]

In a word, Catchpole sees a 're-Judaizing' tendency in the Jerusalem church
just as other scholars have imputed such a tendency to Matthew's Gospel.
Or in Bultmann's words: 'Presumably a regression [sic] had taken place so
that the old scruples and fidelity to the Law had gradually gained ground . . .

This is partly attributable to the personal influence of James, the Lord's brother, and is partly a reaction against the criticism of the Law and the temple-cult on the part of the Hellenistic[– Jewish] Church'.[25]

So the time has come to ask whether James the brother of Jesus authentically reflected Jesus' own outlook, or whether he diverged from it; and this question, in turn, requires an analysis of Jesus' distinctive outlook and his relationship to the various traditions of the elders.

5

Jesus' Distinctive Religious Virtuosity

We know next to nothing about Jesus' formative years, about his childhood. And yet Luke, as we have already noted, relates one episode that provides the key, perhaps, to the formation of Jesus' self-understanding. When he was 12 years of age, we are told, his parents brought him up to Jerusalem for the Passover feast, according to custom. We may assume that they travelled in the company of other pilgrims. On their return journey, discovering that the boy was not among the company, they returned to Jerusalem where they found him in the temple sitting among the teachers, impressing them with his questions and knowledge. When his parents saw him, 'they were astonished; and his mother said to him, "son, why have you treated us so? Behold, your father and I have been looking for you anxiously," And he said to them, "How is it that you sought me? Did you not know that I must be in my Father's house?"' (Luke 2:41ff). Note, '*my* Father's house'! From a very early age, then, Jesus evidently felt that he possessed an especially intimate relationship with God – as *his* Father. It is noteworthy that Luke's Gospel differs in this respect from Matthew's in the opening of the Lord's Prayer. While Matthew says, 'Our Father . . .', Luke says, simply, 'Father . . .'. And in John's Gospel we read that Jesus' compatriots regarded his healing on the sabbath as offensive; and that seeking to justify himself, Jesus answered: '*My* Father is working still, and I am working.' And John comments: 'This was why the Jews sought all the more to kill him, because he not only broke the sabbath, but also called God his Father, making himself equal with God' (5:17ff). One should not dismiss this as a later Christological insertion. The author of John's Gospel seems to be stating a fact here; and scholars are increasingly turning away from the older assumption that where Jesus' biography is concerned, nothing reliable can be learned from the Fourth Gospel.

Earlier I described Jesus as a 'charismatic religious virtuoso', a major characteristic of which is intense religiosity and the feeling of an especially close relationship with the divine. Jesus not only referred to God as *my*

Father, he used an Aramaic term of endearment in addressing God. Edward Schillebeeckx and other scholars have called this the '*Abba*' experience. *Abba* implies 'father dear', it is the word that young children, in particular, used in Jesus' time to address their fathers; and it is still used in Israel today. The word *Abba* appears in its Aramaic form in the Greek text of Mark's Gospel; and as the Greek texts are the earliest we possess, the transliteration in them of Aramaic words is highly significant. In Mark, Jesus is quoted as saying on the eve of his death, 'Abba [and then, translated], Father, all things are possible to thee. Take away this cup from me. Nevertheless not what I will, but what thou wilt' (Mark 14:36). *Abba* is also found twice in the epistles of Paul (Gal. 4:6; Rom. 8:15). Although the one and only time that this Aramaic word appears in the Gospels is in this Marcan passage, scholars cautiously suggest that calling God '*Abba*' was a persistent habit of Jesus' and that we should supply this same Aramaic word behind the Greek wherever the words 'the Father', 'Father' or 'my Father' appear in the Gospels. *Abba* is one of the most authentic words in the texts, in that it was most assuredly used by Jesus. Thus Schillebeeckx writes:

> What we gather in the first instance from the certain knowledge we have of Jesus' praying to God as *Abba* is the unconventional style of Jesus' intercourse with God, its unaffected and natural simplicity, which must have been inscribed on the hearts of the disciples, because this kind of praying to *Abba* at once became generally current in early Christianity.[1]

Luke's account of Jesus at the age of 12 suggests that already at that time he felt himself to be in a uniquely personal relationship with God. There is a counterpoint, however, to his relationship with God as *his Abba*, and that is his relationship with his own parents. His father does not figure at all in the Gospels, and Jesus appears to have been altogether estranged from his family:

> And his mother and brothers came; and standing outside they sent to him and called him. And a crowd was sitting about him; and they said to him, 'Your mother and your brothers [and your sisters] are outside, asking for you.' And he replied, 'Who are my mother and my brothers?' And looking around on those who sat about him, he said, 'Here are my mother and my brothers! Whoever does the will of God is my brother, and sister, and mother.' (Mark 3:31)

The special relationship Jesus believed he had with God the Father, together with his intense religiosity and his idiosyncratic words and deeds, led some of his friends to look upon him as 'mad'. When they heard that he had appointed disciples and given them authority to cast out demons, 'they went out to seize him, for they said, "He is beside himself"' (Mark 3:21). There is reason to believe, then, that neither his family nor his friends understood him, and that some even regarded him as not in his right mind.

As a versatile religious virtuoso, Jesus appears in several roles: healer, exorcist (magician), preacher, teacher, prophet, creator of parables and a Messianic figure. He appears in all these roles and yet in none of them exclusively. He spent the first 30 years of his life in southern Galilee, a period about which we know almost nothing. In the whole of the New Testament only one verse (Matt. 13:55; Mark 6:3) tells us that Jesus was a *tekton*, most likely a carpenter though the word can mean smith or stonemason. It is probable that Jesus followed the trade of Joseph who died, evidently, before Jesus began his ministry. There is no mention of Joseph, in contrast to Miriam (Mary), Jesus' mother, and his brothers Jacob (James) Joseph, Judah (Judas) and Simon. Sisters, though alluded to, are not named.

From the very beginning of his ministry Jesus is looked upon as 'different'. To be sure, he appears frequently in the synagogues of Galilee; he is, after all, a religious Jew. But what he says there and how he says it offends not only the learned but the plain people as well. 'And they were astonished at his teaching, for he taught them as one who had authority, and not as the scribes' (Mark 1:22ff). His healing methods may also have deviated from the traditional ones; for upon healing the leper, he instructed him to 'say nothing to anyone' and to show himself to the priest and offer for his cleansing what Moses commanded. But the leper, contrary to his instructions, talked freely about it and spread the news, 'so that Jesus could no longer enter a town, but was out in the country . . . ' (Mark 1:40ff). The scribes accuse him of being possessed by Beelzebul, and that it is 'by the prince of demons that he casts out demons' (Mark 3:22). To the scribes Jesus' words sound blasphemous, for in healing a paralytic he says, 'my son, your sins are forgiven' (Mark 2:5). In his home country he is looked upon as presumptuous, at the very least. Astonished (i.e., offended?) at what he has to say in the synagogue on the sabbath, they ask, "'Is not this the carpenter, the son of Mary and brother of James and Joses and Judas and Simon, and are not his sisters here with us?" And they took offence at him. And Jesus said to them, "a prophet is not without honour, except in his own country" . . . And he could do no mighty work there' (Mark 6:1–5).

Jesus repeatedly declared that he was able to heal the crippled and the sick, that is, those possessed by demons, only through their belief *in him and his power* (e.g., Mark 10:51–2). This, evidently, was enough to provoke the accusation that his work was done by Beelzebul. As Morton Smith has remarked, these accusations reflect a real difference between his methods and those of the scribes, a difference 'that led to his being charged with magic'. It was alleged 'that Jesus "had" a demon and did his exorcisms by this indwelling demonic power. Since this charge was not brought against the other exorcists they must have been thought to effect their exorcisms by other means, presumably prayer to God . . . Perhaps Jesus did not use such methods, but perhaps he did.'[2] The evidence suggests the former, for in healing a man who was deaf and who had a speech impediment, Jesus took him aside, 'put his fingers into his ears, and he spat and touched his tongue; and looking up to heaven, he sighed and said to him, *Ephphatha*, that is, "Be opened (Mark 7:33ff). Jesus used a similar method with a blind man, spitting on his eyes and laying hands upon him (Mark 8:22ff), in both cases without prayer to God. Likewise in the healing of the demoniac (Mark 5:1ff) there is no prayer; and 'magic' is surely suggested in the story of the woman who had haemorrhaged for 12 years and who 'came up behind him in the crowd and touched his garment. For she said, "If I touch even his garments, I shall be made well." And immediately the hemorrhage ceased . . . And Jesus, perceiving in himself that *power had gone forth from him*, immediately turned about in the crowd, and said, "Who touched my garments?" And when he discovered who it was and why she had done so, he said, "Daughter, your faith has made you well . . ."' (Mark 5:25ff). Jesus' healing of the daughter of the head of the synagogue also entailed no prayer. She appeared to be dead and Jesus simply took her by the hand and said, '*Talitha cumi*', that is, 'Talitha, rise!'. The texts, then, do seem to suggest that Jesus' healing methods were idiosyncratic, diverging from the traditional ones; and it is possible that this divergence, like others soon to be examined, was prompted by the special relationship he believed he had with his '*Abba*'.

Jesus in the Synagogues

The Gospel according to Luke sheds considerable light on the question of why Jesus' sermons in the synagogues not only astonished but offended the people. Luke's treatment of Jesus' experience in Nazareth, during a brief return to his home country, is significantly different from that of the other Synoptics. In Mark (6) and Matthew (13) the main point seems to be that his kin and fellow countrymen had regarded both his words and his actions as pretentious for a mere hometown *tekton*. Accorded no honour in his home country, he can do no 'mighty works' there, 'because of their unbelief'. In Luke, however, we find an account of what Jesus had to say in the synagogue:

And he came to Nazareth, where he had been brought up; and he went to the synagogue, as his custom was, on the sabbath day. And he stood up to read; and there was given to him the book of the prophet Isaiah. He opened the book and found the place where it was written, 'The Spirit of the Lord is upon me, because he has anointed me to preach good news to the poor. He has sent me to proclaim release to the captives and recovering of sight to the blind, to set at liberty those who are oppressed, to proclaim the acceptable year of the Lord'. (Luke 4:16–19; Isa. 61).

This citation of Isaiah is absent from Mark and Matthew. After reading this portion from the prophet and sitting down, Jesus, seeing that all eyes are upon him, says 'Today this scripture has been fulfilled in your hearing'. And those present wondered at his words, saying, 'Is not this Joseph's son?'. It is Jesus' response to this remark, or what might be called his *midrash*[3] on the Isaiah passage, that provokes their anger:

Doubtless you will quote to me this proverb, 'physician, heal yourself; what we have heard you did at Capernaum, do here also in your own country'. And he said, 'truly, I say to you, no prophet is acceptable in his own country. But in truth, I tell you, there were many widows in Israel in the days of Elijah, when the heaven was shut up three years and six months, when there came a great famine over all the land; and Elijah was sent to none of them but only to Zarephath, in the land of Sidon, to a woman who was a widow. And there were many lepers in Israel in the time of the prophet Elisha; and none of them was cleansed, but only Naaman the Syrian.' When they heard this, all in the synagogue were filled with wrath. And they rose up and put him out of the city, and led him to the brow of the hill on which their city was built, that they might throw him down headlong. But passing through the midst of them he went away. (Luke 4:16–30)

As James A. Sanders has convincingly observed,

Luke makes it very clear . . . that the offense taken by the faithful of Nazareth was at Jesus' *midrash* on the Isaiah passage. What in Mark and Matthew, is a rejection by Jesus of the people's *apistia* [unbelief; lack of faith], in Luke is a rejection of Jesus by the people because of his sermon. The puzzled reaction of the people after Jesus reads the passage from Isa. 61, plus 58:6, is shown in their single question, 'Is not this Joseph's son?'.[4]

They are puzzled that one of their fellow villagers takes it upon himself to proclaim that the great day has arrived; familiarity breeds contempt. But their puzzlement soon becomes extreme anger and they turn into a lynching party. What was it that made them so angry? 'In Luke', Sanders suggests, 'it is not Jesus' general wisdom nor even his works which offend the people, as is apparently the case in Mark and Matthew; in Luke it is the specific application Jesus makes of the Isaiah passage.' By the juxtaposition of the acts of Elijah and Elisha and Isaiah 61, Jesus implies 'that the words meaning poor, captive, blind and oppressed do not apply exclusively to any in-group but, on the contrary, apply to those to whom God wishes them to apply. God sent Elijah and Elisha to outsiders, the Sidonian widow and the Syrian leper.'[5] What Jesus' fellow villagers found offensive, then, was not only that he had arrogated to himself this passage of unique prophetic authority, but that he also declared that the *aphesis* (redemption) of which it speaks will include in the End Time those outside Israel. Who will be redeemed is a decision of God alone. Sanders believes that the religiously exclusivist attitude of the Qumranites–Essenes was the foil against which Jesus' *midrash* in Luke 4 was aimed. Be that as it may, Luke 4 strongly suggests that although Jesus appears here to reaffirm the universalism so characteristic of Isaiah, he does so in a manner not designed to endear himself to his listeners.

Jesus in the Gospel According to John

It is John's Gospel that gives us considerable insight into Jesus' idiosyncrasies. Before we enter into substantive matters, however, we need to say a word about the trustworthiness of this Gospel for historical purposes. Earlier we saw that in the nineteenth century New Testament specialists rejected the use of John for scholarly research into the life of Jesus, and that as a consequence the Synoptics gained the dominant position in New Testament studies. In the early decades of the twentieth century, however, scholars began to challenge this deprecation of John. P. Gardner Smith, for example, wrote that 'if in the Fourth Gospel we have a survival of a type of first century Christianity which owed nothing to synoptic developments, and which originated in a quite different intellectual atmosphere, its historical value may be very great indeed'. He then goes on to say that 'where the Fourth Gospel differs from the synoptics it may henceforth be wise to treat its testimony with rather more respect than it has lately received, and perhaps in not a few cases it may prove to be right'.[6] And R. H. Lightfoot has stressed that John 'plants the roots of his gospel most firmly in history and historical facts ... There can be no doubt that the evangelist believed himself to be giving the true interpretation not only of the Christian revelation, but of the historical Lord Himself.' And in the same vein: 'That St. John was altogether indifferent to historical fact is out of the question; *no evangelist* is more insistent than he on the historical truth which he regards as essential to the Gospel.'[7] To take but one example, John 'may be historically more correct than Mark in narrating more than one journey of the Lord from Galilee to Jerusalem in the course of the ministry'.[8]

One conspicuous difference between the Synoptics and John is the latter's use of the term 'the Jews'. In Matthew and Mark this term occurs only in the editorial contexts (Matt. 28:15; Mark 7:3); in Luke we meet it also at 7:3 and

23:51. In these Gospels opposition to Jesus is normally expressed via particular parties, notably Pharisees, Sadducees, or both. But throughout John, Jesus' opponents are 'the Jews', the term occurring some 70 times, while 'the Pharisees' appears barely 20 times and the Sadducees not at all. This, however, should detract not at all from John's trustworthiness. For, as we shall see, not only in John but in the other Gospels as well, it is Jesus' idiosyncratic conduct and his claims of unique authority which made him both popular and unpopular, depending on the circles in which he moved.

Right at the outset we learn from John that when Jesus came to his own home, 'his own people received him not' (1:11); and that those who came from places outside his home were quite sceptical of the claims made for his Messianic status. For when Jesus found Philip and he, in turn, found Nathanael and said to him, 'We have found him of whom Moses in the law and also the prophets wrote, Jesus of Nazareth, the son of Joseph', Nathanael replied: 'Can anything good come out of Nazareth?' (1:43ff). John also reveals, in line with what we learn from the Synoptics, the strained if not estranged relationship that Jesus had with his mother. At the marriage ceremony at Cana in Galilee, when the wine fails, she informs Jesus of the fact and he replies, rather harshly, 'O woman, what have you to do with me?' (2:1ff).

During a visit to Jerusalem Jesus heals a man on the sabbath who had been unable to walk for a very long time. Jesus heals on this occasion simply by saying, 'Rise, take up your pallet and walk'. In this particular instance there is no 'work' involved in Jesus' healing and it is not he who is criticized but rather the man who is cured – for carrying his pallet, i.e., 'working', on the sabbath. We may assume, however, in accordance with what we learn from the Synoptics, that Jesus also used his other methods on the sabbath; moreover, that he healed not only those whose lives were immediately in danger, which was allowed under the Mosaic Law, but the chronically ill as well. John remarks that 'this was why the Jews persecuted Jesus, because he did this on the sabbath'. This is the context in which Jesus replies to his critics by saying, 'My Father is working still, and I am working'. And John comments: 'This was why the Jews sought all the more to kill him, because he not only broke the sabbath but also called God his Father, making himself equal with God' (5:1–18). The inescapable impression we get from John is that Jesus did in fact claim unique authority for himself. His claim was not that he was 'equal with God', since he says 'Truly, truly, . . . the son can do nothing of his own accord' (5:19); and 'I can do nothing on my own authority' (5:30). Rather his claim was that 'the works which the Father has granted me to accomplish, these very works which I am doing, bear me witness that the Father has sent me' (5:36).

Now although there can be little doubt that in 6:41ff, we have the intrusion of christological dogma, there can be equally little doubt that this material contains a historical nucleus. For the embarrassing nature of what John recounts here is proof enough of its authenticity. When Jesus says that he 'came down from heaven', the Jews murmur, 'Is not this Jesus, the son of Joseph, whose father and mother we know? How does he now say, "I have come down from heaven"?' (6:41ff). Whatever it was that Jesus said precisely in the synagogue at Capernaum, it was found to be so offensive that 'many of his disciples, when they heard it, said, "This is a hard saying; who can listen to it?"' (6:60). As a result, soon after this 'many of his disciples drew back and no longer went about with him' (6:66).

There are clear signs in the texts of ambivalence towards Jesus. On the one hand, he seems to be popular – some people, indeed, perceiving him as the Davidic, political-military Messiah who will liberate Israel from Roman domination. For John has the people say, 'This is indeed the prophet who is to come into the world' (6:14). Apparently, however, that is not the role that Jesus saw for himself: 'Perceiving then that they were about to come and take him by force to make him king [i.e., to receive him as the Messianic king], Jesus withdrew again to the hills by himself' (6:15). On the other hand, some of his words and deeds were found to be so offensive that he had to remain in Galilee and could not go about safely in Judea. There is scepticism and confusion about him: if he has a special relationship with the Father, why does he go about in secret instead of coming out in the open and proving who he is? His brothers, no less sceptical than others, urge him to go down to Judea for the feast of Tabernacles: 'Leave here and go to Judea, that your disciples may see the works you are doing. For no man works in secret if he seeks to be known openly. If you do these things, show yourself to the world. For even his brothers did not believe in him' (7:1–5). And 'After his brothers had gone up to the feast, then he also went up, not publicly but in private. The Jews were looking for him at the feast, and saying, "Where is he?". And there was much muttering about him among the people. While some said, "He is a good man", others said, "No, he is leading the people astray" (7.10ff). Jesus, then, was both popular and unpopular and there was considerable confusion about the role he was to play in the life of the nation.

There is no reason to doubt that in the eyes of some of Jesus' contemporaries Jesus was a 'wise man', 'who wrought surprising feats' (Josephus, *Antiq.* 18:63). These phrases, unlike others in Josephus' famous statement about Jesus, most probably are not a later interpolation. Geza Vermes has attempted to situate Jesus among the Galilean *Hasidim* who were believed to possess extraordinary powers due to their special relationship with God. As charismatic individuals, their perceived powers were independent of any institution. The 'unsophisticated religious ambience of Galilee', writes Vermes, 'was apt to produce holy men of the *hasidic* type and . . . their success in that province was attributed to the simple spiritual demands of the Galilean nature, and perhaps also to a lively folk memory concerning the miraculous deeds of the great prophet Elijah'[9] with whom Jesus was, of course, compared. Galilean *Hasidim* (Heb. plural of *Hasid*), like Honi and Hanina ben Doza, conducted themselves in highly individual ways and sometimes in opposition to the prevailing norms. An inevitable tension therefore existed between these charismatics and the representatives of institutional Judaism. Vermes cites two main reasons for the tension: the Hasidic lack of conformity in certain matters of religious practice, and 'the threat posed by the unrestrained authority of the charismatic to the upholders of the established religious order'. Hanina, for example, "not only flouted the rabbinic code of conduct by walking alone at night, but he owned goats which he should not have done in Palestine according to the Mishnah, and even went so far as to carry the unclean carcass of a snake ... The charismatics' informal familiarity with God and confidence in the efficacy of their words was also deeply disliked by those whose authority derived from established channels.'[10] According to the Synoptic evidence, 'sympathetic witnesses of his Galilean activity recognized Jesus as either John the Baptist, Elijah, or a prophet, a view apparently shared by the entourage of Herod Antipas, with the possible hint at the notion of a prophet *redivivus*' (Mark 8:28; Matt. 16:14; Luke 9:19; Mark 6:15; Luke 9:8).[11] And a link with Elijah and Elisha is acknowledged by Jesus when he expressly cites them (Luke 4:25–7).

So we may assume that Jesus was perceived as a performer of 'surprising feats' and that he was a 'wise man', in the words of Josephus. He taught in the temple where his audience hung on every word. They marvelled at what he had to say; but they also asked, 'How is it that this man has learning [or knows his letters], when he has never studied?' (John 7:14). Here we see at least one source of tension between Jesus and the representatives of institutional Judaism.[12] It was not only his 'surprising feats' and his 'magical charisma' that put him at odds with the religious establishment; an equally important factor may have been, in Max Weber's words, his 'reaction to the unique concern for erudition in the law characteristic of Jewish piety. The Christian evangel', Weber continues,

> arose in opposition to this legalistic erudition, as a non-intellectual's proclamation directed to non-intellectuals, to the 'poor in spirit'. Jesus understood and interpreted the 'law', from which he desired to remove not even a letter, in a fashion common to the lowly and the unlearned, the pious folk of the countryside and the small towns who understood the law in their own way and in accordance with the needs of their own occupations, in contrast to the Hellenized, wealthy and upper-class people and to the erudite scholars and Pharisees trained in casuistry. Jesus' interpretation of the Jewish law was milder than theirs in regard to ritual prescriptions, particularly in regard to the keeping of the Sabbath, but stricter than theirs in other respects, e.g., in regard to the grounds for divorce ...

[Jesus'] self-esteem was grounded in the knowledge that he, the non-scholar, possessed both the charisma requisite for the control of demons and a tremendous preaching ability, far surpassing that of any scholar or Pharisee. This self-esteem involved the conviction that his power to exorcise demons was operative only among the people who believed in him, even if they be heathens, not in his hometown and his own family and among the wealthy and highborn of the land, the scholars, and legalistic virtuosi – among none of these did he find the faith that gave him the magical power to work miracles. He did find such faith among the poor and the oppressed, among publicans and sinners, and even among Roman soldiers. It should never be forgotten that these charismatic powers were the absolutely decisive components in Jesus' feelings concerning his messiahship . . .

Jesus recognized two absolutely mortal sins. One was the 'sin against the spirit' committed by the scriptural scholar who disesteemed charisma and its bearers. The other was unbrotherly arrogance, such as the arrogance of the intellectual toward the poor in spirit, when the intellectual hurls at his brother the exclamation, 'Thou fool!'.[13]

When Jesus responds to his scholar-intellectual critics, it is almost always by means of prooftexts from the Scriptures or arguments based upon them. Criticized for healing on the sabbath, he replies: 'If on the sabbath a man receives circumcision, so that the law of Moses may not be broken, are you angry with me because on the sabbath I made a man's whole body well? Do not judge by appearances, but judge with right judgment' (John 7:23–4). But in Judea and in Jerusalem, in particular, he continued to engender confusion. Some said 'This is really the prophet. Others said, This is the Christ [Messiah]'. But some said, 'Is the Christ to come from Galilee? Has not the Scripture said that the Christ descended from David, and comes from Bethlehem,[14] the village where David was? So there was a division among the people over him' (John 7:40ff).

In John (ch. 11) we read the narrative concerning Lazarus, who was near death or mistaken for dead, and how Jesus revived him. In this instance Jesus' 'surprising feat' is accomplished by prayer:

'Father, I thank thee that thou hast heard me. I knew that thou hearest me always, but I have said this on account of the people standing by, that they may believe that thou didst send me.' When he had said this, he cried with a loud voice, 'Lazarus, come out'. (11:41ff)

Those who witnessed this event, now coming to believe in him, reported the news to the chief priests and the Pharisees who convened the council and said:

'What are we to do? For this man performs many signs. If we let him go on thus, everyone will believe in him [as the Davidic Messiah], and the Romans will come and destroy both our holy place and our nation?' But one of them, Caiaphas, who was high priest that year, said to them, 'You know nothing at all; you do not understand that it is expedient for you that one man should die for the people, and that the whole nation should not perish' . . . So from that day on they took counsel how to put him to death. (11:45–53)

In these terms, Jesus' revival of Lazarus appears to have been a turning point; since it was in consequence of this event that the Council convened, fearing that the crowds would take Jesus' 'surprising feats' as a sign of his Messiahship, and that this, in turn, would provoke extreme punitive measures on the part of the Romans. Jesus was now at the height of his popularity. Great crowds, hearing that Jesus was coming up to Jerusalem, 'took branches of palm trees and went out to meet him, crying "Hosanna! Blessed is he who comes in the name of the Lord, even the King of Israel!"' (John 12:12ff). Look, 'the world has gone after him', the religious leaders remarked, their fears now greater than ever as to how the Roman authorities would react. The multitude, viewing Jesus' entry to Jerusalem as a 'triumphant' one, waved branches in his honour, as an expression of their expectation of the national liberty which he would win for them. And later this gave an added opportunity to the Roman soldiers in their mockery of him. But as we shall see in Part III of this present work, though the fears of the Jewish leaders were justified – in the light of previous Roman reactions to Messianic demonstrations – neither they nor the multitude had grasped the meaning of Jesus' entry as he himself had conceived it.

As we reflect on the Gospel of John and that of the Synoptics, we can see rather clearly why Jesus was at once popular and unpopular. He was often among the people and his message was strongly related to his own person. He believed himself to be uniquely connected with the kingdom he preached. He was a highly successful healer and his chief concern was with the needy and the outcasts. He believed himself sent to the sick (Matt. 9:12), to the 'last' (Luke 19:10), and to the poor (Matt. 11:5). He ate with tax collectors and sinners (Matt. 9:11 and parallels). This naturally made for the popularity of Jesus among the simple folk. Perhaps it would be safe to say that his popularity was mainly among the poor, the sick, the down and out and the outcasts. The fact that he had a large adherence from among such elements must have been one reason for the tension between him and the authorities. But he was also unpopular with many in the crowd, as we have seen in our analysis of Luke 4:16ff. He said things which offended the religio-national sentiments of his audience; and he offended by the unique emphasis he placed on the importance of his own person and by his claim of the right to forgive sins. Doubtless, John records historical fact when he states that many of Jesus' disciples went back and walked no more with him

6:66). Thus it is probably true, as Jacob Jocz has observed, that 'Jesus was popular and unpopular at the same time. His power of personality, his beauty of speech, his lofty teaching, his care for the simple and lowly were an attraction. But only the small group round the twelve and a few outsiders, men and women, formed the inner circle of discipleship. The rest remained outside . . . '.[15]

6

Jesus and the Torah (the Law)

The Sabbath

In Mark 2:23ff, we hear the Pharisees criticizing Jesus, holding him responsible, as it were, for the conduct of his disciples. It was a sabbath day and they were in the field plucking grain. 'Look', say the Pharisees to Jesus, 'why are they doing what is not lawful on the sabbath?' The first observation we need to make here is that it is not Jesus but his disciples who are accused of violating the sabbath. A second observation, equally important, is that Jesus disagrees that a violation of the sabbath has in fact taken place, and he defends his disciples' conduct by citing Scripture: 'Have you never read what David did', he replies to the Pharisees, 'when he was in need and was hungry, he and those who were with him: how he entered the house of God, when Abiathar was high priest, and ate the bread of the Presence, which it is not lawful for any but the priests to eat, and also gave it to those who were with him?' (Mark 2:25–6). This exchange is fairly typical of all of Jesus' encounters with his critics and intellectual adversaries: he either provides prooftexts from the Scriptures or arguments based upon them in order to defend his outlook. We can therefore say that although there were definite religio-ideological differences between Jesus and some of the Pharisees, he rejected the accusation that his disciples had violated the sabbath. It is noteworthy, moreover, that Jesus' method of healing by command alone – 'Stretch out your arm' – is the only cure placed unanimously by the Synoptics on a sabbath day (Mark 3:1–5; Matt. 12:9–13; Luke 6:6–10). Speech would not be construed as 'work' infringing the law governing the day of rest. And even when he heals by word alone, he defends his conduct by means of an argument: 'Is it lawful on the sabbath to do good or to do harm, to save life or to kill?' (Mark 3:4).

There seem to have been other occasions, however, when Jesus went beyond healing by word alone on the sabbath. In Luke 13:10ff we read about the woman who had had an infirmity for 18 years: 'she was bent over and could not fully straighten herself. And when Jesus saw her, he called her and said to her, "Woman, you are freed from your infirmity". And he laid his hands upon her, and immediately she was made straight, and she praised God' (Luke 13:10–13). In response to the indignation of those present in the synagogue, Jesus defends his actions by pointing out the inconsistency in theirs: 'You hypocrites! Does not each of you on the sabbath untie his ox or his ass from the manger, and lead it away to water it? And ought not this woman, a daughter of Abraham whom Satan bound for 18 years, be loosed from this bond on the sabbath day?' (Luke 13:15ff). In John's Gospel Jesus also defends his healing on the sabbath by calling attention to the inconsistencies in current practices: 'Moses gave you circumcision (not that it is from Moses, but from the fathers), and you circumcise a man [i.e., a male infant] upon the sabbath. If on the sabbath a man receives circumcision, so that the law of Moses may not be broken, are you angry with me because on the sabbath I made a man's whole body well? Do not judge by appearances, but judge with right judgement' (John 7:22–4). And in Matthew, in response to the question, 'Is it lawful to heal on the sabbath?', Jesus says: 'What man of you, if he has one sheep and it falls into a pit on the sabbath, will not lay hold of it and lift it out? Of how much more value is a man than a sheep! So it is lawful to do good on the sabbath' (Matt.12:9ff). In Jesus' response to his Pharisaic critics we can discern a social element. As a child of the Galilean countryside who had never visited Sepphoris or any other large city of the Galilee, he was bound to have his differences with some of the scholars who had grown up in the intellectual environment of the 'polis' of Jerusalem. Members of such urban circles asked, 'What good can come out of Nazareth?' But, as Max Weber observed, 'Jesus' knowledge of the law and his observance of it was representative of that average lawfulness which was actually demonstrated by men engaged in practical work, who could not afford to let their sheep lie in wells, even on the Sabbath.[1]

Both Jewish and Christian scholars, basing themselves on the earliest strata of the Talmud, have argued convincingly that Jesus' religious philosophy was congruent with that of the liberal Pharisees. Take, for example, Jesus' famous epigram found in Mark 2:27: 'The sabbath was made for man, not man for the sabbath . . .' Many scholars are in agreement that in practice the rabbis' teachings were in basic accord with this principle. The rabbis based themselves on Leviticus 18:5: 'You shall . . . keep my statutes and my ordinances, by doing which a man shall live . . .' The commandments were given that man might *live* by them. This text provided the scriptural ground for the rabbinic approval of many acts, which in and of themselves would have been violations of the sabbath, were they not necessary for the preservation of human life (TB[2] Yoma 85b). Indeed, it was universally accepted among the rabbis that the sabbath law was in certain emergencies to be disregarded. Some based their rulings on Lev.18:5, others on Exod.31:16: 'the people of Israel shall keep the sabbath, observing the sabbath throughout their generations, as a perpetual covenant'. This was taken to mean that one may profane a particular sabbath in order to preserve a human being so that he may observe many sabbaths. And they saw even further justification for this policy in Exodus 31:14: 'You shall keep the sabbath, because it is holy unto you.' *Unto you*, they argued, is the sabbath given over, and you are not given over to the sabbath. Thus the general rule emerged that for the preservation of human life, the sabbath law is waived. This rule emerged quite early and certainly no later than the period of the Maccabean revolt. The Book of Maccabees (I.2:39ff) informs us that the religious authorities sanctioned self-defence on the sabbath; and Josephus provides us with an enlightening account of the circumstances that gave rise to this policy. The Maccabean uprising was formally launched with the now famous battle-cry of Mattathias: 'Whoever is zealous for our country's laws and the worship of God, let him come with me!' 'So saying', wrote Josephus,

he set out with his sons into the wilderness, leaving behind all his property in the village. And many others also did the same, and fled with their children and wives into the wilderness, where they lived in caves. But when the king's officers heard of this, they took as many soldiers as were then in the citadel of Jerusalem, and pursued the Jews into the wilderness; and when they had overtaken them, they tried at first to persuade them to repent and choose a course which was for their own good, and not to bring upon the king's men the necessity of treating them in accordance with the laws of war; the Jews, however, did not accept their terms, but showed a hostile spirit, whereupon they attacked them on the sabbath-day and burned them in the caves, just as they were, for not only did the Jews not resist, but they did not even stop up the entrances to the caves. And they forebore to resist because of the day, being unwilling to violate the dignity of sabbath even when in difficulties, for the law requires us to rest on that day. And about a thousand with their wives and children died by suffocation in the caves; but many escaped and joined Mattathias, whom they appointed their leader. And he instructed them to fight even on the sabbath, saying that if for the sake of observing the law they failed to do so, they would be their own enemies, for their foes would attack them on that day, and unless they resisted, nothing would prevent them from all perishing without striking a blow. These words persuaded them, and to this day we continue the practice of fighting even on the sabbath whenever it becomes necessary (*Antiq*.12:271–7).

The preservation of life (Heb. *Pikuah Nefesh*) is so well established a principle in the Mishnah that it is to be applied even in cases of doubt: 'If a man has a pain in his throat, they may drop medicine into his mouth on the sabbath, since there is doubt whether life is in danger, and whenever there is

doubt whether life is in danger this overrides the sabbath' (Mish. Yoma 8:6).
Now, where Jesus appears to have differed with the Pharisees, even the most
liberal, is in his willingness to heal on the sabbath even when there was no
apparent danger to life. In John 7:23, as we have seen, Jesus defends his
action with the analogy of circumcision, the most conspicuous relaxation of
the sabbath law. Israel Abrahams has called attention to the fact that 'In
[TB] Yoma 85b the very words of John 7:23 are paralleled, and the saving of
life derived by an a fortiori argument from the rite of circumcision.'[3] The
principle underlying the relaxation of the sabbath law for circumcision is
this: although as a rule surgery is prohibited on the sabbath, the sabbath is
'waived' in order to perform the great *mitzvah* [obligation to God] of
circumcision. Jesus, however, went beyond the Pharisaic position in that he
treated the chronically ill on the sabbath. He attended to maladies,
infirmities and other ailments for which the treatment could be postponed
without fear of life-threatening consequences. Jesus' justification of his
actions is based on the assertion that the Pharisees would permit the relief of
an animal's distress on the sabbath – a principle which is firmly a part of the
Pharisaic–Rabbinic tradition (*Tosefta* Sabbath 15; TB Sabbath 128b; Heb.
Tsaar baal haim). How much stronger then is the case for relieving a human
being's distress on the sabbath.

The impression is therefore unavoidable that Jesus' outlook was highly
distinctive. For him the chief criterion for the validity of a specific *halakhah*
(ordinance) is its compatibility with the love command. When Jesus refers to
the well-known verse from Hosea 6:6, 'For I desire mercy, and not sacrifice,
and the knowledge of God rather than burnt offerings' (Matt.12:7), Jesus is
asserting that David took the freedom to violate sacred food but that the
priest had to overlook the breach because God requires *hesed*, i.e., love and
mercy. Analogously he implies that the Pharisees ought to overlook his
disciples' plucking (or rubbing grain, or both) to assuage their hunger. Jesus
also applies the well-known hermeneutical rule of the rabbis called in
Hebrew *Kal vehomer*, which deduced the weightier from the less weighty and
vice versa. He argues that if one will waive the sabbath to save an animal,
then one may certainly do so to heal a human. Apparently the man who
suffered from dropsy (Luke 14:1–6) was in no immediate danger of losing
his life; he had been ill for some time, and he could have waited for
treatment one more day. But it was Jesus' attitude that one should never
delay an act of mercy. Similarly he applies the *Kal vehomer* principle when he
argues, in effect, that if one may set right one organ on the sabbath, then one
may surely heal the whole body. Jesus' critics and interrogators find it
difficult to respond to his arguments. As Phillip Sigal has observed, 'The
important point to notice in all of this is that Jesus does not simply negate the
challenge by rejecting the Sabbath, or by countering that the *Pharisaioi* offer

arguments of no validity.'⁴ Jesus does not simply dismiss them or shrug them off..He does not concede that either he or his disciples are in violation of the sabbath; instead he presents alternative interpretations, often citing prooftexts. Neither Jesus, nor his disciples and followers, took the sabbath laws lightly. This is borne out by the fact that after the crucifixion they postponed taking care of him until after the sabbath. In none of the sabbath controversies is Jesus revealed as denying the validity of the sabbath observance; in all of these controversies he is revealed as having a less rigid and otherwise distinctive attitude towards the sabbath law. The question remains, however, whether Jesus' attitude in this respect was unique and original to him, or whether it was common to the more liberal Pharisees of his day. Some scholars, citing the Talmud, have argued the latter position; other scholars have protested that it is methodologically problematic to use the Talmud as a source for the Jewish practices and ordinances in the period prior to AD 70. To do justice to the question of the nature and extent of Jesus' originality, we have to examine his attitude towards other issues.

Dietary Laws (Kashrut) and Hygiene

Chapter 7 of the Gospel According to Mark raises several key issues concerning Jesus' attitude towards the 'tradition of the elders'. The chapter opens by relating that several Pharisees had gathered together with Jesus and some scribes who had come from Jerusalem. The Pharisees and scribes observed that some of his disciples ate with hands unwashed. Then follows a parenthetic remark by the evangelist: '(For the Pharisees and all the Jews, do not eat unless they wash their hands, observing the tradition of the elders; and when they come from the market place, they do not eat unless they purify themselves; and there are many other traditions which they observe, the washing of cups and pots and vessels of bronze.) And the Pharisees and the scribes asked him "Why do your disciples not live according to the tradition of the elders, but eat with hands defiled?"' (7:1–5). The first observation to be made here is that it is *not* Jesus who is accused of this lapse, but rather the disciples; and, indeed, not all of his disciples but only *some* of them (7:2). The second observation is that 'all the Jews' (verse 3) may be an inaccuracy. The debate continued well into Talmudic times whether the washing of hands before eating was obligatory for all Jews. Nevertheless, it is clear from Mark and the other Gospels that already in the first century many pious Jews followed the tradition of the elders in this respect – notably Jesus himself and most of his disciples, since the Pharisees accuse only *some* of not doing so.

How does Jesus reply to his questioners? He does not directly defend the behaviour of those who failed to wash their hands, but changes the subject

X / instead. He not only accuses them of hypocrisy, but worse. After quoting from Isaiah 29:13 he says, 'You leave the commandment of God, and hold fast the tradition of man' (Mark 7:6–8). As Jesus proceeds to explain this statement, it becomes apparent that from his standpoint some of the Pharisaic teachings appeared to contradict the law of Moses:

> And he said to them, "You have a fine way of rejecting the commandment of God, in order to keep your tradition!' For Moses said, 'Honour your father and mother'; and 'He who speaks evil of father or mother, let him surely die'; but you say, 'If a man tells his father or his mother, What you would have gained from me is *corban*' (that is, an offering to God) – then you no longer permit him to do anything for his father or mother, thus making void the word of God through your tradition which you hand on. And many such things you do (Mark 7:9–13).

Matthew's treatment of this event is significantly different. Like Mark he has the questioners ask Jesus why the disciples violate the tradition by not washing their hands before eating; and like Mark Matthew has Jesus reply with a reprimand of the Pharisees for transgressing the commandment of God for the sake of their tradition. Matthew then has Jesus draw a lesson from this. In Phillip Sigal's words,

> that a vow, contrary to the Torah, which proceeds from a person's mouth defiles a person, not some exterior agent that enters a person; that is, the source of human sin is within oneself. When the disciples want a better response, Jesus replies with a sermonette on the source of the distortion of the ethical imperative, the human heart, as in Genesis 8:21, and he emphasizes that when eating with unwashed hands, placing the food into one's mouth with [an] impure hand, does not lead to ethical impurity or sin, for the food ends up in a sewer, but the human heart designs sin. At no point does Jesus speak of dietary practices.[5]

Mark, however, does make a transition to dietary matters. The disciples request a clarification of Jesus' parable, and he replies, 'Do you not see that whatever goes into a man from the outside cannot defile him, since it enters, not his heart but his stomach, and so passes on?' And Mark inserts the editorial comment: '(Thus he declared all foods clean.)' (7:19b). Thus Mark, in Sigal's words again, 'proceeds to redact the metaphorical, parabolic *haggadah* [homily] of Jesus into a *halakhic* revolution: that Jesus has abolished *kashrut*, the dietary practices. Mark is speaking here from later Christian perspective just as he must explain to a predominantly Gentile church unversed in Judaism, what the purity practices were all about (verses 3–4) . . .'[6]

We have to choose between Mark and Matthew in this regard; and there can be no doubt that it is Matthew's version, not Mark's, that is supported by the other evidence of the New Testament. For as we have seen, when Peter fell into a trance and heard the voice urging him to eat 'all kinds of animals and reptiles and birds of the air', he replied, 'No Lord; for I have never eaten anything that is common or unclean' (Acts 10:9–14). If Peter never ate anything regarded as unclean under Jewish law, is it possible to believe that Jesus 'declared all foods clean'? If Jesus had believed or said such a thing, why would not Paul have relied on him when he dismissed the need to observe the food laws? And why was James the brother of Jesus among the most ardent advocates of the written and oral Law? It was in the presence of the followers of this same James, let us remember, that Peter and Barnabas were afraid to eat with Gentiles, keeping themselves apart from the uncircumcised and abstaining from forbidden foods (Gal. 2:12–13). Judging from the book of Acts, then, no one would have supposed that Jesus had set aside any dietary laws. On the contrary, Peter in Acts 10:14 has never heard of any such declaration; and despite Peter's vision (Acts 10:10–16; 11:5–10), the Jerusalem apostles retained food prohibitions for Gentile converts (15:29; 21:25). Yet Mark (7:19) wants us to believe that Jesus had declared all foods clean. It is also noteworthy in this connection that if Luke based himself on Mark, as many scholars believe, he omitted every passage that would modify or abrogate a Mosaic ordinance (Mark 2:27, 7:1–23; 10:2–12, 12:31b–34).

If we compare the Marcan and Matthean versions of the matter in question, we can see that the latter conveys Jesus' concern with what should take precedence. Christopher Rowland has decribed this concern well: 'In Matthew', writes Rowland,

it would appear that Jesus thought the issue of external cleanness trivial compared with moral uncleanness. If this emphasis is the original one (which has been lost in Mark's Gospel because of concern for the Gentile Christians and their rejection of the food laws), then what we have is an emphasis by Jesus on the words and deeds of an individual as being the important evidence of his character rather than that which he received from outside himself. The Matthean version is not so much a rejection of the food laws as a statement about the supreme importance of man's behaviour and his inner motives and desires as a test of his character.

. . . the evidence of the Gospels does not allow us to conclude that Jesus was against the law of Moses. The tradition shows him interpreting the Torah, even though he frequently comes to very different conclusions from those which were commonly held. Even so, these conclusions are more often than not based on the words of the Scripture and follow the traditional pattern of argument and exegesis.[7]

Romans 14:14ff sheds some light on the problems that already had emerged in Paul's time as a consequence of the presence of Gentile converts in the Jewish–Christian communities outside Palestine. It is clear that these passages in

Paul's letter were written in response to a conflict that had arisen over the food laws between the Jewish and Gentile Christians. Paul is trying to mediate between them: 'If your brother is being injured by what you eat, you are no longer walking in love. Do not let what you eat cause the ruin of one for whom Christ died . . . Do not, for the sake of food, destroy the work of God. Everything is indeed clean, but it is wrong for any one to make others fall by what he eats; it is not right to eat meat or drink wine or do anything that makes your brother stumble' (Rom. 14:14–21). Somewhat later, the author of Mark's Gospel, writing for a Roman audience, faced the same issue and found it expedient to draw the editorial conclusion for his readers that Jesus had not intended that they should adopt Jewish scruples in this matter. So if Jesus in fact said what is attributed to him in Mark 7:18ff, and Matthew 5.17ff, it was certainly no attack upon the law. It was rather a reaffirmation of the love commandments and the prophetic teaching concerning the heart. Like the prophets before him, Jesus believed that real defilement is an inward matter.

The Issue of Divorce

On the matter of divorce, the Deuteronomic law states:

> When a man takes a wife and marries her, if then she finds no favour in his eyes because he has found some indecency in her, and he writes her a bill of divorce and puts it in her hand and sends her out of his house, and she departs out of his house, and if she goes and becomes another man's wife, and the latter husband dislikes her and writes her a bill of divorce and puts it in her hand and sends her out of his house, or if the latter husband dies, who took her to be his wife, then her former husband, who sent her away, may not take her again to be his wife, after she has been defiled; for that is an abomination before the Lord . . . (Deut. 24:1–4)

It would appear, according to Josephus, that this law was still in effect in the first century. For he writes: 'Some time afterwards Salome had occasion to quarrel with Costobarus and soon sent him a document [i.e., a bill of divorcement] dissolving their marriage, which was not in accordance with Jewish law. For it is (only) the man who is permitted by us to do this, and not even a divorced woman may marry again on her own initiative unless her former husband consents. Salome, however, did not choose to follow her country's law but acted on her own authority and repudiated her marriage' (*Antiq.* 15:259–60). Now in Mark 10:2ff we read that the Pharisees came up and, in order to test Jesus, asked: 'Is it lawful for a man to divorce his wife?' The very asking of this question suggests that the law had come under review, so to speak, within the Pharisaic movement. Was Jesus being asked to take a stand towards the respective positions of the two major Pharisaic schools? In any event he replied to their question thus:

> 'What did Moses command you?' They said, 'Moses allowed a man to write a certificate of divorce, and to put her away.' But Jesus said to them, 'For your hardness of heart he wrote you this commandment.' But from the beginning of creation, 'God made them male and female'. 'For this reason a man shall leave his father and mother and be joined to his wife, and the two shall become one.' So they are no longer two but one. What therefore God has joined together, let not man put asunder' (Mark 10:2–9).

This saying of Jesus has been widely regarded by scholars as a prime example of his complete opposition to the law of Moses. Not atypical in this regard is David R. Catchpole, who writes, 'Jesus' ruling on divorce is a ruling against Moses and therefore against Pharisaism'.[8]

In order to see clearly why this statement is misleading, we need to take note of the fact that although Jesus disagrees here with a Mosaic injunction, he is not, strictly speaking, rejecting this specific Mosaic law but rather explaining why it was made: 'For your hardness of heart he wrote you this commandment.' Moreover, he bases his disagreement on the Scripture. For when he says, 'from the beginning of creation, 'God made them male and female' . . . What therefore God has joined together, let not man put asunder' – this is based on Genesis 1:27, 2:24 and 5:2. And as Christopher Rowland has correctly observed,

> as far as Jesus was concerned, the *whole* of the Pentateuch was the product of Moses' pen. When we realize this, we see that his reference to the story in Genesis 1:27 and 2:24 is a reference to another part of the Torah and acceptance of that in preference to the law in Deuteronomy. It should not surprise us that Jesus prefers a part of the Torah dealing with the situation as it was at creation. After all, the perfection of the universe at creation is often a paradigm in Jewish texts for the character of the world in the kingdom of God. Thus the ethics of the kingdom of God require a return to that perfect state which God had always intended for his creation.[9]

Evidently, Jesus not only knew the Hebrew Scriptures as he did the palm of his hand, he gave considerable thought to the ethical significance of every part of it. In this respect Jesus is in line with the prophetic tradition. Witness the fact that hundreds of years earlier the prophet Malachi anticipated Jesus' position: 'For I hate divorce, says the Lord the God of Israel . . .' (Malachi 2:16).

When the Pharisees say to Jesus that the law of Moses allows divorce, and when he replies, 'For your hardness of heart he wrote you this commandment' (Mark 10:5), some scholars suggest that in prohibiting divorce absolutely as he does in Mark (though not in Matthew), Jesus provides a ruling that is more considerate of the interests of the woman, and therefore more compassionate. In response to such an interpretation we should note, first, that even the Deuteronomic law gives no absolute power to the man. The husband's right of divorce was abrogated in two cases (Deut. 22): if he ravished a virgin or if he falsely accused his wife of pre-nuptial sexual intercourse. In the first case the man was compelled to wed the woman and 'not put her away all his days', and in the second case he was also prohibited from ever divorcing his wife. But the most telling evidence against this notion – that Jesus' attitude towards divorce somehow considers the interests of the woman – is found in the texts. When his disciples ask for additional clarification, Jesus replies: 'Whoever divorces his wife and marries another, commits adultery against her; and if she divorces her husband and marries another, she commits adultery' (Mark 10:11).

In Matthew we have a somewhat different version of this encounter, which runs parallel to Mark's in all respects but one. In Matthew, Jesus' prohibition of divorce is not absolute: 'And I say to you: whoever divorces his wife, except for unchastity, and marries another commits adultery' (Matt. 19:9). Here as elsewhere, discrepancies between Mark and Matthew have given some New Testament specialists an opportunity to press their claim that where the question of the Law is concerned, the words which Matthew places in Jesus' mouth must be read as a 're-Judaization of Jesus' original message. Matthew's divergence from Mark is to be explained, so these scholars argue, as a concession to Jewish accusations of antinomianism in the early church. Thus Herbert Braun writes: 'Jesus himself unconditionally forbids a man to divorce his wife (Mark 10:11; Luke 16:18). Matthew (5:32; 19:9) breaks through this unconditionality with an exception, according to which a man is able to get a divorce after all, namely, when his wife commits adultery. The casuistic treatment of the question has begun.'[10] One may begin to comment on this statement with an obvious question: If adultery is a violation of one of the Ten Commandments, why is it casuistry, albeit 'Christian casuistry' as Braun calls it, to specify adultery as a condition for divorce? The Deuteronomic law does in fact specify that it is 'because he has found some indecency in her' (24:1), that he writes his wife a bill of divorce. The Hebrew word translated as 'indecency' (ervah) definitely suggests illicit sexual intercourse. So it is true that Matthew's condition is in line with Deuteronomy. Braun acknowledges that 'Like all Judaism, the Jesus tradition rejects adultery'.[11] Can we doubt that this tradition authentically reflects Jesus' own views? And if Jesus did in fact reject adultery, why does Braun question the genuineness of Matthew 5:32 and 19:9? Why does he deprecate those passages as evidence of casuistry? One might wish to argue that Jesus would have counselled forgiveness for an adulterous act under some circumstances? But would he have favoured the preservation of the marriage relationship regardless of the acts of sexual indecency and disloyalty committed by one or the other? After all, Jesus is reported by Mark (10.19) to have included adultery as a violation of the Decalogue; and in Matthew Jesus states that even a covetous look at another man's wife is to be regarded as an adulterous act (Matt. 5:27). In an effort to save his thesis that Matthew's treatment of the question is casuistical, Braun writes: 'As Jewish as Jesus' decisions are in respect to adultery, he is just as unjewish [sic] in his attitude towards divorce.'[12]

Braun believes that Jesus' attitude favours the wife. But as we have already seen, Mark 10:12 speaks of both the man and the woman as adulterers if they divorce and remarry. How does Braun deal with this problem? He assigns Mark 10:11 to Jesus himself, and 10:12 to the early church – surely a highly subjective and arbitrary way of dealing with evidence embarrassing to one's thesis. He presses his thesis by alleging that the 'Jewish texts are full of a clear animosity toward women. For instance it recommends that a man should not speak very much with his own wife, to say nothing of another woman. This animosity [?] is totally absent from the synoptic Jesus tradition.'[13] This is a strange assertion in light of the Synoptics' portrayal of Jesus' relationship with his own mother. And in Braun's own examples of Jesus' relationship with women (Mark 14:3–9; Luke 7:36–50) we find them anointing his head, washing his feet and otherwise serving him, while he, on his part, seems to follow Braun's version of the Jewish tradition by not speaking to these women very much at all.

Braun insists that Jesus' teaching about divorce, in which he presumably went beyond existing Jewish presuppositions, 'is still an expression of the protection and regard that should be directed to women who were unprotected and despised under Jewish marriage law'.[14] Braun not only brings no evidence to support this canard, he conveniently ignores the male chauvinism in the early church. For if male chauvinism is the issue here, it certainly was not combated in the earliest Christian teachings. Paul, for example, says, 'I want you to understand that the head of every man is Christ, the head of a woman is her husband . . .' (1 Cor. 11:3). He enjoins that 'the women should keep silence in the churches. For they are not permitted to speak, but should be subordinate . . .' (1 Cor. 14:34).

So if Matthew qualifies the divorce 'ruling' with the phrase 'except for unchastity', and thus departs from Mark's absolute prohibition of divorce, who is closer to Jesus' own view? It would seem that some scholars have ignored the problems and ambiguities involved in the argument that in Mark Jesus' stance on divorce is an example of his complete opposition to the law of Moses. For even if we assume that Mark is more authentic, we have to recognize that 'in forbidding divorce Jesus did not directly defy the Mosaic law. It is a general principle that greater stringency than the law requires is not illegal. The *haberim* and the Essenes . . . took on themselves stringent requirements not in the Mosaic law, and they doubtless did so on religious grounds.'[15] Jesus, similarly, may have sought to exceed the stringency and righteousness of the Mosaic provision for divorce, but his position involved no hint of its abrogation, or a denial of its divine status. It is noteworthy that something of a parallel to Jesus' saying may be found in third-century rabbinic statements to the effect that when someone separates from the wife of his youth, the altar itself sheds tears over him – alluding to Malachi 2:16. If, therefore, Jesus diverged from certain traditions to a noticeable degree, he nevertheless did not say anything 'which would lead to disobedience of the law, and he cannot be said to be opposing it'.[16]

7

Who was the First Evangelist?

What is the relationship between Matthew's Gospel and Jesus' own outlook? This all-important question requires that we pause to consider the 'Matthew or Mark' issue, which was touched on earlier in the discussion of Matthew's trustworthiness, especially in regard to Jesus' attitude towards the Law (see chapter 4). As we noted, the majority of New Testament specialists assign temporal priority to Mark, arguing that he was a direct literary source for both Matthew and Luke. The words Matthew attributes to Jesus in the Sermon on the Mount (5:17ff), these scholars argue, far from being Jesus' *ipsissima verba*, express the very opposite of his true outlook. These words and all others in Matthew favourable to the Law are explained away by this school of thought in one of two ways or both: either as a defence against anti-Christian Pharisaic allegations that Christianity has lowered moral standards: or as a Jewish-Christian reaction to the antinomian tendency within the church. In their present form, therefore – so the argument goes – many of Jesus' sayings in Matthew bear the signs of the post-resurrection church and a degree of 're-Judaization'. These same scholars question the authenticity of what they call 'harsh sayings' about Gentiles and tax-collectors (5:46ff; 6:7; 18:7; 21:31ff). In the Sermon on the Mount itself they try to distinguish between those utterances that are the product of the church's so-called 're-Judaization', and those which, owing to their depth and penetrating quality, may be regarded as Jesus' own words. If, as is our purpose here, we are interested in grasping Jesus' own religious outlook, it is unavoidable that the 'Matthew–Mark' question be addressed. To do so adequately we need to review further the historical process by which Mark came to replace Matthew as, purportedly, the first and most reliable Gospel.

When the texts of the first three Gospels are presented in parallel columns so that they may be 'seen together' (hence 'synoptic'), as was first done by Johann Jacob Griesbach in 1774–6, they disclose many similarities. At the same time, however, they reveal an abundance of sharp differences, which extend through whole chapters. This peculiar phenomenon of agreement and discrepancy constitutes the 'Synoptic problem'.[1] There are only two possible solutions to the Synoptic problem, as was already recognized in the eighteenth century by Johann Gottfried Eichorn. Either the three Gospel writers relied on one another, or they made use of a common source. The earliest solution proposed in that period rejected the likelihood of inter-dependency and opted instead for an 'ur-gospel', i.e., an earlier, primary tradition, either oral or written, which served as a common source for the Synoptic authors. How then did scholars account for the significant differences between these authors? They attempted to explain the disparities as the result of the wide dissemination of the tradition which was modified and transformed in the course of transmission. The proponents of the written ur-gospel hypothesis were unanimously agreed that the original source employed by the Synoptic authors was written in the Aramaic language. But no Aramaic text was ever found. Besides, there were nagging doubts about a common source, given the extensive differences between Matthew, Mark and Luke, extending at times through entire chapters. If the three authors used a common basic text, why are there such disparities between them? As no satisfactory answer to this question was provided, the ur-gospel theory, in both its written and oral forms, was eventually abandoned.

An alternative view then emerged positing a 'usage-relationship' of some kind between the authors of Matthew, Mark and Luke. Although there were at first several theories of such utilization, in the end scholarly discussion has concentrated on two possibilities: the priority of Matthew, known as the 'Griesbach (or Owen–Griesbach) hypothesis'; or the priority of Mark, known as the 'Marcan hypothesis'. The central question was posed as an alternative: either Matthew and Luke depended on Mark, (the Marcan hypothesis), or Mark relied on them (Owen–Griesbach). The issue was whether Mark's or Matthew's Gospel was first chronologically. Griesbach's thesis ran thus: when Mark wrote his work he had before him not only Matthew but Luke as well; and he selected and excerpted from them whatever he wished to preserve of the words and deeds of Jesus. This view had already been published by Henry Owen in his *Observations on the Four Gospels* (London, 1764). Owen characterized the Gospel of Mark as a compilatory 'abridgement of St. Matthew and St. Luke'. 'That St. Mark followed this plan', wrote Owen, 'no one can doubt, who compares his Gospel with those of the two former Evangelists. He copies largely from both: and takes either the one or the other perpetually as his guide. The order, indeed, is his own, and is very close and well connected' (p.50).

The Owen–Griesbach source-theory found immediate recognition and became the dominant view informing all the major New Testament commentaries of the early nineteenth century. In Germany, distinguished representatives of the Griesbach hypothesis included not only F.C. Bauer and his so-called 'Second Tübingen School', but Bauer's most famous student, David Friedrich Strauss, whose pioneering *Leben Jesu* (1835) was based on the Griesbach thesis. It is important to note that with his thesis Griesbach had intended no denigration of the Second Evangelist. The Gospel of Mark, he stressed, was to be regarded as a new version of the Gospel, even if its author did make use of Matthew and Luke as sources; for Mark's 'aim was neither to copy out their books nor to summarize them, but with their guidance to compose a new narrative adapted to his readers'.[2]

This observation has been largely ignored in the century-long debate with Griesbach that began in the 1830s to 1840s. It was then that the originators of the Marcan hypothesis set about trying to prove the opposite, namely, that Matthew and Luke had used the Gospel of Mark as their source. But to appreciate the magnitude of the task they faced, we need to note the following:

1. There are 180 instances in which one finds 'minor additional details in Mark that extend beyond the text of Matthew and Luke, including passages where either Matthew or Luke are lacking' (p.11).
2. 'Of these 180 cases of additional details in Mark, more than half affect the text of Matthew and Luke simultaneously, while the rest of the cases touch upon only that Evangelist whose order Mark followed.'
3. There are 35 instances of minor additional details in both Matthew and Luke that extend beyond Mark.
4. There are also 35 instances in which Matthew and Luke concur in expressions and wording, contrary to Mark (pp.18–19).
5. There are 22 instances in which Matthew and Luke concur in their divergences from Mark's word form.

Thus the advocates of the Marcan hypothesis had to provide very convincing answers to the following questions if the Griesbach hypothesis was to be replaced:

1. Where did the extensive additional substantive material shared by Matthew and Luke alone come from?
2. How could it be that the additional substantive material in the Gospel of Mark failed to appear in Matthew and Luke, if Mark had been their source?
3. How can it be explained that in 180 cases Matthew and Luke, independently and without knowledge of each other, joined in leaving out and ignoring the identical phrases and sentences of the Gospel of Mark – if this had been their source?
4. How was it possible that both the First and the Third Evangelist,

without having contact with each other, and in spite of their separate styles of work, nevertheless in 35 cases added to the text of Mark in exactly the same places and in exactly the same phrasing?
5. What caused both Matthew and Luke, in another 35 cases, independently to agree in replacing a word which, according to the hypothesis, they found in the text of Mark, with the same similar-sounding new word?
6. What caused Matthew and Luke, independently and without personal contact, in 22 cases to make exactly the same small modification in an identical manner to a word they both had in common in the text with Mark (pp. 21–2).

Moreover, if Mark was the source for Matthew and Luke, where did the non-Marcan material common to the First and Third Gospels come from? The originators of the Marcan thesis could never quite agree in their answers to this fundamental question. For this reason only a few scholars, at first, were won over to their cause. But in 1863 Heinz Julius Holtzmann (1832–1910) presented a 'two-source theory' in an attempt to bolster the foundations of the Marcan hypothesis. 'Holtzmann proceeded in this manner', writes Stoldt: 'he did not say that Matthew and Luke used the canonical Gospel of Mark as a source. Rather, he posited two fundamental sources, a historical source and a *logia* [i.e., a 'sayings'-source] which he designated with the Greek capital letters Alpha and Lambda; . . . we shall call them A and L (p.70). Thus 'Holtzmann erected a theoretical superstructure with two imaginary entities which he endowed with the character of primary sources: A and L. He asserted that the first one corresponded to the ur-Mark, and that the second one was identical with the *logia* collection, the only literary proof of which was Papias' well known note: "So then Matthew composed *ta logia* in the Hebrew [or Aramaic] language." This is the sole literary support for the presumption of a sayings-source of any kind' (p. 74).

For Holtzmann, the hypothetical ur-Mark was so fundamental that it constituted the ultimate source not only for the canonical Gospel of Mark, but also for all of the corresponding parallel texts in the Gospels of Matthew and Luke, as well as the Lukan Sermon on the Mount. The so-called 'logia-source', in contrast, is quantitatively quite insignificant. Its only essential contents are a series of sayings from the Lukan travel narrative, since Holtzmann has excluded the extensive complex of logia of both Sermons on the Mount, as well as all the logia in the Gospel of Mark, including the discourses and parables. He maintained that Matthew and Luke drew this latter material in its entirety from the Gospel of Mark and not from the sayings-source. Thus Holtzmann's sayings-source 'has only minimal formative weight of its own. Moreover, it plays no role in

influencing the structure and composition of the First and Third Gospels
. . .' (p. 88). Twenty years later, under the pressure of criticism not from
defenders of the Griesbach thesis but precisely from other proponents of
Marcan priority, Holtzmann withdrew from his own ur-Mark theory and
acknowledged that the distinction between an ur-Mark and Mark must be
abandoned. And a decade or so after that Paul Wernle, the 'consummator of
the two-source theory (an ur-Mark and a sayings-source), remarked that
'Evidence for a longer ur-Mark has never been produced and cannot be
produced . . . There is no compelling reason to postulate a shorter or longer
ur-Mark as distinct from a canonical Mark. From this point of view the
ur-Mark hypothesis simply collapses." (pp. 92–3).

Wernle, however, succeeded no better than his predecessors in placing
the Marcan hypothesis on a firm footing. A detailed critique of Wernle's
highly subjective theory and method may be found in Stoldt's painstaking
analysis. For our purposes, however, one fairly typical example of the 'rigour'
of Wernle's method will suffice. Comparing Luke with Mark, he asserts that
virtually all of Mark's narrative material is contained in three segments of
Luke. But on the same page he acknowledges 12 exceptions[3] and writes that
apart from these exceptions all the passages of Mark are contained in Luke.
Stoldt comments on the amazing audacity of a scholar who can make such a
claim in view of 12 highly significant 'exceptions', one of which spans one
and a half chapters.

Wernle, however, also innovated. It was he who renamed the hypothetical
common sayings-source, designating it by the letter 'Q', from the German
word *Quelle*, for 'source'.

> It is not unreasonable to suppose [wrote Wernle] that from the moment of its
> genesis the sayings collection underwent continuous historical development
> until it was taken up into Matthew and Luke. As Jesus' legacy to the
> community, it belonged to every single individual, and everyone had the right
> to make improvements [sic] or additions. Probably only a very few equally long
> copies were in existence. Between the first written copy (Q) and the collection
> which Matthew (Q^{mt}) and Luke (Q^{lk}) found, stood Q^1, Q^2, Q^3; for us the
> effort to differentiate between these three would be in vain. The Judaic form
> (Q^j) denotes a single stage on this path [Early? Late?]. This assumption alone
> provides an unforced [?] diagnosis of what we find in our Gospels. (p. 112)

And Stoldt aptly comments that

> in Wernle's hands this renaming of the *single* 'sayings' collection' leads to the
> emergence of no fewer than seven 'Q' sources and this formal change of name
> actually indicates a redefinition of the substance of the collection. It is evident
> that Wernle's unverifiable, hypothetically postulated multiple source 'Q' left

open all hypothetical possibilities because of its unlimited potential for expansion. It contained seven allegedly detectable versions and also had supposedly been in a constant state of flux, and it even had a 'history'. (p.113)

The notion of a 'sayings-source' is itself quite arbitrary, as if Jesus' sayings were somehow collected and recorded separately from the accounts of his deeds. But if a basic distinction cannot be maintained between 'discourses' and 'accounts', then, as Stoldt rightly observes, 'the whole Gospel of Mark must also fall into the category of "discourses" and be ascribed to source "Q". This is true because in almost every story in the Gospel of Mark there is an important series of sayings' (p. 114). This whole two-source theory only makes sense 'under the assumption that one source was a historical source and the other a discourse source, and that Matthew and Luke drew upon the former for the historical part of the Gospels and upon the latter for logia material. But since it now turns out that this clearcut distinction is only theoretical . . ., this whole two-source system becomes questionable. It does not stand up in the face of the fact that it is a matter of *mixed sources* in which the only difference between historical and logia is one of emphasis' (p. 116). Besides, this blurring of the distinction between the two sources served the interests of Wernle and his followers; for had they proposed the existence of a distinct and separate sayings-source, it would be quite incomprehensible why Mark himself did not obtain all his sayings from 'Q', as, presumably, did Matthew and Luke. But the truth is that a definite separation of the two alleged sources, a historical one and a logia source, was not maintained and, as a consequence, became a system of arbitrary stop-gaps. Not to mention the 'impossible editorial procedures Matthew and Luke would have had to undertake to obtain their logia from Mark whenever he could supply them, obtaining the others from "Q", but abandoning it whenever Mark provided more logia' (p. 117).

If there was one logia source, why did Matthew and Luke use it so differently – which is especially striking in their treatment of the Sermon on the Mount? While Matthew presents it as a compact entity, Luke divides it into parts with different phrasing and meaning. And Stoldt asks, 'How could such a discrepancy come about, if both evangelists drew from the same source – the logia source? How was this astonishing phenomenon to be reconciled with the existence of a uniform source?' (p. 118). Wernle presented a 'solution' from the standpoint of the Marcan hypothesis by asserting that there was not one 'Q' but several. But how may this be reconciled with Papias' simple note which mentions only *one* logia collection? Furthermore, Papias' fragment contains not only this statement: 'So then Matthew composed *ta logia* in the Hebrew [or Aramaic] language'; the statement continues thus: 'and each interpreted it as he was able'. This raises an obvious question: For whom did Matthew prepare this compilation of Jesus' sayings in the Hebrew language? Certainly not for the Greeks or even Greek-speaking Jews. The 'only remaining possibility', Stoldt convincingly observes, 'is that he compiled and recorded it for his Judaeo-Christian compatriots and fellow believers. For what purpose? For the purpose of proselytizing among the Jews' (p. 119). This suggests that Matthew's Gospel reflects an early stage of Judaeo-Christianity, and therefore rather reliable reminiscences.

Another argument for the Marcan or two-source theory has been called 'the proof from order'. This was first proposed by Christian Hermann Weise, who placed the main weight of his argument on the composition and arrangement of the whole. He was followed by Heinz Julius Holtzmann and William Wrede who agreed that the validity of the Marcan hypothesis ultimately rests on the proposition that the sequence of the narratives in Mark determines the sequence in Matthew and Luke. But a close comparative analysis shows that there is no such common sequence held in common by the three Synoptic writers. In Stoldt's words: 'nowhere does the Gospel of Mark appear in the other two Gospels as an intact and continuous narrative; rather, it runs parallel to the others, always only temporarily and partially, in changing intervals and in quite different lengths. Sometimes it runs parallel to Matthew for a passage, sometimes to Luke, sometimes to both, occasionally to neither. Insofar as all three do not coincide, the parallelism of one of them to Mark ceases as soon as it begins with the other' (p. 136).

So if there are parallels, they are only partial and temporary. But even if parallels are acknowledged, there is still the question of whether the proponents of Marcan priority are justified in asserting that it is Mark who is always followed by the others. After all, the parallels, in and of themselves, prove nothing. The alternative hypotheses that need to be tested and proved, if possible, are: is Mark being followed, or is he the follower? When one evangelist deviates from another and then returns, who is following whom?[4]

But what about this notion of a presumed sequence common to the three Gospels? Luke (6:20–8:3) is a narrative block of one and a half chapters for which no equivalent whatever is to be found in Mark. Worse still, Luke's travel narrative (9:51–18:14) is an 'interruption' of the so-called common thread of narration that extends for no fewer than nine chapters and for which there is no real equivalent in Mark. Mark's Gospel also has an extended narrative of almost two chapters (6:45–8:26) which finds no parallel in Luke. The advocates of Marcan priority have dubbed this the 'Marcan gap in Luke'. So tenaciously do these scholars hold to their theory that embarrassing facts are explained away by finding fault with the texts. 'The existence of the so-called "Marcan gap in Luke",' writes Stoldt, 'repeatedly so distressed advocates of the Marcan hypothesis that they took refuge in the *ultimum refugium* of all proponents of a floundering hypothesis;

they argued that only a "defective copy" of Mark was available to Luke' (p. 137). That Mark's text was 'defective' was first argued by Edward Reuss in his *Geschichte der Heiligen Schriften des Neuen Testaments* (1842, p. 174); and he was followed in this respect by Rudolf Bultmann, who wrote: 'I shall not deal here with the question of whether Luke deliberately left out the section Mark 6:45–8:26 or whether he – as appears more likely to me – did not find it in his copy of Mark' (*Die Geschichte der synoptischen Tradition*, 1957, p. 387n.; cited in Stoldt, p. 137). It is a fact, then, that Luke and Mark have no common story line. Substantial divergences from Mark's narrative also occur in the first half of the Gospel of Matthew (4:24–13:58).

All of this points up, for Stoldt, the apparent error of the advocates of Marcan priority: they begin with an *a priori* tenet, and then select their evidence accordingly. They select for comparison from the Gospels of Matthew and Luke only those parts for which equivalent contents can be found in the Gospel of Mark. Even then, however,

> The Sermon on the Mount – with its partial equivalent, the Sermon on the Plain in Luke – as well as the centurion's pericope, John the Baptist's question, Jesus' sermon about John the Baptist, and the sermons of John the Baptist himself, all together constitute clear ruptures of the Marcan story line, quite apart from the fact that the extensive travel narrative of Luke cannot be fitted at all into a continuous thread of narration. (p. 139)

There is no order in Matthew and Luke that follows or coincides with that in Mark. The order is imposed from above by eliminating those portions of the Gospels of Matthew and Luke which find no parallels in Mark, and by regrouping the remaining portions according to the order of Mark. The inescapable fact seems to be that far from there being a common narrative line in the first three Gospels, there are only occasional parallels – sometimes between Mark and Matthew, at other times between Mark and Luke.

Let us accept, for the moment, the assumption of Marcan priority. What this means for the advocates of this theory is that Matthew and Luke both had before them the Gospel of Mark, using it as a model for their respective texts, which they wrote independently and without knowledge of each other. If that were the case, how would one explain Matthew's and Luke's varying departures from Mark, taking turns, as it were, in following Mark? These varying parallels and departures remain inexplicable. 'What utterly enigmatic understanding', asks Stoldt, 'would have prompted the First and Third Evangelists to sense, without knowledge of each other, when the other departed from the narrative sequence of Mark, and what uncanny para-psychological contact could, from time to time, have sent out the magical impetus for them once more to take their turns accompanying Mark? This whole conception is – well, let us just say: scarcely believable' (p. 142).

If, however, instead of assuming Marcan priority we approach the matter with the Owen-Griesbach hypothesis, the reason for the convergences and divergences between the three Evangelists becomes quite clear. It was Mark who revised the Gospels of Matthew and Luke, employing them as his model and selecting freely between them. 'In so doing he followed sometimes the narrative sequence of one and sometimes that of the other, or – whenever they coincided – both at the same time' (p. 142).

It is not easy to explain why, in spite of all the cogent objections that have been raised against the Marcan hypothesis, it still remains the dominant one among New Testament specialists. Stoldt has argued that scholars cling to this view, consciously or not, out of ideological considerations. Originally it was a reaction against the watershed study by David Friedrich Strauss, whose *Life of Jesus* (1835), based on the Griesbach thesis, argued that the Gospels contain not history but myths. The challenge thus laid down by Strauss could only be met by proving the opposite, namely that the Gospels were not myth but history. What this task necessarily entailed, then, was to reject the Griesbach hypothesis. The Gospel of Mark as compared with that of Matthew and Luke appeared to be the freest from the legendary material, lacking the whole pre-history and post-history – i.e., the genealogy and birth narratives, the resurrection narratives and the ascension narrative. Hence, inasmuch as Mark possessed the fewest legendary accretions, it could be assumed (in line with Enlightenment, rationalist presuppositions) that what he gave us was history, not myth.

Although the theory of Marcan priority has been supported by the majority of New Testament specialists for some time now, it has always met with resistance and opposition. The entire Second Tübingen School unanimously rejected the Marcan, two-source theory, and it remained highly controversial in Germany, its original home, until the end of the First World War. It was only after the war that the theory received additional, and what has proved to be decisive, sanction through the founders of 'form criticism', Martin Dibelius and Rudolf Bultmann. 'Form criticism' was, in essence, a new source-hypothesis designed to explore the obscure and empty space between the historical Jesus and the extant accounts of his experiences. The result of this movement, which has had considerable influence on British and North American scholars, was a fragmentation of the texts into what are purported to be original pericopes. Marcan priority was preserved by arguing, as did Dibelius, that Mark, in dealing with the life of Jesus, 'joined together, as he saw fit, fragments of the tradition preserved in the communities'.[5] And Bultmann, similarly, proposed that 'in Mark one can still clearly recognize ... how the oldest tradition consisted of individual parts and that the continuity is secondary'.[6] Insofar, then, as form-criticism and other related methods presuppose the Marcan priority or two-source theory, it is simply arguing in a circle to assert that the two-source theory has been confirmed by form criticism! On the other hand, neither have the defenders of the Griesbach hypothesis succeeded in tying up all the loose ends of their theory. W.R. Farmer, for example, has vigorously argued the proposition that Mark wrote after Matthew and Luke and was dependent on both. And yet, as Stoldt has observed, 'Farmer was no more able to present proof for the partial dependence of Luke upon Matthew than Griesbach had been in his time.' (p. 247).

There are signs in North American scholarship of a serious reopening of the debate between the proponents of the opposing theories.[7] One must observe, however, that the Marcan priority or two-source theory has led to an abundance of rather unconvincing assertions concerning the nature of 'Q'. As Stoldt, again, observes, 'there is hardly a problem concerning Q which has not been raised and to which an answer could not be found in the literature even though these answers are quite diverse and conflicting. Only one question remains unanswered: *Where is the literary evidence for Q?*' (p. 249). And yet, Stoldt's strong rebuttal of the two-source theory notwithstanding, he believes that neither was Griesbach entirely right. In 'the exaggerated formulation', writes Stoldt, 'that "The whole gospel of Mark was taken from those of Matthew and Luke", he [Griesbach] was not right . . . But there is no doubt about the temporal posteriority of the Gospel of Mark. Thus Henry Owen and Johann Jacob Griesbach correctly recognized that Matthew and Luke formed the textual basis for Mark. And Griesbach in fact proved this with a textual analysis carried out with philological precision' (p. 259). The Gospel of Mark represents a new intellectual creation limiting itself to the presentation of the kerygmatic activity of Jesus, omitting the legendary pre-history and post-history. Finally, Stoldt acknowledges that the adherents of the Griesbach thesis have yet to provide a good answer to this question: 'Where did Matthew and Luke get their material?' (p. 260). This is still a mystery – although, as we noted earlier, John Rist's suggestion, of the independence of Mark and Matthew, has much to commend it: they based themselves, as did perhaps the other two Evangelists, on oral traditions. And the possibility that these oral traditions were supplemented by notes should not be ruled out.

In any case, given the controversial and unresolved nature of the debate concerning Matthew versus Mark, there is no good reason to challenge the trustworthiness of Matthew in his characterization of Jesus' attitude towards the Law. As we saw in chapter 6, there is nothing in Jesus' attitude toward the sabbath, the dietary laws and the question of divorce that can be construed as a repudiation of the Mosaic laws; and the various utterances which Matthew attributes to Jesus, far from being a manifestation of a presumed 're-Judaization', are entirely congruent with everything else we have learned about Jesus as a pious Jew. Furthermore, there is good reason to believe that where the nature of first-century Judaism is concerned, Matthew is more reliable than Mark.

Additional Questions about the Marcan Priority Thesis

Some scholars point to certain specifics in Mark as evidence of priority, which might just as easily serve to support the priority of Matthew. Phillip Sigal has called three such instances to our attention. The first has to do with the word *grammateus*, 'scribe'. This word appears 21 times in Mark, 19 of which are found in contexts where the author exhibits hostility toward this group. This hostility may be taken as evidence that Mark is early and that it reflects the tension between the scribes and Jesus; but the hostility may also be taken as evidence for the lateness of Mark, reflecting the church's angry reaction to Jewish criticism, and the church's efforts at de-Judaization.

Sigal's second example is the word *nomos* ('law'). This word, he writes, 'never occurs in Mark, and when Mark refers to a Torah precept, e.g., the fifth commandment (7:10), he attributes to Moses rather than to God what Matthew attributes to God (15:4). Is this Matthew improving on Mark, or is it Mark at a later date seeking to downgrade the status of Judaic revelation, a process clearly seen in the Epistle of Barnabas and Justyn Martyr's *Dialogue with Trypho?'* The third example is Matthew 24:20, where

> Jesus tells the disciples to pray that the eschaton will not happen during the winter, or on the Sabbath. This clearly addresses a time when the Sabbath was still of some significance to an expectant Judaic church. But some decades later, as the Sabbath became of less urgency in a growing Gentile-dominated church, Mark omits the Sabbath and has Jesus only advise the disciples to pray that it will not take place in winter (Mark 13:18). There are no grounds for believing this to be a Matthean interpolation. If Jesus spoke at all on this subject he would more naturally have included the Sabbath than not included it. And if he did speak this around [the year] 30 when his living ministry was within Judaism, Mark would find it perfectly appropriate to revise this teaching in a later, end-of-the-century setting where the seventh-day Sabbath was being abolished.[8]

All that 'Mark wants to depict', Sigal continues, 'is Jesus' fate on the cross as the central fact of Christian faith. Mark is no longer interested in influencing the course of Judaism, and revises the portrait of Jesus the protorabbi so evident in Matthew and Luke. He eschews the idea of Jesus as a new Moses, but cannot entirely dismiss the tradition of Peter which reflects that Jesus was seen as a protorabbi (e.g., Mark 9:5). That Matthew's remained the most popular Gospel only indicates that the church was not yet ready for Marcan revisionism.'[9]

Pierson Parker, a distinguished proponent of the Griesbach thesis, insists on the secondary character of the Second Gospel because it 'simply cannot be the work of any Jew or Jewish-Christian, and certainly not of Peter or his companion'.[10] The author of Mark, Pierson demonstrates, apparently knew little about Judaism and Palestinian geography. In Mark 1:13 we read that Jesus, during his wilderness temptation, 'was with the wild beasts'. And Parker comments: 'Well, Jesus might in the wilderness have seen some scorpions or vipers, but the only beasts thereabout were a few goats. Had he gone up into the hills at night, he perhaps would have heard the far-away howl of a jackal or a hyena; but even these would not have been "with" him.' In Mark 6:2lff, we are told that Herod Antipas 'gave a banquet for his courtiers and officers and the leading men of Galilee; and that during the festivities Herod ordered John the Baptist beheaded and the head brought in on a platter. This suggests that the banquet was held not far from the stronghold in which the Baptist was incarcerated and executed. Josephus informs us that this stronghold was in Machaerus, located some 100 miles from Tiberius in Galilee. And Parker asks: 'Did the "chief men of Galilee" walk, or ride their donkeys, all that way to a party? Or did our author just have no idea where Tiberius and John's jail were?' And at Mark 7:31 we read, 'Then Jesus returned from the region of Tyre, and went through Sidon to the Sea of Galilee, through the region of the Decapolis.' Parker rightly remarks that anyone trying to trace that itinerary on a map, would have great difficulty making sense of it. There are not only these and other geographical oddities in Mark – suggesting that he never saw Palestine at all – there are also signs of his ignorance of the Hebrew and Aramaic languages. Mark 5:41 states that '*Talitha cumi*' meant 'Little girl, I say to you, arise'. But the Aramaic phrase contains nothing equivalent to 'I say to you'. And Mark 7:11 states that the Hebrew word *Korban* means 'gift', whereas it actually means 'sacrifice' in the religious sense. In Mark 10:46 we encounter the name 'Bartimaeus, a blind beggar, the son of Timaeus', which means literally, 'the son of Timaeus, the son of Timaeus'. Did the author of this Gospel not know that *bar* means 'son' in Aramaic? At 15:34 the author makes the totally implausible statement that Jesus cried in Aramaic, *Eloi, Eloi*, and that the bystanders thought that he was calling Elijah. Matthew's statement (27:46), on the other hand, that Jesus cried in Hebrew, *Eli, Eli* (my God, my God), is more than likely. The Second Evangelist also makes serious errors with respect to basic Jewish beliefs. Jews did not call David 'our father' as in Mark 11:10; nor did they believe that the eschatological kingdom was of David, but rather of God or of Heaven.

Parker provides a considerable amount of additional evidence to support the proposition that the Second Evangelist rather consistently represents the Gentile point of view in the early church; and Gentile Christianity being historically later than Jewish Christianity, one may deduce that Mark's stance represents a later view than that of Matthew. Parker concludes that Mark 'evidently got caught up in the Jewish–Gentile controversy, and was a strong partisan for the Gentile side. He therefore grew highly impatient with the leadership of Peter and the Twelve . . . His own understanding of Jesus' homeland and background was not robust. His Aramaic was so sketchy as to be almost non-existent, though he liked to include Aramaic words that seemed to him of supernatural import. His Greek was Italianate . . . He was a . . . Gentile, Italian theologian.'[11]

The distinguished German scholar Martin Hengel insists on the priority of Mark. And yet some of the characteristics which Hengel discerns in Mark would seem to speak against Marcan priority. He states, for example, that Mark's writing 'does not fit well into the earliest period of ferment after the birth of Christianity, when . . . [the people] were expecting an imminent end with burning hearts. In the early period of this eschatological enthusiasm . . . there had been hardly any thought of a "Jesus biography", but only of the proclamation by word of mouth of the new message of the coming of the crucified Messiah as Son of Man and judge of the world within a limited area in Syria and Palestine.'[12] Hengel also acknowledges that 'For Mark, the question of the validity of the ritual law, over which there was such a fierce struggle at the time of Paul, is in principle no longer a problem and has clearly been resolved in favour of the mission to the Gentiles. The work is in fact obviously written for Gentile Christians.'[13] Moreover, Hengel places the origin of the Second Gospel in Rome, not Syria–Palestine. And like Pierson Parker, Hengel recognizes the Second Evangelist's ignorance of Palestine: 'One factor in particular which tells against Palestine and Syria is the complete ignorance of the situation in Judea between 66 and 69 . . . the Gospel of Mark, not least Mark 13, is written at a clear geographical distance from Palestine, for Gentile Christians, who have no inkling of the real political situation there.' Hengel also reminds us of the numerous Latinisms in the Gospel, pointing to its origin in Rome. Nevertheless, Hengel believes that the Second Gospel 'was written by a Jewish Graeco-Palestinian, John Mark, who was a missionary companion of Peter for some time'.[14] In striking contrast to Parker's view, Hengel maintains that Mark understood Aramaic which 'is evident from the correct[?] Aramaic quotations in his gospel'. Acknowledging, however, that Mark's apparent knowledge of Judaism and Palestine is not above criticism, Hengel attempts to explain this feature of the Gospel by asserting that 'Mark does not mean to provide a historically accurate account in the modern sense, but presents Jewish customs polemically and tendentiously, i.e., in a vague and exaggerated way'.[15]

Clearly Pierson Parker and Martin Hengel, two highly respected New Testament specialists, are miles apart in their assessments of the author of Mark. As representatives of the Griesbach and two-source hypotheses respectively, they bring dramatic proof of the fundamental disagreements between the two sides. Surely the work of Pierson Parker, W.R. Farmer and Hans-Herbert Stoldt, to mention just a few of the critics of the theory of Marcan priority, have provided sufficient grounds not only for re-opening the debate, but for adopting a different scholarly attitude towards Matthew's Gospel. Farmer's first methodological rule and its underlying logic needs to be taken seriously. 'Assuming', he writes, 'that the original events in the history of the Christian movement took place in Palestine, within predominantly Jewish circles, and that by the time the gospels were written, Christianity had expanded outside of Palestine, and outside of circles which were predominantly Jewish in orientation: *That form of a particular tradition found in the Gospels, which reflects an extra-Palestinian, or non-Jewish provenance is to be adjudged secondary to a form of the same tradition which reflects a Palestinian or Jewish provenance.*'[16] It follows that the more Jewish Gospel of Matthew and the policy of the Jerusalem congregation under the leadership of James the brother of Jesus, may most faithfully reflect Jesus' own outlook. This would mean that Matthew was not a product of an alleged 're-Judaizing' process, but rather that Mark was the beginning of a long *de*-Judaizing process. Farmer has asked a highly significant question in this regard: How come Matthew has had so much influence on the church, and Mark so little?[17] One obvious answer that immediately suggests itself is that Matthew contains the Sermon on the Mount, the Beatitudes and the Lord's Prayer. That is to say, that Matthew, more than any other Evangelist reveals Jesus' originality and creative genius. It is in Matthew that we see Jesus as a charismatic religious virtuoso with his feet firmly planted in the Judaism of his time; and it is also in Matthew that we see quite clearly Jesus' divergence from some of the traditions of his time. Therein lies his originality, in his creative divergence from *some* of the traditions of the elders.

8
Jesus' Originality
and Creative Genius

Chapters 5 to 7 of Matthew's Gospel are usually referred to as the Sermon on the Mount (SM). To anyone reading it free of presupposition it will appear as a unified entity. Some influential scholars, however, have denied the thematic unity of the SM, treating it as a 'collection of unrelated sayings of diverse origins, a patchwork'.[1] Some scholars have maintained that the SM and other components of Matthew were derived from three main sources: from Mark, probably written in Rome: from the so-called 'Q', a written or oral collection of Jesus' sayings, c.AD 50; and a source named 'M', probably originating with the earliest Jewish-Christian community in Jerusalem. We have already considered the basic problems besetting the theory of Marcan priority and the hypothetical source, 'Q'. Besides, such hypercritical dissections of the SM amount to a denial that it was a sermon at all.

Another related factor contributing to the fragmentation of the SM is the application to it of 'form criticism'. This is a method designed by New Testament specialists for the examination of the forms which the traditions about Jesus had presumably assumed before they were written down. What was the determining condition, form critics ask, that accounted for the present form and content of a tradition? Most often the answer given is that it was the needs of the church – in preaching, teaching, proselytizing etc. – that determined what was transmitted. Some form critics attribute not only the preservation of the tradition but its very creation to the church, thus denying, in effect, that the SM and the other sayings in Matthew are authentic reflections of Jesus' own stance. The net result of such methods has been to create an extreme scepticism with regard to the possibility of grasping a highly plausible conception of the Jesus of history.

W.D. Davies and others have rightly challenged this scepticism on the following grounds. The Jews of Jesus' generation were long accustomed to the faithful learning and transmitting of tradition. From early childhood whole passages from the Scriptures as well as the sayings and other utterances of famous sages were memorized and repeated and passed on to the next generation. The Mishnah itself, written down for the first time *c.*AD 200, is a perfect example of such sayings and teachings that existed primarily or exclusively in their oral form for hundreds of years. We may assume that Peter, James the brother of Jesus and Paul were in frequent communication with the earliest Christian communities, and that the traditions transmitted to and within those communities were supervised, so to speak, by the apostles. It was therefore not a vague, improvised folk tradition, developing over a long period of time, that lies behind the New Testament texts, but 'an ecclesiastical one, which developed intensively in a brief period' (p. 417). It was, after all, in the interest of the earliest church to remain as faithful as possible to Jesus' original teachings. So although the needs of the emerging church had some influence on the tradition in the course of its transmission, there is no reason to suppose that none of Jesus' actual words survived. Davies proposes that the very fact that definite words and utterances were attributed to Jesus testifies to the seriousness of the early church's determination to anchor its tradition in him. That the church somehow created whole sayings of its own accord, arbitrarily ascribing them to Jesus, is scarcely credible. It is therefore not unreasonable to suppose that it is the ethical teachings of Jesus himself, and not merely those of the early church, that are recorded in Matthew.

As we have already noted, the Gospels regard Jesus as a teacher or rabbi, among other things. He was addressed as 'teacher' by his disciples, by his learned adversaries and by the crowds. This conception prevailed in the early centuries of the church's history, when Jesus was frequently designated as 'teacher'. That the church fathers regarded this designation as fully appropriate is clear. The same understanding of Jesus as a teacher, albeit a 'false' one, emerges from the Talmudic literature. Davies calls attention to the fact that 'In one passage an actual word of his is cited (TB Shabbat 116 a-b, although this may be a late interpolation) and it is possible that Christian emphasis on Jesus as an ethical teacher who had his own interpretation of the law, because he was the Messiah, led to the suppression of much Jewish speculation on the Messiah as the inaugurator of a New Law' (p. 419).

But if Jesus was a rabbi, it is also evident from everything we have learned about him so far that he differed significantly from the other Jewish teachers and learned Pharisees of his era. We may safely assume that the others studied in the already established academies of Jesus' older contemporaries, Hillel and Shammai, to name only the most famous. Paul, as we have seen, though born in the Diaspora, was early sent by his father to Jerusalem to receive a thorough Jewish education. In a Hebrew (or Aramaic) speech attributed to him in Acts (ch. 22) Paul states: 'I am a Jew, born at Tarsus in Cilicia, but brought up in this city [i.e., Jerusalem] at the feet of [Rabbi] Gamaliel, educated according to the strict manner of the law of our fathers, being zealous for God as you all are this day.' The usual pattern was that after one started as a pupil, as did Paul, and mastering the Scriptures and the traditional oral commentaries, one became a teacher with pupils of one's own. Although such teachers showed individual ingenuity in their interpretation of the Scriptures, they took the greatest care in passing on faithfully what they had received. Jesus, however, as we will recall, is described in John 7:15 as *agrammatos*, as one who had learning but who had never studied – in an academy, that is. We know of no distinguished teachers of Jesus, and there is no evidence that Jesus was trained in any of the 'academies' (Heb. *yeshivot*) as was Paul. One of the reactions from those who heard Jesus' words was that 'he taught . . . as one who had authority, and not as the scribes' (Mark 1:22). The source of his authority, as he understood it, differed from that of the rabbis. Jesus offered his teachings with the unique, 'But I say to you . . .', and he cited Scripture directly to justify his position, something a Pharisaic teacher would not normally do without basing himself on previous rabbinical authorities. As I have emphasized, Jesus' self-understanding appears to have been that he had an especially intimate relationship with God and, hence, an authoritative involvement with the Scriptures. Another distinguishing feature of Jesus' teaching was that he taught not only in the synagogues, but also in the open air, by the sea (of Galilee) and on the hills (e.g., Mark 4:1ff; 5:1ff). His audience consisted not only of his own pupils (i.e., disciples) but of the crowds as well. Davies asks the highly significant question of whether Jesus had a 'school' of his own. Can the Greek word *oikos* in Mark, literally 'house', be taken to mean 'school'? In Hebrew the major schools or academies in Jesus' time were in fact called 'houses' – *Bet Hillel* (the House of Hillel), *Bet Shammai* (the House of Shammai). Was there a *Bet Yeshu* or House of Jesus as well? It is interesting in this connection that Mark 2:18 compares Jesus' disciples both with those of John the Baptist and those of the Pharisees. Where discipleship to Jesus apparently differed from that among the Pharisees was in the personal devotion to him and the indifference to worldly things that it called for. To become a Pharisaic or rabbinic pupil (Heb. *talmid*) meant primarily a life devoted to studying the twofold law, but no severing of ties with worldly callings. Many of the early rabbinical teachers had manual occupations as did their students; Jesus, in contrast, appears to have given up the trade he most probably learned from his father. Later we shall explore Jesus' conception of the 'Kingdom of Heaven' and the role he believed he would play in bringing it about. But, as Davies stresses, the eschatological character of Jesus as a teacher must not obscure his affinity with the rabbis.

The fact that Jesus is so often questioned about the Law, both in public and in private, also strongly suggests that there was considerable interest in his distinctive outlook. Notice that he was questioned about such issues as the sabbath, washing of hands before eating, perhaps dietary regulations, and whether it was lawful, i.e., in accordance with the Torah, to pay tribute to the Roman government. The evidence as a whole, then, strongly indicates that Jesus had a 'school' of sorts around him which, despite its distinctiveness, none the less had definite rabbinic features. 'We need not doubt', Davies concludes, 'that those chosen to be with him learned from him, treasured his words and passed them on. The emergence of the words of Jesus in so many . . . documents of the early church is not accidental . . . The continuity was preserved by the *talmidim* [pupils] of Jesus and their successors . . . in the early church. All of which makes it credible that the "words" of Jesus were preserved and transmitted with some degree of faithfulness' (p. 424).

The Am Ha-aretz

W.D. Davies and other scholars have made the assumption that the majority of the Jews in the countryside of Palestine in the first century 'lived their lives in disregard of the claims of the Law. They constituted the *am ha-aretz*, the "people of the land", who were held in contempt by the religious' (p. 425). This conception is most likely untrue, judging from Josephus' description of both Jewish religious education in his time and the people's basic respect for the Torah. On this the New Testament is in agreement with Josephus. For outside of the 'publicans and sinners', the rest of the plain people with whom Jesus came into contact are portrayed as God-fearing people who observed the sabbath and the holy days, attended synagogue and abided by the dietary laws. Jesus was the son of a craftsman and he emerged from the plain people, so to speak. He most probably received his elementary Jewish education in the village school of Nazareth. Does the New Testament give us any reason to suppose that the other children of Nazareth, Capernaum or any of the other villages of Galilee, had received a lesser education? No doubt the religious understanding of the highly learned individuals differed from that of the plain people. But does that justify characterizing the people of the countryside as disobedient to the Law? Who frequented the synagogues in which Jesus taught, if not the plain people?

Many of the earliest rabbis were drawn from the people, working with their hands by day, and studying, discussing and teaching in the evenings and on the sabbaths and festivals. Any antagonism between them and the multitude is out of the question. There is no evidence in the rabbinic literature that any large portion of the population, whether in Judea or in Galilee, consisted of poor and despised persons who did not observe the ethical and ritual requirements of the Law. If anyone failed to observe the Law, it was the rich rather than the poor. Doubtless the 'tax-collectors' of the Gospels were rich as were, in all likelihood, the other 'sinners'. Strange though it may seem, the *am ha-aretz* of the Talmud may even have referred to the comfortable and prosperous, since it is the *am ha-aretz* who are criticized for not meticulously tithing their land. It goes without saying that the great majority of the people could not have been as learned as the rabbinical scholars; but it does not follow that they were not observant on that account. If there did exist a section of the populace with whom the rabbinic teachers were at odds, it was the 'sinners' of the New Testament, a very small fraction of the nation. As we earlier noted in our analysis of the Pharisees, they were the leaders of the people. As Josephus stresses again and again, the Pharisees had 'the multitude' on their side.

Hillel was, of course, from among the humble and the poor. Shemaiah, the predecessor of both Hillel and Jesus, said: 'Love labour and hate mastery . . .' (Mish. Aboth 1:10). It is true that Hillel said 'an *am ha-aretz* cannot be a *Hasid*' (Mish. Aboth 2:6). Properly translated, this means that 'an ignorant man cannot be saintly'. What Hillel meant here was certainly no denigration of labouring men and women. He pointed, rather, to a simple truth: that those who devote themselves exclusively to worldly pursuits, without making time for pursuits of the spirit, will be one-sided human beings lacking the spiritual qualities of the *Hasid*. So Mishnah Aboth 2:6 needs to be supplemented by Hillel's sayings in 2:5: 'Keep not aloof from the congregation . . .' And by 2:8 as well, where Johanan ben Zakkai, who received the tradition from Hillel and Shammai, used to say: 'If thou hast wrought much in the Law claim not merit for thyself . . .' And, finally, by 2:2: 'Raban Gamaliel [the third] the son of Rav Judah the Patriarch said: Excellent is study of the Law together with worldly occupation, for toil in them both puts sin out of mind. But all study of the Law without [worldly] labour comes to naught at the last and brings sin in its train. And let all those who labour with the congregation labour with them for the sake of Heaven . . .'

Clearly a man of Hillel's humility and tolerance could not have denigrated a whole class of people. And, indeed, if we read Hillel's saying in context, it is quite obvious that the designation '*am ha-aretz*' is not a social class concept at all: A brutish man dreads not sin, and an ignorant man [Heb. *am ha-aretz*] cannot be saintly, and a shamefast man cannot learn, and the impatient man cannot teach, and he that engages overmuch in trade cannot become wise; and where there are no men strive to be a man' (Mish. Aboth 2:6). It is not a social class, but certain types of *individuals* who are being admonished here. The so-called *am ha-aretz* is a crass, materialistic individual preoccupied and absorbed only with the sensate elements of his environment. How could the Pharisees or earliest rabbis, who themselves were often poor, despise the poor? The evidence in the rabbinic literature points in precisely the opposite direction. C.G. Montefiore cites two important passages in this regard:

T.B. 81a: 'Pay ye special regard to the sons of the poor, for from them cometh forth Torah.'

T.B. Sanhedrin 96a: 'Pay ye special regard to the sons of the *amme ha-aretz* [plural], for from them cometh forth Torah.'[2]

And in Mishnah Aboth 3:11, Rav Dosa ben Harkinas said: 'Morning sleep and midday wine and children's talk and sitting in the meeting-houses of the ignorant people [Heb. *Amme-ha-aretz*] put a man out of the world.' Again here, *amme-ha-aretz* is properly translated as 'ignorant people', thus avoiding any social class connotation. In Joshua 1:8 we read: 'This book of the law shall not depart out of your mouth, but you shall meditate on it day and night, that you may be careful to do according to all that is written in it.' So the question arose among the rabbinical teachers of how to abide by this injunction (T.B. Menahot, 99b):

> R. Ami said: From the words of R. José we learn that, even if a man has studied no more than a single section [Heb. *perek*] in the morning and a single section in the evening, he has fulfilled the precept inculcated in Josh. 1:8. R. Johanan said in the name of R. Simeon ben Yohai, even the morning and evening recital of the *Shema* (Deut. 6:4–9) suffices. Yet it is forbidden to announce this in the presence of *amme ha-aretz*. But Raba said, it is a duty to announce this in the presence of the *amme ha-aretz*.

And C.G. Montefiore comments: 'The motive for the difference in attitude towards the *amme ha-aretz* is given by Rashi:[3] do not tell them the minimum, lest they make it a maximum for their children – so runs one view; tell them the minimum, for it will lead them into a frame of mind in which they will accustom their children to study the Torah. In neither view is there a display of animus or contempt; the motive in both views is solicitude for the good of the *am ha-aretz*.'[4] Even the impatient and perhaps less tolerant Shammai said: 'Make thy [study of the] Law a fixed habit; say little and do much, and receive *all* men with a cheerful countenance' (*Mish. Aboth* 1:15).

In sum, an *am ha-aretz* is an ignorant *individual* who fails to educate himself and his children and who neglects or violates the ethical and ceremonial precepts of the twofold Torah. Doubtless it was such individuals with whom Jesus ate and for which he was criticized by some of the Pharisees (Matt. 9:11). And as Montefiore remarks, it is part of Jesus' distinctive glory that he tried to win such individuals back.

In trying to grasp his distinctiveness and originality we must recognize that Jesus innovated by the radical nature of his ethical demands and by the love, mercy and compassion of his daily deeds. In these terms the Sermon on the Mount (SM) is of a piece with what comes before it in Matthew's Gospel: he went about all Galilee not only teaching and preaching, but 'healing every *inner righteousness plus outer observance of the law—*

disease and every infirmity among the people' (Matt. 4:23–5). And the same underscoring of the mercy of his acts reappears in Matthew following the SM, in chapters 8–9. As regards the SM itself, we need to clarify wherein lies Jesus' originality. For the ideas expressed there have ample precedent in the Scriptures and did not originate with him. Even Jesus' command to love one's enemy (Matt. 5:44) is anticipated in Proverbs: 'If your enemy is hungry, give him bread to eat; and if he is thirsty, give him water to drink' (Prov. 25:21). And Jesus' blessing of the 'poor in spirit' is expressed much earlier in Isaiah 66:2: 'Thus saith the lord . . . this is the man to whom I will look, he that is humble and contrite in spirit . . .'

The key to Jesus' originality lies in two elements of the SM, both of which are brought out in Matthew 5:17–20. There we find a direct, unqualified and unequivocal affirmation of the Law: 'Think not that I have come to abolish the law and the prophets; I have come not to abolish them but to fulfil them.' This is the first element; and insofar as scholars deny that this statement accurately reflects Jesus' own stance, they fail to grasp his outlook authentically. The second element is expressed in 5:20: 'For I tell you, unless your righteousness exceeds that of the scribes and Pharisees, you will never enter the kingdom of heaven.' It is this sentence, as we shall see, that epitomizes Jesus' outlook and mission.

Matthew's Gospel, persistently stressing the profound dependence of the New Testament on the Hebrew Scriptures, never loses 'from view the actual situation of the historical Jesus, with its definite Jewish background and setting'.[5] In Matthew Jesus not only affirms the continuing validity of the Torah, his attitude towards it is positive throughout: 'The scribes and Pharisees sit on Moses' seat; so practice and observe whatever they tell you' (23:3). And although the same passage accuses the Pharisees of hypocrisy, it clearly indicates that insofar as they teach the Law they deserve respect. From 23:23 we learn that Jesus accepted the Pharisaic tithing ordinances even with regard to small plants. Moreover, he instructs the healed leper to show himself to the priest and to make the offering Moses commanded (8:4). He tells the rich young man to keep the commandments given in the Law (19:17–19). And when we read that his purpose is not to tear down the law but to fulfil it, this represents in 'a deep sense' 'the attitude not only of Matthew but also of Jesus. For him the Law revealed the will of God; his purpose was not to fight that revelation but to affirm it, and to give it fuller expression. He did not think his work hostile to the Law of God as given in the Old Testament. That Law was a real divine revelation and it carried authority.'[6] Of course! How could it have been otherwise?

If therefore we take for granted and bear in mind that Jesus' attitude towards the Law could not have been anything but positive, we will easily understand why it is an egregious error to refer to Matthew 5:21–48 as

to overflow the cup

'antitheses', as some New Testament specialists have done; and why David Daube and W.D. Davies are certainly right in insisting that these utterances by Jesus, far from being antitheses, call for a heightened obedience to the deepest intent of the Law. What Jesus is calling for here is 'radical' in the original sense of the word: going to the root of things. Jesus is going to the root of the Law and probing for the ultimate will of God so that it may be obeyed. For if such radical obedience were achieved, Jesus believed, it would hasten the coming of the Kingdom. Hence these statements by Jesus are corollaries of his admonition that in order to enter the Kingdom of Heaven one must exceed the righteousness of the scribes and Pharisees. We have no ready-made term for Jesus' pronouncements in 5:21–48; but far from being 'antitheses' to the Law, they are a call for an intensified and deepened commitment to the Law and, hence, to the will of God:

> You have heard that it was said to the men of old, 'You shall not kill; and whoever kills shall be liable to judgement'. But I say to you that everyone who is angry with his brother [without cause?] shall be liable to judgment; whoever insults his brother shall be liable to the council and whoever says, 'You fool!' shall be liable to the hell [Gehenna] of fire. So if you are offering your gift at the altar, and there remember that your brother has something against you, leave your gift there before the altar and go; first be reconciled to your brother, and then come and offer your gift. (5:21–4)

> You have heard that it was said, 'You shall not commit adultery'. But I say to you that everyone who looks at a woman lustfully has already committed adultery with her in his heart. (5:27)

> It was also said, 'Whoever divorces his wife, let him give her a certificate of divorce'. But I say to you that everyone who divorces his wife, except on the ground of unchastity, makes her an adulteress . . . (5:31)

As we noted at length in chapter 6, Jesus' stance on the question of divorce is no repudiation of the Law. The intent behind it is a call for greater compassion and commitment.

> Again you have heard that it was said to the men of old 'You shall not swear falsely, but shall perform to the Lord what you have sworn'. But I say to you, Do not swear at all, either by heaven, for it is the throne of God, or by the earth, for it is his footstool, or by Jerusalem, for it is the city of the great King . . . Let what you say be simply 'yes' or 'no' . . . (5:33–7)

This demand of Jesus' is virtually indentical to the Essenes' avoidance of oaths as described by Josephus: 'Any word of theirs has more force than an oath; swearing they avoid, regarding it as worse than perjury, for they say that one who is not believed without an appeal to God stands condemned already' (*War* 2:135).

> You have heard that it was said, 'an eye for an eye and a tooth for a tooth'. But I say to you, Do not resist one who is evil. But if anyone strikes you on the right cheek, turn to him the other also . . . (5:38ff)

This, of course, is one of the most famous of Jesus' pronouncements. It has been taken as a deprecation of the 'primitive' *lex talionis* of the Mosaic law. However, Nietzsche's proposition concerning the 'inversion' of values gives us a profound insight into the historical process that culminated in Jesus' 'pacific' teachings. 'Now it is plain to me', wrote Nietzsche, 'that the source of the concept "good" has been sought and established in the wrong place: the judgment "good" did not originate with those to whom "goodness" was shown! Rather it was "the good" themselves, that is to say, the noble, powerful, high-stationed and high-minded, who felt and established themselves and their actions as good, that is of the first rank, in contradistinction to all the low, low-minded, common and plebeian.'[7] 'All that has been done on earth', Nietzsche continues,

> against 'the noble', 'the powerful', 'the masters', 'the rulers', fades into nothing compared with what the *Jews* have done against them; the Jews, that priestly people, who in opposing their enemies and conquerors were ultimately satisfied with nothing else than a radical revolution of their enemy's values, that is to say, an act of the *most spiritual revenge* . . . It was the Jews who, with awe-inspiring consistency, dared to invert the aristocratic value-equation (good=noble=powerful=beautiful=happy=beloved of God) and to hang on to this inversion with their teeth . . . saying, 'the wretched alone are the good; the poor, impotent, lowly alone are the good; the suffering, deprived, sick, ugly alone are pious, alone are blessed by God . . .'[8]
>
> . . . This Jesus of Nazareth, the incarnate gospel of love, this 'Redeemer' who brought blessedness and victory to the poor, the sick, and the sinners – was he not this . . . bypath to precisely those *Jewish* values and new ideals?[9]

Now there appears to be considerable truth in the proposition that from the time of Moses' repudiation of the values of the Egyptian 'house of bondage', Judaism developed as the negation and inversion of the ideals of polytheism.[10] And Jesus' repudiation of force and violence in Matthew 5:38ff may also be understood in this light. Jesus' teachings may be viewed as a continuation and accentuation of this inversion process, in his case, a rejection of the Roman (i.e., pagan) ideals of war, power and might. At the same time his teachings were, most probably, a repudiation of the ideas of some of Jesus' Jewish contemporaries – namely, those who showed hatred towards the Roman oppressors and their collaborators, and who advocated the use of force and violence against them.

An 'inversion' of this kind appears also in the next of Jesus' utterances:

> You have heard that it was said, 'You shall love your neighbor and hate your enemy'. But I say to you, Love your enemies and pray for those who persecute you, so that you may be sons of your Father who is in heaven; for he makes the sun rise on the evil and on the good, and sends rain on the just and on the unjust. For if you love those who love you, what reward have you? Do not even the tax-collectors do the same? And if you salute only your brethren, what more are you doing than others? Do not even the Gentiles do the same? You, therefore, must be perfect, as your heavenly Father is perfect. (5:48)

There is a real problem and puzzle here; for while the Hebrew Scriptures do of course teach that one should love one's neighbour, nowhere do they say that one should hate an enemy. On the contrary, Proverb 25:21, as we earlier noted, enjoins the opposite: it is precisely by giving your enemy in need food and water, that 'you will heap coals of fire on his head, and the Lord will reward you'. The most plausible hypothesis, then, is that Jesus aimed the statement 'Love your enemies' against those of his contemporaries who, like the Zealots, showed hatred towards the Romans and towards those Jewish leaders who aided and abetted them.

A close and careful look at these passages (Matthew. 5:21–48) makes it quite evident that Jesus taught no new 'laws' to replace the old. Nor did he propose any so-called 'antitheses' to the Mosaic legislation. Much has also been made, as we have seen, of Jesus' pronouncement on divorce. It seems clear, however, that if Jesus had intended to repeal the Deuteronomic law and replace it with another, he would have said so. Josephus informs us that 'it is an ancestral custom of ours to have several wives at the same time' (*Antiq.* 17:14). And as A.E. Harvey has noted, if the repeal of the Deuteronomic law had been Jesus' intention, 'he would surely have had to support it with further legislation; in particular, it would have been illogical to eliminate divorce without also eliminating polygamy, which though seldom practised, was still permissible under the law of Moses'.[11] Harvey makes another illuminating observation about these verses in Matthew. Throughout, Jesus says, 'You have heard . . .' or 'It was said . . .' *not* 'It is written . . .' or 'You have read . . .'. Hence, it is a near certainty that Jesus' pronouncements are not a divergence from the *written* Law of Moses itself, but rather from certain current interpretations of that Law. In other words, Jesus is here diverging from some of the traditions of the *Oral* Law, or what the Gospels call the 'tradition of the elders'. It is the form, perhaps, of these passages, that has misled commentators. 'If it were not the form', writes A.E. Harvey, which appears to place the speaker in opposition to the Law of Moses, it is unlikely that the content of the [so-called] antitheses would have caused us so much trouble. In no case would the following of Jesus' precepts have placed a person actually outside the law. To refrain from anger rather than merely avoiding homicide; to refrain from lustful looks rather than merely avoiding adultery; to renounce the option of divorce rather than to invoke the protection of the law when a divorce is desired; to refrain from swearing altogether rather than merely to be punctilious in the performance of an oath; to abjure any form of compensation for insult or injury rather than to seek damages at law; and to include your personal enemies among the neighbours to whom you are bidden to show love – all these injunctions can be regarded as an application, rather than a repeal, of the existing law, and in fact analogies are to be found in the work of [Jewish] teachers who would never have been suspected of any lack of reverence for the Law of Moses.[12]

Although many scholars continue to resist this view, they have come to acknowledge 'that the brunt of Jesus' criticism in the Gospel as a whole is directed not against the law itself, but against the prevailing interpretation and practice of it'.[13]

The Beatitudes

The ideals of humility, meekness, mercy and peace expressed in the Beatitudes (Matt. 5:3–10) are all essential elements of the teachings of the Prophets and the Psalms. In Isaiah (i.e., Deutero- and Trito-Isaiah) we read:

> For thus says the high and lofty one who inhabits eternity, whose name is Holy: I dwell in the high and holy place, and also with him who is of a contrite and humble spirit, to revive the spirit of the humble, and to revive the heart of the contrite. (57:15)

> The spirit of the Lord God is upon me, because the Lord has anointed me to bring good tidings to the afflicted [or poor]; he has sent me to bind up the broken-hearted, to proclaim liberty to the captives, and the opening of the prison to those who are bound; to proclaim the year of the Lord's favour, and the day of vengeance of our God; to comfort all who mourn . . . (61:2–3)

> But this is the man to whom I will look, he that is humble and contrite in spirit, and trembles at my word. (66:2)

> You shall see, and your heart shall rejoice; your bones shall flourish like the grass; and it shall be known that the hand of the Lord is with his servants . . . (66:14)

And in the Psalms we read:

Refrain from anger, and forsake wrath!

. . .

The meek shall possess the land, and delight themselves in abundant prosperity.

. . .

The Lord upholds the righteous; he knows the day of the blameless . . .

. . .

The righteous shall be preserved forever . . . and possess the land, and dwell upon it forever.

. . .

Mark the blameless man, and behold the upright, for there is posterity for the man of peace. (Ps. 37)

Truly God is good to the upright, to those who are pure in heart. But as for me, my feet had almost stumbled . . . For I was envious of the arrogant, when I saw the prosperity of the wicked. (Ps. 73:1–3)

Who shall ascend the hill of the Lord? And who shall stand in his holy place? He who has clean hands and a pure heart, who does not lift up his soul to what is false, and does not swear deceitfully. (Ps. 24:3–4)

Thus when Jesus says, 'Blessed are the peacemakers' (Matt. 5:9) and assigns so high a value to peace, meekness, humility and mercy, he is reaffirming time-honoured values found in the Scriptures. But he is also expressing the ideals and sentiments of his countrymen who, rejecting the ways of the armed Zealot rebels, waited for God to bring in the Kingdom without the military assistance of men. Jesus' relationship to the Zealots is an issue I shall explore later at length. For the present, however, we can observe that the Beatitudes seem genuinely to reflect the feelings of certain sections of the populace who had grown weary of the violence and who yearned for peace. This group was alternatively called the poor, the meek, the mourners, those who hunger and thirst for vindication, the pure in heart, the merciful, the peacemakers and those who are persecuted for righteousness sake. Their reward was to come with the Kingdom of Heaven (Heb. *Malkhut Shamayim*), which would bring them full vindication. The eight Beatitudes are unified by scriptural background, content and stylistic composition. George W. Buchanan has called attention to this unity which, he believes, 'argues against the assumption that the Matthean Beatitudes are secondary to Lukan Beatitudes or that they were composed in any jigsaw fashion, based on non-biblical, hypothetical sources [i.e., 'Q']. The close identification of the Matthean Beatitudes with Second Isaiah and Psalms 24, 37, and 73, shows that Mathew 5:5 should be translated, "Blessed are the meek, for they will inherit the land", meaning the promised land. Matthew 5:6 should be rendered: "Blessed are those who hunger and thirst for vindication, for they will be satisfied".'[14]

The Lord's Prayer

The Sermon on the Mount contains the 'Lord's Prayer', the sole religious 'service' or solemnity that Jesus authorized. He rejected the ostentatious piety of those who 'love to stand and pray in the synagogues and at the street corners, that they may be seen by men', and he urges his disciples and followers to do otherwise: 'when you pray, go into your room and shut the door and pray to your Father who is in secret; and your father who sees in secret will reward you.' And then, significantly, Jesus says: 'And in praying do not heap up empty phrases as the Gentiles do; for they think that they will be heard for their many words. Do not be like them, for your Father knows what you need before you ask him.' Then, telling his listeners to pray 'like this', Jesus composes and recites a direct, simple and succinct prayer that is truly remarkable for the universality of its appeal and the brevity with which it conveys its earnestness and devotion:

> Our Father who art in heaven, Hallowed be thy name. Thy kingdom come, Thy will be done, on earth as it is in heaven. Give us this day our daily bread; and forgive us our debts, As we also have forgiven our debtors; And lead us not into temptation, But deliver us from evil. (Matt. 6:5–13)

It has long been recognized among students of first-century Judaism that there are many affinities between the language of the Lord's Prayer and that of both the Hebrew Scriptures and rabbinic prayer. Some scholars have painstakingly demonstrated that every word and phrase of Jesus' prayer can be traced to biblical and rabbinic sources. A few examples: 'Our Father who art in heaven' is an expression found in many Jewish prayers. One such prayer, recited on Mondays and Thursdays before returning the Torah scroll to the ark, opens several times with the introductory clause: 'May it be thy will, O our Father who art in heaven.' In one of the most widespread Jewish prayers, the 'kaddish', we find, 'may thy name be hallowed and may thy kingdom come. Exalted and sanctified be his great name in the world which he created according to his will, and may he bring about his kingdom.'[15] The phrase, 'Thy will be done, as in heaven, so on earth', appears in the 'short prayer' of the early *Tanna*,[16] Rav Eliezer: 'What is the short prayer? Rav Eliezer said: Do thy will in heaven, and on earth, give comfort to those who fear thee, and do what is right in thy sight.'[17] The expression, 'Give us this day our daily bread' is found in a similar form not only in the Hebrew Scriptures ('Feed me with mine allotted bread', Prov. 30:8), but in a variant of Rav Eliezer's 'short prayer' as well: 'may it be thy will, O our God, to give to everyone his needs and to every being sufficient for his lack'. In the 'Shemoneh-Esreh' prayer (i.e., 'Eighteen Benedictions'),

'Forgive us our debts' is the sixth blessing. And in Ben Sirach (28:2–5) we find 'Forgive thy neighbour's sin and then, when thou prayest, thy sins will be forgiven; man cherisheth anger against man, and doth he seek healing (or forgiveness) from the Lord?' Finally, the phrase, 'lead us not into temptation' occurs in a Talmudic prayer: 'Lead us not into sin or iniquity or temptation.'[18]

The outstanding Jewish scholar Joseph Klausner thus concludes that the Lord's Prayer 'can be divided up into separate elements, every one of which is Hebraic in form and occurs in either the Old Testament or the Talmud'. Klausner nevertheless recognizes and acknowledges that Jesus created something new and original:

> ... Jesus gathered together and, so to speak, condensed and concentrated ethical teachings in such a fashion as to make them more prominent than in the Talmudic *Haggadah* and the *Midrashim*, where they are interspersed among more commonplace discussions and worthless matter ...
>
> Although there is in the Mishnah, an entire tractate devoted exclusively to ethical teaching, viz., *Pirke Aboth* [the Ethics of our Fathers], it is but a compilation drawing on the sayings of many scores of *Tannaim* ... ; *but the ethical teachings of the Gospel, on the contrary, came from one man only and are, every one, stamped with the same peculiar hallmark. A man like Jesus, for whom the ethical ideal was everything, was something hitherto unheard of in the Judaism of the day.*[19]

There is, then, no denying Jesus' originality. For it should be underscored that although portions of the Lord's Prayer have parallels in other Jewish prayers, taken as a whole, it is a unique entity. The Lord's Prayer may therefore be considered Jesus' original creation: an extraordinarily beautiful, private prayer of the truly devout.

Jesus' Parables

Jesus' originality lies also in another facet of his teaching method – his use of allegory and parable. A parable discloses the nature of something through a comparison with something else; it illustrates a moral attitude or a religious principle. Some New Testament specialists have assumed that the parables attributed to Jesus in the Gospels are rather innovations of the Christian communities that developed only after his death. It may be true that the early communities preserved, collected and arranged Jesus' sayings, and perhaps even created a setting for them, 'sometimes modifying their form, expanding here, allegorizing there, always in relation to its own situation between the cross and the *Parousia*'.[20] Nevertheless, when the parables are translated back into Aramaic, Jesus' mother tongue, their original Palestinian colouring becomes obvious. A form of heightened prose, they exhibit alliteration, plays on words, and images drawn from the daily life of Palestinian Jews in the time of Jesus. As a teacher of ethics calling on all and sundry to repent because God's Kingdom was imminent, he preferred short, pithy, colourful utterances, the kind with which the *Pirke Aboth* (the Sayings, or Ethics, of the Fathers, in the Mishnah) are filled. Parables and proverbs, in particular, are characteristic of folk wisdom; and we may assume that there was a large, common treasure of wise, homiletic sayings both among the people and the rabbis. Jesus no doubt drew upon these, but also added to the common treasure. Indeed, he was a great artist of the parable. The Gospel parables bear the unmistakable mark of an original and exalted personality; and even if Jesus was not the original author of them all, his adaptation was accomplished with extraordinary skill.

All the parables of 'growth' are most probably authentic. They are above all related to the coming of the Kingdom of God, a mysterious and miraculous process, as is life itself. The question of how it would come about remains something of a mystery, and becomes a source of confusion and misunderstanding, as we shall see, for both the disciples and the crowds. The meaning of Jesus' parables was by no means always clear, even to his most intimate associates. They revealed and concealed at one and the same time. As Jesus began to teach beside the sea of Galilee, for example, he spoke to the large crowd in the parable of the sower who went out to sow; and when he finished speaking and was alone, 'those who were about him with the twelve asked him concerning the parables. And he said to them, "To you has been given the secret of the Kingdom of God, but for those outside everything is in parables; so that they may indeed see but not perceive, and may indeed hear but not understand; lest they should turn again and be forgiven." And he said to them, "Do you not understand this parable? How then will you understand all the parables?"' (Mark 4:1–13). Jesus then proceeds to explain the parable of the sower. His reply to those about him is truly enigmatic: he speaks in parables so that the crowd will see and hear but not understand. Why? Even his disciples do not quite understand. It appears that Jesus deliberately addressed the crowd in parables precisely because it concealed as much as it revealed. He 'did not speak to them [the crowd] without a parable, but privately to his own disciples he explained everything' (Mark 4:33–4). Yet there is very good reason to believe that not only the crowds but the disciples too remained confused to the very end. How the Kingdom would come about and the role their master was to play in it never became clear to them. We may go a step further and suggest that perhaps Jesus himself was unclear about these matters. The 'Kingdom of God', he says, 'is as if a man should scatter seed upon the ground, and should sleep and rise night and day, and the seed should sprout and grow, *he knows not how*. The earth produces of itself, first the blade, then the ear, then the full grain in the ear. But when the grain is ripe, at once he puts in the sickle, because the harvest has come' (Mark 4:26–9). And Jesus continues: 'With what can we compare the Kingdom of God . . . ? It is like a grain of mustard seed, which, when sown upon the ground, is the smallest of all the seeds on earth; yet when it is sown it grows up and becomes the greatest of all shrubs, and puts forth large branches, so that the birds of the air can make nests in its shade' (Mark 4:30–2). It seems evident, then, that 'Jesus cannot speak adequately about the coming of the Kingdom of God unless he primarily uses the form of parable as a revelation which conceals'.[21]

Scholars are pretty much in agreement that all of Jesus' parables are full of 'the secret of the Kingdom of God' (Mark 4:11) – that is, the belief that the eschaton is in the process of realization. The crisis is imminent, the final crisis of history, and the opportunity must be seized before it is too late. But *how* must it be seized? That is the question to which Jesus' parables and proverbs never provided a clear and unambiguous answer. If Jesus thought of himself as a 'sower of seeds', as a sower of a mustard seed that will become the greatest of shrubs; as a teacher calling for a righteousness that would exceed that of the scribes and Pharisees; as a sower of seed upon good soil so that his word would bear fruit 'thirtyfold and sixtyfold and a hundredfold' (Mark 4:20) – if Jesus thought of himself in this way, then it is almost certain that neither the crowds nor the disciples quite understood how the opportunity was to be seized before it was too late. The reason for their confusion can only become clear after we have adequately examined the complexity of the concept of the Kingdom of Heaven and the role of the Messiah in it.

9

The Kingdom of Heaven
and the Role of the Messiah

At the heart of the Messianic idea in Israel was the hope of a better future. The hope became a definite expectation with the eighth-century prophets of social justice. The expectation was worldly in that the radical changes foreseen were to take place in this world; but the expectation was also transcendent in that the transformation of the world was to be the work of God. The God-ordained revolution was to affect not only the destiny of the nation but that of all humanity. This was certainly true of the vision of Isaiah, the most universalist of the prophets:

> It shall come to pass in the latter days that the mountain of the house of the Lord shall be established as the highest of the mountains, and shall be raised above the hills; and all the nations shall flow to it, and many people shall come, and say: 'Come let us go up to the mountain of the Lord, to the house of the God of Jacob; that he may teach us his ways and that we may walk in his paths.' For out of Zion shall come forth the law, and the word of the Lord from Jerusalem. He shall judge between the nations, and shall decide for many peoples; and they shall beat their swords into ploughshares, and their spears into pruning hooks; nation shall not lift up sword against nation, neither shall they learn war anymore. (Isa. 2:2–4)

Isaiah's vision is one of the earliest sources of the idea that in the 'latter days' humanity would enter a new era, in which there would be a radical break with the past: peace, justice and happiness would prevail. From the standpoint of the prophets of social justice, God would judge Israel on the basis of its social and moral conduct. It was their expectation, therefore, that the new era would come about as God's gracious response to the moral purification and cleansing of the nation.

Whereas in the biblical period hopes for salvation centred on the nation, in the post-biblical period a concern for individual salvation emerged, its earliest manifestation being the belief in resurrection. As we noted earlier the book of Daniel (c. 167–165 BC) exercised a profound influence on the formation of the Messianic idea. Reflecting the distress that befell the nation with the wicked actions of Antiochus Epiphanus, the author foresees a coming deliverance in which God himself will sit in judgment of the kingdoms of this world and take away the power of the evil ones forever. But 'the saints of the Most High' will receive the new kingdom, and all peoples and nations will serve the saints who will possess it for evermore (Dan. 7:9–27; 2:44). The new element in Daniel is the promise that 'many of those who sleep in the dust of the earth shall awake, some to everlasting life, and some to shame and everlasting contempt' (12:2). It is in this remarkable book that the hope for a bodily resurrection is plainly expressed, a hope that became a firm article of faith for the Pharisees and the people. The future of Israel is envisioned as a worldly kingdom in which all the saints who have fallen asleep will awake and participate.

After Daniel, judging from the apocryphal and apocalyptic books, the Messianic idea assumed a new form.[1] The age prior to the Messianic era was to be a time of extreme suffering, conflict and confusion. This is expressed in Baruch and 4 Ezra and in the New Testament as well. The age of suffering draws to a close with the reappearance of the prophet Elijah, whose central mission is to restore peace on earth (Malachi 4:5) and to prepare the way for the coming of the Messiah. In the Psalms of Solomon he appears as an extraordinary but fully human being, descended from the house of David, and endowed by God with special gifts and powers so that he may become the ruler of the earthly kingdom. In 4 Ezra and the Parables of Enoch, on the other hand, the Messiah's appearance takes on a supernatural character; and in the latter work one also finds the phrase 'son of man', an application of Daniel's image (7:13) to a Messianic figure, a chosen instrument of God called 'the Elect'. With the appearance of the Messiah, the wicked, hostile powers will assemble themselves for an assault against him, but they will be destroyed by God himself. The Messianic kingdom will include the restoration of the independence of Israel, the Holy Land, the renewal of Jerusalem and the ingathering of those who were dispersed by the wicked, pagan empires. In the Messianic era all nations will acknowledge the God of Israel, as was prophesied by the prophets (Isa. 2:2ff; Micah 4:1ff; 7:16ff; Jer. 3:17; 16:19ff; Zeph. 2:11; 3:9; Zech. 8:20ff; Deut. Isa. 55:5; 56:1ff).

How did Jesus view himself and how was he viewed by others in relation to the traditional Messianic ideas in Israel? This most central question is also the most difficult to answer because the evidence in the New Testament is contradictory. In Mark we read that when Jesus' name had become known, some said that he was John the Baptizer raised from the dead; others said he was Elijah, and still others believed that he was a 'prophet like one of the prophets of old' (6:14–15). After his arrest, when he is brought before the high-priest, Jesus is asked: 'Are you the Christ [i.e., Messiah], the son of the Blessed?' And Jesus said, 'I am; and you will see the son of man sitting at the right hand of Power, and coming with the clouds of heaven' (14:61–2). But when Pilate asked Jesus whether he was King of the Jews, i.e., the Messiah, Jesus replied: 'You have said so' (15:2). In Matthew, Jesus never says 'I am' in reply to the high-priest's question. Instead, he says, 'You have said so', adding, however, 'But I tell you, hereafter you will see the son of man seated at the right hand of Power, and coming on the clouds of heaven' (26:64). His reply to Pilate is also, 'You have said so' (27:11). When Pilate presumably offers the crowd an opportunity to choose either Barabbas or Jesus for release, he says: 'Whom do you want me to release for you, Barabbas or Jesus *who is called Christ*' (27:17). This is significant in that together with other evidence to be presented shortly, it suggests that some people did in fact call Jesus 'Messiah'. Later, the Roman soldiers mock him, saying, 'Hail, King of the Jews!' (27:29). Finally, the titulus stating the charge against him read: 'This is Jesus, the King of the Jews' (27:37).

In John there is a highly revealing passage strongly suggesting that, however Jesus may have viewed himself, the crowds looked upon him as 'the prophet who is to come into the world!': 'perceiving then that they were about to come and take him by force to make him king, Jesus withdrew again to the hills by himself' (John 6:14–15). John also relates that a great crowd who had come to the feast heard that Jesus was coming to Jerusalem. So they took branches of palm trees and went out to meet him, crying, "Hosanna! Blessed be he who comes in the name of the Lord, even the King of Israel"' (John 12:12–13). That Jesus had a popular following is also attested by the words John places in the mouths of the Pharisees observing the scene: 'look, the world had gone after him' (12:19). In John, Jesus' reply to Pilate suggests that if some of the crowds viewed Jesus as a Messianic figure in the Davidic, political-military sense, Jesus' self-understanding may have been quite different: 'my kingship is not of this world; if my kingship were of this world, my servants would fight' (18:36). Finally, there is the statement in Acts 1:6 strongly indicating that after the Passion the disciples had the expectation that a tangible political change would result from Jesus' return: 'So when they [the apostles] had come together, they asked him, "Lord, will you at this time restore the kingdom to Israel?".'

So we see that while the crowds and, most probably, the disciples definitely perceived Jesus as fulfilling the political-military Messianic role, Jesus' self-understanding in this regard is anything but clear and unequivocal. The fascinating episode at Caesarea Philippi has some bearing on the question before us. There Jesus asks his disciples, 'Who do men say that I am?' 'And they told him, "John the Baptist; and others say, Elijah; and others, one of the prophets." And he asked them, "But who do you say that I am?" Peter answered him, "You are the Christ." And he charged them to tell no one about him' (Mark 8:27–30). In the same conversation, however, when Jesus went on to tell them that the son of man must suffer many things and be rejected and killed, this alarms Peter who rebukes him. Why does it alarm Peter? Most probably because Peter's conception of the Messiah was not one in which he would suffer and be killed. In response to Peter's alarmed reaction Jesus says, 'Get behind me Satan [i.e., 'adversary']! For you are not on the side of God, but of men' (Mark 8:31–3). It is as if Peter is tempting Jesus to accept the role which the crowds and the disciples prefer: a triumphant Messiah-King who would restore the independence of Israel. Most of the disciples and followers no doubt shared this expectation, as is clear from the request of the sons of Zebedee: 'Grant us to sit, one at your right hand and one at your left, in your glory' (Mark 10:35ff; cf. Matt. 20:20). But what about Jesus himself? How do we interpret his question, 'Who do men say that I am?', and his reasons for asking it? Cullen Murphy has described this question as one of

the most resonant in the whole of the New Testament. It is the question, it seems, of a man who wishes to disturb but who is also himself disturbed; of a man who has somehow found himself in deeper waters than anticipated; of a man at once baffled and intrigued by a destiny that he may have begun to glimpse but of which he is not fully aware. And thus, seeking guidance, seeking perhaps to know the range of possibilities, Jesus puts the question to his followers.

It may be that Jesus went to his death not knowing quite who he was, regardless of what other men thought. He certainly went to his death with public opinion sharply divided and with his own disciples profoundly confused.[2]

Yes, it could hardly be expressed better: public opinion was sharply divided, the disciples were profoundly confused, and Jesus himself was never quite certain of the role he felt himself called upon to fulfil. Public opinion was divided in that he was at once popular and unpopular: unpopular to the extent that he diverged from the traditions of the elders and offended certain sections of the Pharisaic movement; popular, however, with those to whom he reached out with his personal concern, healing them and promising salvation if only they will change their ways. We cannot describe who the latter were in precise sociological terms; but the strong impression we receive from the Gospels is that it was the highly distraught and distressed folk of Galilee on whom Jesus had the greatest impact. It was they who clung to the undying hope that some world-shaking, supernatural intervention was due at any moment. This was the social background of the disciples as well.

But even among the crowds who followed Jesus and within his own entourage, his message was interpreted differently by different individuals. To some he appeared as the anointed one, a Davidic worldly prince who would lead the people in their expulsion of the pagan empire and the restoration of the kingdom to Israel. These were the crowds who tried to 'take him by force to make him king' (John 6:15). On the margins of the crowds that viewed him in a Messianic role were those who were ambivalent and unsure. Jesus' emphasis on peace articulated the deep yearnings of the pacifist elements among the plain people of Galilee; but this emphasis could hardly have endeared him to those of his fellow countrymen who were sympathetic to the Zealots. Indeed, we need to address the important question of whether there were points of contact between Jesus and the Zealots; for there are serious scholars who have made a strong case for such points of contact. Before we address this issue, however, we need to clarify further the Jewish conception of the Kingdom of Heaven.

There can be little doubt that Jesus envisaged an imminent, divine intervention in the world, a dramatic world-renewing judgment similar to the 'latter days' pictured in the apocalyptic writings. This was to entail a catastrophic change, consummating the old era and inaugurating the new through some sort of Messianic agency. Jesus' ethical teachings must be seen in the context of his eschatological expectation. His call to repentance, like John's before him, and the urgency with which he called for a higher righteousness, were conditioned by the extraordinary situation which he believed was 'at hand'. It was Albert Schweitzer who did much to validate the eschatological element of the Gospels by demonstrating that it was not the product of the later church, but of Jesus himself. Jesus' indifference to family and property resulted from his acute sense of the transitional nature of the present historical order.

Today there are few New Testament specialists who would disagree with Schweitzer on his main point, namely, that a flood of light is thrown upon Jesus and his teaching when we bear in mind that he expected the end of an age and the dawn of a new. But the recognition of the eschatological context of Jesus' words and deeds should not blind us to the *this-worldly concerns of any and all Messianic ideas in Jesus' time*. All Messianic ideas, without exception, looked forward to the reconstitution of the world in accordance with the highest ethical ideals of Judaism. Jesus' Messianic outlook was no exception. We may safely assume that he knew the world would continue, albeit in a reconstituted form. In these terms the ethical ideals he taught were intended not just for the 'interim', in Schweitzer's sense, but for eternity.

Jesus spoke in both prophetic-Messianic and in apocalyptic terms. He proclaimed the coming of the 'Kingdom of Heaven' and hoped that his own words and deeds of healing would hasten its realization. But he certainly understood that the Kingdom could be realized nowhere else but in this world. In his saying concerning the temple, that he could destroy it and build it up again in three days (John 2:19; cf. Matt. 26:61; Mark 14:58), he envisioned the future as a continuation of history, but on a qualitatively higher level. He announced the imminent 'end-time', but went on to teach as if the world will go on. This is no contradiction from the standpoint of Jewish prophecy and eschatology. God will intervene and there will be a radical break with the past, but then the world will go on with humanity having achieved a higher form of social and moral righteousness. Jewish eschatology, as we have seen, far from being exclusively otherworldly, was always historical and transcendental at one and the same time. Allowance for the symbolic nature of its forecasts enables us to see that its chief concern was with the future of Israel and humanity. For the author of the book of Daniel, for example, 'the actuality corresponding to the victory of the "son of man" over the "beasts" is a victory of the Jews over the Seleucid monarchy, and the subsequent erection of a Jewish empire. It had not happened [yet] when he wrote, but it had for him the actuality of an impending historical event.'[3] A similar view prevailed in Jesus' time towards the Roman empire. To return to Jesus' saying about the temple, it clearly signifies the continuation of history: 'The manifest disintegration of the existing system', writes C.H. Dodd, 'is to be preliminary to the appearance of a . . . new community to embody it. And yet, it is the same temple, first destroyed, that is to be rebuilt. The new community is still Israel; there is continuity through the discontinuity . . .'[4] Or as Amos N. Wilder has observed in this regard, if Jewish eschatology in Jesus' era 'had taken a sheerly transcendental direction, it would have been a complete reversal and denial of the main stream of Jewish religion. No religion has ever been so completely realistic in its concerns for man's [sic] life in this world. The commanding, age-old and original concern of the prophets and psalmists of Israel was for a purified and holy kingdom, an Israel disciplined and ministering to the world. Their interest was in the social-historical future of man.'[5] Any attempt to reduce Jesus' teachings to some sort of other-worldly transcendentalism therefore fails to situate him properly in his religio-cultural context.

Some scholars have nevertheless insisted that Jesus' conception of the Kingdom must be understood 'as something through and through *spiritual*. Just as much as the Fatherhood of God, the Kingdom of God is a personal relation between God and the individual human being.'[6] Manson thereby denies the worldly aspect of the Messianic expectation. To support his view Manson cites a parable from the rabbinic literature. In this parable God is likened to a king who enters a province and states that he will be king; to which the people reply, 'What hast thou done for us that thou shouldst reign over us?' In reply the parable proceeds to relate what God had in fact done for Israel: 'The omnipresent (*makom* = God) brought Israel out of Egypt, he divided the sea for them, he brought down *manna* for them, he caused the spring to flow for them, he brought the quails to them, he waged war with the Amalek for them. He said to them: I will be king over you. They said to him: Yes, yes.'[7] But this passage conveys the very this-worldliness of God's kingship that Manson wishes somehow to deny. Did the promise of eternal life make the Kingdom 'through and through spiritual'? The idea of bodily resurrection, as we have seen, was first expressed in the book of Daniel; but Daniel's concerns were no less worldly on that account. Nor were the concerns of the Pharisees, for whom resurrection was a fundamental article of faith. There can be no doubt that Jesus stood in the tradition of Jewish eschatology. 'It is not possible', writes Hans Conzelmann, 'to interpret the kingdom as a spiritual entity, as a kingdom of inwardness. It manifests itself – for Jesus, just as for Jewish apocalyptic – as a visible world transformation.'[8] If we bear this in mind, we gain some insight into the reason for the scepticism with which Jesus' claims were met among many of his contemporaries. He refused to give a sign, and they saw no outward sign. They were prepared to believe, perhaps, that the Kingdom was near; but all they had to do was to look around them to see that poverty, illness, sin, wickedness and oppression continued to exist. The Kingdom was supposed to bring an end to these things; therefore it was not yet here.

Jesus and the 'Son of Man'

In the Hebrew Scriptures the word 'Messiah', meaning literally 'the anointed one' (Gr. 'Christ'), was applied to Israel as the elect people (Hab. 3:13), chosen by God to fulfil his purpose. The early kings of Israel were also referred to as the 'anointed of God'. In time, however, it came to denote an ideal king, a descendant of David, who would come to deliver Israel and reign in righteousness: 'Lo, your king comes to you; triumphant and victorious is he, humble and riding on an ass, on a colt the foal of an ass. I will cut off the chariot from Ephraim and the war horse from Jerusalem; and the battle bow shall be cut off, and he shall command peace to the nations; his dominion shall be from sea to sea, and from the River to the ends of the earth' (Zech. 9:9–10). It is this passage from Zechariah that is cited in the Gospels when Jesus sends two of his disciples into a village near Jerusalem to obtain such a colt, on which he then enters the city (Matt. 21:1ff; Mark 11:1ff; Luke 19:28ff). The passage from Zechariah as well as this episode in the Gospels creates a problem of interpretation, for as we can see, the Messianic figure is described in Zechariah as triumphant, victorious and humble at one and the same time. What was Jesus' intention in entering Jerusalem on a colt? Some of the crowds seem to have looked upon his entry as the triumphant one of the Messiah, as forecast by the prophet. But perhaps this question is best postponed for a later context in which Jesus' relationship to the Zealots is explored (see chapter 10).

'Son of God' may also have been a Messianic title, probably based on Psalm 2:7: 'I will tell of the decree of the Lord: He said to me, "You are my son, today I have begotten you. Ask of me, and I shall make the nations your heritage, and the ends of the earth your possession. You shall break them with a rod of iron, and dash them in pieces like a potter's vessel."' Here the imagery is consistently militant. The statement in Matthew (3:17; 17:5), 'this is my beloved son, with whom I am well pleased', was probably drawn from the psalm.

'Son of man', a third phrase appearing in the Gospels, is very difficult to interpret, as is Jesus' use of it. We earlier noted the ambiguity of Jesus' reply to the high-priest's question: 'I adjure you by the living God, tell us if you are the Christ [Messiah], the son of God.' And Jesus replies: 'You have said so. But I tell you, hereafter you will see the son of man seated at the right hand of Power, and coming on the clouds of heaven' (Matt. 26:63–4). The phrase 'son of man', occurring in the Gospels only on the lips of Jesus himself, is a translation of the Aramaic *bar nasha*, which means simply 'man' or 'human being'. In the Hebrew Scriptures 'son of man' (Heb. *ben adam*) is often a poetic synonym for 'man' (e.g., Ps. 8:4). In the book of Ezekiel, where the phrase occurs more than 90 times, it describes the prophet himself as a lowly and insignificant individual whom God nevertheless sees fit to address. Some scholars believe that Jesus took the title from the book of Ezekiel and, hence, that Jesus was similarly expressing his humility. Other scholars believe it more likely that Jesus derived the phrase from the book of Daniel (7:13–14), where the vision of the four beasts is described, and the author adds, 'I saw . . . one *like* unto a son of man . . .'. In Daniel, as already noted, the phrase 'son of man' represents 'the saints of the Most High', i.e., the community of the faithful, the people of God.

There are scholars who have proposed that at first Jesus employed the phrase in the community sense which we find in Daniel, and that he therefore intended by it not only himself, but also the community of his disciples. There are instances, however, in which Jesus may be referring to himself alone. In Matthew 9:6 (Mark 2:10), for instance, he says, 'the son of man has authority on earth to forgive sins'. In Matthew 12:8 (Mark 2:28), 'the son of man is lord of the sabbath'. He may be referring to himself; but the meaning could also be 'communal' – that the human being is lord of the sabbath. Nevertheless, notwithstanding a persistent ambiguity, Jesus does seem to employ the phrase in order to refer to himself: e.g., 'Foxes have holes, and birds of the air have nests; but the son of man has nowhere to lay his head' (Matt. 8:20); 'but I tell you that Elijah has already come, and they did not know him, but did to him whatever they pleased. So also the son of man will suffer at their hands' (17:12). 'Truly, I say to you, there are some standing here who will not taste death before they see the son of man coming in his Kingdom' (16:28). This 'coming' (Gr. *parousia*) would usher in the Kingdom of Heaven.

It is, however, problematic to regard the phrase 'son of man' as a Messianic title. Geza Vermes has stressed that in the Aramaic context '*bar nasha*' ('son of man') is a circumlocution in which a speaker alludes to himself not as 'I', but in the third person, implying reserve or modesty. Furthermore, in none of the passages in Jewish literature scrutinized by Vermes, 'not even in the Jewish Messianic exegesis of Daniel 7, does the expression '*Bar nasha*' figure as a title'.[9] Vermes notes, in addition, that 'the famous Enochic 'son of man' about whom New Testament scholars have speculated so much, appears to be missing from the pre-[A.D.] 70 text of the Aramaic Enoch'.[10] It is entirely possible then, as Vermes suggests, that the apocalyptic 'son of man' may be a phantom, an invention of New Testament specialists. We may therefore seriously question the existence of a special 'son of man' concept in the Judaism of Jesus' time; and it is noteworthy that an increasing number of scholars now embrace the self-reference meaning of the phrase, which enables the speaker to make his point with greater delicacy.

C.F.D. Moule concurs with Vermes in this regard. Moule writes that the 'son of man',

> the 'human figure' of Daniel 7:13 need not have been understood by Jesus (if he did use it) as . . . an essentially supernatural figure. In Daniel 7 itself, . . . it simply represents or symbolizes the persecuted loyalists (no doubt, of Maccabean days) in their ultimate vindication in the court of heaven. Or, if there is anything supernatural about it, it belongs to the vindicated state only, of what, in origin, is very much on earth. And it is this symbol that Jesus adopted to express his vocation and the vocation to which he summoned his followers. It was with reference to Daniel's 'apparently human figure' that Jesus used the term '*the* son of man' (almost nowhere outside the Christian tradition is the definite article used); and, having once adopted the phrase, he was able to apply it alike to his authority, . . . his impending death, and to his ultimate vindication.[11]

The reason for excluding I Enoch 37–71 (the 'Similitudes') and 4 Ezra 13 as antecedents to the Gospel usage, Moule continues, is that unlike Daniel 7, 'these works cannot be proved to be early enough to have been used by the Evangelists, let alone Jesus. It is a well-known fact that the Similitudes are the only part of I Enoch so far *un*represented at Qumran.' It may some day turn up there; 'but, unless and until it does, it is unscientific to assume an early date for this, the only section of Enoch that is relevant to "the son of man" . . .'[12]

What appears in Daniel, in Aramaic, is *not* '*the* son of man', but simply *kevar nash*, equivalent to the Hebrew *keven adam*, meaning 'something like a man or human being'. For Moule, this is a symbol for the persecuted pious and faithful; but other scholars, without good grounds, interpret the figure in Daniel's vision as a permanent, supernatural member of the heavenly court. Finally, Moule calls attention to two notoriously difficult problems:

> the strikingly limited occurrence of the term 'the son of man,' and the comparative rarity with which the figure of the suffering Servant is applied to Christ. Why . . . is there in early Christian apologetic outside the gospels no application to Jesus of a full-length testimonium from Daniel 7? Or again, Isaiah 53 is almost the only Old Testament passage which seems to recognize innocent suffering as possessing redemptive power. Why, then, are direct references to Isaiah 53 in the gospels so very rare? Why are the occurrences scarcely less meagre in the whole of the rest of the New Testament? And – most surprising of all – why are the explicit *redemptive* phrases from Isaiah 53 only quoted once or twice at all?[13]

The Jewish mind had no conception of a suffering Messiah with redemptive powers – powers that would become manifest through his death. We should recall how obstinately the apostles rejected Jesus' prediction of his own passion (Luke 9:45); and that prior to it, the expectation of Jesus' followers was probably expressed by Cleopas when he said, 'we had hoped that he was the one to redeem Israel' (Luke 24:21). It was only after the resurrection appearance that the disciples could be convinced of the notion of a suffering-and-dying Messiah. It is also quite indisputable that Paul had a very hard time trying to persuade his fellow Jews 'that the Christ must suffer' (Acts 26:23). For the Jews of Jesus' time, Isaiah 53 had its original meaning: it referred to the people of Israel, not to an individual. Furthermore, it was fundamental to the Jewish faith that thanks for redemption was owed to God, not to his chosen instrument, however extraordinary an individual he might be (Ps. 107:1–2). We should not assume, therefore, that Jesus saw himself destined to be the heavenly judge of the world. It was the belief in the resurrection that gave rise to that idea. It 'was in the first instance primitive tradition which, through faith in the risen Jesus who will come to judge the world, added the name of majesty even to those sayings of Jesus in which it did not originally occur'.[14] Thomas Sheehan cites Thessalonians 1:1 as one of the earliest written statements about Jesus, showing that the 'Christian community had already elevated the prophet beyond his own understanding of his status and had endowed him with two titles, "Lord" and "Christ", neither of which he had dared to give himself'.[15] Certainly not 'Lord', given the constraints of monotheism.

Finally, we must note that the difference in meaning between 'imminent' and 'present' has been blurred by some New Testament specialists. 'Despite the fact', writes Christopher Rowland, 'that the consensus of New Testament scholarship accepts that Jesus believed that the kingdom of God had already in some sense arrived in Jesus' words and deeds, the fact has to be faced that the evidence in support of such an assumption is not very substantial.'[16]

The Question of Bethlehem

In the book of the prophet Micah we read: 'But you, O Bethlehem Ephratah, who are little to be among the clan of Judah, from you shall come forth for me one who is to be the ruler of Israel' (5:1–3). On the basis of Micah and other scriptural passages, Bethlehem was the place in which the Messiah's birth was expected (Isa. 11:1; Jer. 23:5; 33:15; Zech. 3:8; 6:12). Was Jesus born in Bethlehem? Clearly this question has a bearing on how he was perceived by others and even on how he perceived himself. If he was not born in Bethlehem and this fact was known, it would not be surprising that any Messianic claims made on his behalf would be greeted with extreme scepticism: for example, 'Search and you will see that no prophet is to rise from Galilee' (John 7:52).

Both Matthew and Luke name Bethlehem as the place of Jesus' birth. But both Evangelists betray the fact that it was out of theological considerations that they made this assertion; the details provided by them are quite discrepant. According to Luke (2:1–52), it is the census imposed by Caesar Augustus that brings Jesus' parents to Bethlehem, after which they return to their home in Nazareth. Matthew (2:1–33), on the other hand, states that Jesus' parents live in Bethlehem, and only after their flight to Egypt and their refuge there, does Nazareth become their new home. Nor can we be certain that he was born in Nazareth inasmuch as the oldest texts vary between the designations 'the Nazarene', and 'the Nazirite', the latter phrase having nothing to do with Nazareth at all, but rather referring to a religious order bound by a vow to be temporarily set apart from the rest of the community for service to God. It is noteworthy that James the brother of Jesus is said to have been a Nazirite: he drank no wine nor strong drink, ate no meat, never cut his hair, attired himself in cotton, never woollens, possessed only one garment, and spent much of his time fasting and praying in the temple.[17] James and his companions requested that Paul should pay the expenses of the Nazirites for the shaving of their heads, which remained shaved while under a vow, and that he too, should purify himself with them and enter the temple (Acts 21:18–26).

To return to the question of Bethlehem, Luke's account, on the face of it, appears to be reliable; but the great historian Emil Schürer long ago gave several sound reasons for questioning that account:

1 Historical sources other than Luke do not record a general imperial census in the reign of Augustus.[18]
2 The conditions of a Roman census would not have required of Joseph to travel to Bethlehem, nor would Mary have been obliged to accompany him there.[19]
3 It is highly unlikely that a Roman census was carried out in Palestine during the reign of King Herod, since in that period the country was still an independent kingdom, though under the ultimate suzerainty of Rome. It is quite likely, however, that Quirinius, the governor of Syria (and northern Palestine) organized a Judean census in AD 6/7, for by that time the land had become a Roman province.
4 Josephus says nothing about a Roman census in Palestine during the reign of Herod. Indeed, he describes the census of AD 6/7 as a new and unprecedent imposition that provoked the rise of the Zealot movement under the leadership of Judas of Galilee (*War* 2:117–18).
5 'A census held under Quirinius could not have taken place in the time of Herod, for Quirinius was never governor of Syria during Herod's lifetime.'[20]

All this points to a theological-apologetic function of the census in Luke. It was created to link Jesus' birth with Judah, and the Davidic line of descent.

And while we are on the subject of Luke's account, a word is in order about the extraordinary circumstances surrounding Jesus' birth, which must also be considered legendary. Paul (Gal. 4:4) still knows nothing about a special birth from a virgin. Luke is the first Evangelist to portray Jesus' mother Mary as a virgin (1:34ff), but he contradicts himself in 2:1–14, where he describes Mary as Joseph's 'betrothed, who was with child', and where the motif of the virgin was originally lacking. Matthew (1:18–25) elaborates the motif, asserting that Joseph did not have intercourse with his wife Mary until after the birth of Jesus. This legend, having no apparent Jewish roots, seems to apply to Jesus a feature drawn from the world of the Hellenistic-oriental saviour figures.

Part III

The Road to Golgotha

10

Jesus the Revolutionary?

Jean-Jacques Rousseau was among the earliest commentators on the life of Jesus from a rational standpoint. In a letter dated 1769 he referred to Jesus as a 'Hebrew sage' and ranked him alongside the 'Greek sage', Socrates. For Rousseau, Jesus' main aim was to deliver the Jews from the Roman yoke and to make them free. Jesus' ethical teachings were thus intended to reawaken enthusiasm for freedom, but without arousing the suspicions of the Romans. The Jews, however, did not understand Jesus, who was by nature too gentle a soul to push through a political revolution.

At about the same time Hermann Samuel Reimarus (1694–1768), a professor of oriental languages at Hamburg, set forth a similar thesis in his pioneering and epoch-making work *Vom Zwecke Jesu and Seiner Jünger* (*On the Mission of Jesus and His Disciples*). Reimarus was the first scholar to interpret Jesus not as a 'son of God' or as a prophet or lawgiver, but as a Jewish Messiah. He stressed that neither Jesus nor his disciples had any need to explain the 'Kingdom of Heaven', since it was a familiar and widely current conception among the Jews of that period. The keynote of Jesus' message was 'Repent! for the Kingdom of Heaven is at hand!' – a call which attracted to him large numbers of Jews who despised the Roman tyranny and believed in the coming of the Messiah. Jesus took the Mosaic laws for granted and, at the most, only underscored for his fellow countrymen that in order to prepare themselves for the Kingdom, a fastidious observance of the ceremonial laws was not enough. What was essential was a high ethical standard of conduct in everyday life. Jesus instructed his disciples to preach the gospel of the Kingdom not to the Gentiles but 'to the lost sheep of the house of Israel' (Matt. 10:6).

For Reimarus it was clear that Jesus was a pious Jew in all respects, the sole difference between his teaching and that of his contemporaries being that while he taught that the Messiah had already appeared, they believed that he was yet to come. He tried to enlarge his following through his impressive healing feats and by sending his disciples to preach throughout the communities of Israel, for he believed that they 'will not have gone through all the towns of Israel, before the son of man comes' (Matt. 10:23). But when they met with little success, Jesus decided to test his powers in Jerusalem. As he entered the city he was acclaimed by some of the crowds as the Messiah ('Hosanna, Son of David!'), which emboldened him to attack the money-changers in the temple courtyard. His following was large enough to strike the Romans as a politically dangerous group, but too small to prevent his arrest and execution at their hands. His cry on the cross at Golgotha,[1] 'My God, my God, why hast thou forsaken me?', proves that he neither wished nor expected to die; and that he disappointedly looked upon his death as the end of his work. God, he saw at the end, had not helped him to establish an earthly kingdom and to deliver his people from the Romans.

Jesus and the Zealots

After Reimarus, the political interpretation of Jesus' mission received little or no support until early in the twentieth century when it was revived by Robert Eisler.[2] Basing himself on the Slavonic version of Josephus' writings, Eisler proposed that John the Baptist was a Zealot leader dedicated to the liberation of the Holy Land from the Romans. At first Jesus had preached a higher righteousness; but his growing eschatological fervour, his lack of success in Galilee, and, finally, the provocative incident of the Roman standards in Jerusalem (see Mark 13:14), all combined to draw him to Jerusalem. There, persuaded by his friends, Jesus led an armed insurrection which, Eisler maintained, is reflected in Mark 15:7. To cries of 'Hosanna', Jesus and his followers triumphantly entered the city, forcefully occupied the temple and seized the tower of Siloam, as reflected in Luke 13:1–4. The rebellion was, however, crushed by the Romans, who arrested and executed Jesus as a rebel.

More recently, in the 1960s, the late S.G.F. Brandon vigorously defended the thesis that Jesus was intimately associated with the movement of Jewish freedom fighters called the Zealots. Brandon's revival of the Reimarus thesis has caused quite a stir in New Testament studies, provoking a debate that continues to the present time. The questions at issue are extraordinarily important and merit full consideration. Therefore I shall first provide an exposition of Brandon's thesis.[3]

Brandon's Thesis

Brandon develops his argument through a critical reinterpretation of our major sources of information, which he regards as fundamentally problematic. The New Testament gives us a tendentious view of the events leading to the execution of Jesus; and Josephus, our chief informant for the history of the period concerned, misrepresents the nature of the Zealot movement. Brandon accepts the priority of Mark's Gospel, arguing that it is pivotal in that its tendentious apologetic was largely followed by the other Evangelists. Mark set the pattern by representing the Jewish leaders as somehow compelling a reluctant Roman governor to condemn a man whom he believed to be innocent. If we bear in mind that each Gospel, though drawn from traditional material, was designed to meet the needs of the community of which the author was a member, we can view Mark's Gospel as a response to the distinctive circumstances of the Christian community in Rome. What then were the particular needs to which Mark was responding? A remarkable clue occurs in the list Mark provides of the 12 apostles whom Jesus appointed to preach and cast out demons (3:14–16). Mark, in naming them, designates one 'Simon, the *kananaios*'. No translation of the strange title of this apostle is given, despite the fact that *kananaios* would have been perfectly meaningless to Mark's Greek-speaking audience.[4] The absence of an explanation is all the more conspicuous in the light of Mark's usual practice of explicating for his Gentile readers Hebrew and Aramaic words as well as Jewish customs (e.g., 3:17; 5:41; 7:3–4; 15:22, 34). Then why the silence concerning 'kananaios'? The reason, Brandon believes, is quite evident: if Mark had translated this Aramaic word into Greek, he would have had to write *Zelotes*, thus disclosing that one of Jesus' disciples was a Zealot, a member of the Jewish resistance movement against Rome. Rather than do this, he departed from his custom of translating for his Gentile readers.

Why did he suppress the fact that Jesus had selected a Zealot for an apostle? The answer, Brandon believes, is that the disclosure would have been embarrassing and perhaps even dangerous. Brandon therefore surmises that the Zealots were 'in the news' at the time, which, in turn, suggests a date for Mark's Gospel of about AD 70, the close of the Jewish revolt that shook the foundations of the Roman Empire.

The significance of Mark's suppression of the Zealot connection is further brought out by one of the central issues he chose to deal with, as being of special concern to his fellow Christians in Rome: What was Jesus' attitude towards the paying of taxes to Rome? That he chose this issue in a short gospel is significant, since there were many other spiritual issues he could have taken up. Jesus' response, 'Render to Caesar the things that are Caesar's, and to God the things that are God's' (Mark 12:13–17), is ambiguous when isolated from what Brandon maintains was its original context; but it is doubtful that the ambiguity was deliberate on Jesus' part. 'To argue as some scholars have done', writes Brandon, 'that Jesus intentionally made his answer ambiguous to avoid involvement with a dangerous political issue, is neither realistic nor does it do credit to Jesus. It is not realistic because such an evasion would at once have been detected, and Jesus would have been pressed to define the contrasted 'things' of God and Caesar. Moreover, one who claimed to be, or was regarded as the Messiah, could not have hedged on an issue so fundamental for his countrymen.'[5]

In the context of contemporary Judea there would have been no doubt of what were the things of God as opposed to the things of Caesar: the Zealots and their sympathizers opposed the paying of taxes to Rome because it meant turning over the wealth of the Holy Land to a pagan lord. Indeed, the Zealots opposed not only the paying of tribute, but the very presence of the Romans in the Holy Land. Brandon therefore proposes that Jesus' pronouncement was wholly in line with the Zealot outlook and that it was thus understood by those originally present. Notwithstanding the ambiguity and irony in the pronouncement, Jesus ruled decisively *against* the paying of tribute: Caesar could have what is his, but certainly not the Holy Land or its wealth. Brandon finds confirmation for this view in Luke's Gospel, where it is reported that the Jewish authorities charged Jesus before Pilate, saying, 'we find this man perverting our nation, and forbidding us to give tribute to Caesar, and saying that he himself is Christ [Messiah] a king' (Luke 23:2). But Mark, out of concern with the hostile and dangerous situation facing the Christians in Rome, presents Jesus' statement as if it were an attestation of his loyalty to the Roman overlords.

What we must keep in mind is that Christianity at this time is perceived as a predominantly Jewish movement. Hence it is understandable why Mark reports a strange incident occurring at the moment of Jesus' death – an incident that serves his purpose of trying to dissociate Christianity from its Jewish roots. As Jesus died, according to Mark,

> the curtain of the temple was torn in two, from top to bottom. And when the centurion, who stood facing him, saw that he thus breathed his last, he said, "truly this man was a son of God!". (15:38)

How would the Gentile Christians have understood this statement and how would they have known that the temple in far-off Jerusalem had had a special veil or curtain? Josephus, who had arrived in Rome in the retinue of Titus, described in detail the triumphal march of the victorious Roman armies in AD 71 (*War 7*: 132–52); and he reports that among the spoils of the temple on display were the temple curtains, which were eventually deposited in the imperial palace. In the face of such evidence of the decisive defeat of the Jews, the Gentile Christians would have recalled Paul's doctrine that with the death of Christ the Old Covenant had come to an end, to be supplanted by the New. The Roman victory as a historical fact was conveyed in the

Gospel as Providential: the rending of the temple veil in the final moment of the Saviour's life. Moreover, Mark's linking of the end of the temple, and therefore of cultic Judaism, with the Roman centurion's declaration of the divinity of Jesus, was an astute move. For it assured his Gentile readers that it was not a Jew but a Gentile who first perceived Jesus as the son of God. Thus, in Brandon's words, 'the Roman Christians were encouraged to see in the Flavian triumph not a disturbing reminder that they worshipped a Jew executed for sedition against Rome, but inspiring evidence that Rome had fulfilled God's purpose, adumbrated in the rending of the temple veil and the centurion's confession'.[6]

In Mark we also find a definite denigration of the Jewish leaders of the Jerusalem Christian community. They not only fail to understand the true nature of their master, but one of them betrays him to his enemies (14:10ff); their leader, Peter, denies knowledge of him (14:66–72); and they all desert him in Gethsemane (14:50). Why Mark thus portrayed both the disciples and Jesus' own family (Mark 3:31–5), is certainly no insignificant question. Brandon's explanation is inferred from the situation facing Mark and his fellow Christians after the Jewish catastrophe of AD 70. Out of weakness and fear Mark expressed the resentment of the Gentile community against the control which the mother church in Jerusalem had exerted over it. For Brandon, then, Mark's Gospel has the effect of severing Jesus from his Jewish roots: his own family regards him as mad; his Jewish disciples cannot understand him; and virtually all the other Jewish actors in the drama – Pharisees, Herodians and chief priests – are portrayed as if they are plotting to destroy him from the very beginning of his ministry (Mark 3:6). And finally, it is the Jewish leaders who arrest and condemn him, forcing a reluctant Pilate to execute him (14:43–15:11). A definite anti-Jewish theme is therefore evident in the Gospel of Mark, which depicts Jesus as rejected by the Jewish people and as rejecting them in turn. Mark's Gospel was thus tendentiously designed 'to explain away the problem of the Roman execution of Jesus and to present him as loyal to Rome; and to show that Jesus, though born a Jew, had no essential connection with the Jewish people and their religion, and that a Gentile was the first to perceive the truth, to which the Jews were blind, that Jesus was the son of God.'[7]

The main cause for concern within the early Christian movement after AD 70 was the politically embarrassing and dangerous fact that Jesus had been executed by the Romans for sedition. How the Romans looked upon the Christian movement is exemplified in a statement made by the Roman historian Tacitus:

Christus, the founder of the name, had undergone the death penalty in the reign of Tiberius, by sentence of the procurator Pontius Pilate, and the pernicious superstition was checked for a moment, only to break out once more, not merely in Judea, the home of the disease, but in the capital itself [i.e., Rome] where all things horrible or shameful in the world collect and find a vogue. (Tacitus, *Annales*, XV:44).

That the Roman government suspected the Christians of being a subversive movement is also a major theme of early Church history. On the assumption of Marcan priority, Brandon asserts that Matthew, Luke and John followed Mark's lead in depicting Jesus' execution for sedition as the result of Jewish malice. Whereas Mark, however, was mainly concerned to portray Jesus as pro-Roman, the other Evangelists developed, or even created, the theme of his pacifism. For Brandon, the pacific teachings we find in the Gospels originated not with Jesus himself, but with the early church and the Evangelists. To understand how the idea of the *'pacific Christ'* emerged, Brandon argued, one must begin by focusing on Galilee, the birthplace of both Jesus and the Zealot movement.

The Zealot movement was founded when Jesus was a boy of about 12 years of age, old enough to grasp the significance of the Roman census of AD 6/7 and the disturbances that resulted from it (see chapter 2). It was in that year that the Roman emperor Augustus incorporated the Holy Land into his empire and dispatched his legions to enumerate the inhabitants of the land and to extract tribute. Augustus divided Herod's kingdom between his three sons, appointing Archelaus as ethnarch, and Antipas and Philip as tetrarchs. Antipas received for his province Peraea and Galilee (*War* 2:94–5). The reaction in Galilee was immediate, and from it emerged the resistance movement known as Zealotism, essentially religious in its inspiration and aims. It found practical expression in armed opposition to the Romans. In line with the precedent of the Maccabees, the Zealots made war against both the heathen enemy and its Jewish collaborators. The basic principle inspiring this movement, as we have seen, was the *absolute* sovereignty of God over Israel. This principle precluded the acceptance of any heathen human being as lord, and it entailed a steadfast refusal to yield any of the Holy Land's wealth to a foreign ruler who claimed lordship. Resistance to the existing regime necessarily involved hardship and suffering, but the Zealots were ready to die a martyr's death in the belief that their sacrifices would ultimately call forth God's intervention to save Israel.

Jesus grew up in this environment and it is difficult to see, on logical grounds, writes Brandon, 'why he should not have sympathized with the Zealots and felt hostile towards the Romans and those Jews who, for worldly gain, cooperated with them'.[8] Furthermore, it is significant that Jesus not only had a Zealot as a disciple, he nowhere condemns the Zealots. This argument from silence is valid, Brandon believes, because Mark and the other Evangelists record Jesus' deprecatory remarks about the other Jewish parties – e.g., Pharisees, Sadducees and Herodians. The silence of the Gospels concerning the Zealots may indicate a relationship between Jesus and the resistance movement which the Evangelists preferred not to reveal. Mark tries to explain away Jesus' execution as a rebel, but the execution of Jesus for sedition appears to be a fundamental fact: the *titulus*, over the cross, stated: 'The King of the Jews'. We know from Josephus that many Jewish rebels and Messianic pretenders had met such an end. That the Romans executed Jesus for sedition therefore suggests that they regarded him as politically dangerous.

All four Evangelists agree that the Jewish authorities had subjected Jesus to some form of interrogation before handing him over to the Roman governor. Such a procedure becomes intelligible if we assume that the Jewish leaders had a responsibility for maintaining law and order among their own people, but no authority to execute on a capital charge. According to the book of Acts the Jewish leaders had those whom they regarded as offenders, for example, Peter and John, whipped or imprisoned; as for Stephen, he was stoned by a mob (Acts 4:21, 28, 40; 7:45ff). And the Fourth Evangelist puts these words into the mouths of the Jewish leaders, in their response to Pilate: 'It is not lawful for us to put any man to death' (John 18:31). If, therefore, the Jewish leaders, after interrogating Jesus, turned him over to Pilate, the evidence they produced must have persuaded him that the charge justified the penalty.

What was it about Jesus that prompted their action? They appear to have been fearful of the consequences if Jesus and his followers were allowed to continue their activities: 'If we let him go on thus, everyone will believe in him, and the Romans will come and destroy both our holy place and our nation' (John 11:48).

What was the nature of Jesus' activities which, the Jewish leaders feared, would provoke a harsh Roman reaction? For Brandon it was the so-called 'cleansing of the temple', which, he maintains, was actually an assault upon the sacerdotal aristocracy. The temple was a central institution involving enormous economic resources, both in terms of revenues and the large body of officials and servants it employed. Those who controlled the temple possessed considerable power and influence. Brandon rejects the view of Joseph Klausner and others who interpret Jesus' attack upon the money-changers as an act of indignation against petty individuals. It was rather a radical challenge to the authority of the sacerdotal aristocracy, and a revolutionary action against Rome, for the high-priest's secular authority was a mainstay of the Roman government in Judea. Brandon also rejects the Evangelists' depiction of the attack as an event in which Jesus acted alone. Jesus was not alone, argues Brandon; the 'cleansing' took place either on the same day or on the day after the Triumphal Entry into the city. He was accompanied by his disciples and powerfully supported by the crowd. So it is most likely that the action was carried out with the aid of an excited crowd and was attended by violence. The Gospels, however, say nothing about either the temple police or the Roman troops, stationed in the Antonia fortress, intervening, as they did when Paul was threatened in the temple courts (Acts 21:31ff). Brandon therefore realizes that if the 'cleansing' was as tumultuous an affair as he proposes, the apparent absence of Roman intervention needs to be explained: 'The fact that Mark and Luke mention, in another connection, that there was an insurrection in the city at about this time, which involved bloodshed (Mark 15:7; Luke 23.19, 25), makes it legitimate to wonder whether this attack by Jesus on the temple trading system, . . . tantamount to an attack on the sacerdotal aristocracy, was a far more serious affair than the gospels show and whether it caused those authorities to plan his arrest, and thus forestall Roman action.'[9]

In Mark 14:56, Jesus is accused of having said, 'I will destroy this temple that is made with hands, and in three days I will build another, not made with hands.' Brandon accepts that some such utterance is likely and that it is congruent with his reconstruction of the 'cleansing' events. With both this utterance and his actual attack upon those who controlled the temple, Jesus anticipated the actions of the Zealots in AD 66. Immediately upon gaining control of the temple, they selected a new high-priest by the ancient method of drawing lots, thus putting an end to his appointment by the temporal power, whether Roman or Herodian. There can be little doubt, Brandon argues, that Jesus shared the outrage of the Zealots towards the sacrifices offered daily for the well-being of the emperor – sacrifices which the lower priests, influenced by Zealotism, brought to an end in 66. If, therefore, Jesus' attack had a revolutionary significance, it is quite easy to understand why he was delivered to Pilate charged with sedition against Rome.

The Jewish conception of the Kingdon of Heaven (and the role of the Messiah), Brandon maintains, further supports his reconstruction of the events that took place in Jerusalem during the so-called 'cleansing of the temple'. The prevalent Jewish view entailed a complete rupture with the existing world order, in which Israel was in bondage to the heathen power of Rome. Jesus wished to bring the people to a state of moral and spiritual readiness for the Kingdom; but there was an obstacle – those who waxed fat from their control of the temple and from their cooperation with the heathen power that enslaved God's people. It is quite likely, according to Brandon, that there was an insurrection in the city coinciding with Jesus' attack. The Romans had evidently suppressed both the insurrection and the Jesus coup, capturing some of the insurgents, including Barabbas (Mark 15:6–7). Jesus, recognizing his failure and filled with foreboding, left the city at nightfall and escaped with his disciples to the country beyond (Mark 11:19; 14:18ff). The escape may have been pre-arranged, since Judas Iscariot knew where they were to rendezvous and was able to inform the authorities in time to allow the organization of an arresting force. Brandon notes that both the disciples and the arresting party were armed, suggesting that the latter expected armed resistance. Jesus felt safe in the daytime, Brandon surmises, but unsafe at night without the crowds and the main body of his supporters. Perhaps he was prepared to resist arrest and return the next day to continue his activities; on the other hand, he may well have recognized that the tide of events had turned against him and that a withdrawal to Galilee was in order. Whatever was Jesus' intention, Brandon is confident that armed resistance was offered, but that the Evangelists' portrayal of it as one isolated sword-stroke may be accurate (Matt. 26:51–2). Realizing that resistance was futile, Jesus resolved to surrender.

For Brandon, then, the Triumphal Entry and the aftermath was one obvious justification for the charge against Jesus of political Messianism. The Gospels describe him as deliberately planning an entry into the Holy City which would fulfil the prophecy of Zechariah (Mark 11:1–7; Matt. 21:1–7; Luke 19:29–35; cf. Zech. 9:9). Hence the entry appears to be a demonstration by Jesus of his assumption of Messiahship, an action calculated to challenge both the Jewish leadership and the Romans. He surely must have known that in the contemporary consciousness Messiahship carried an unavoidably political connotation. The fact that he was apprehended at night, after the betrayal of Judas, suggests that Jesus had no intention of giving himself up voluntarily as a sacrificial victim to his enemies. The additional fact that Jesus was crucified between two Zealots indicates that Pilate linked him with the insurrection that had coincided with Jesus' activities in the city.

It is possible – Brandon's argument continues – that Jesus, following John the Baptist as his charismatic successor, took over the mission of preparing Israel for the coming of the Kingdom of Heaven. Josephus reports that the Baptist was executed owing to the crowds that gathered to him and, hence, the political fears he had aroused in Herod (*Antiq.* 18:117–19). Jesus too, had early drawn crowds to himself with his reputation as a 'wonder-worker'; the enthusiasm thus generated may very well have given his movement an impetus which he could have resisted only with difficulty.

Basing himself on an interesting article by H.W. Montefiore,[10] Brandon interprets Mark 6:30ff as a preparation for revolt. 'Sheep without a shepherd' is taken to mean 'an army without a general'. In this light it is possible that Jesus went out to the desert because he was undecided whether or not to associate himself with the Messianic movement. That the men sat down in companies of 50 and 100, according to Mark, suggests a military operation. Thousands of *men* do not gather in the wilderness without good cause; and Brandon finds it difficult to see this gathering as anything but a preparation for an uprising. Jesus, however, resists the attempt to make him into a political and military Messiah. As for Mark's handling of the episode, H.W. Montefiore thinks that either the event's full significance had eluded him, or that he simply preferred not to disclose to his readers in the Roman Empire Jesus' involvement in such affairs. John 6:15, as earlier noted, also relates that the crowds tried to take Jesus by force and make him king. So, Brandon asks, if Jesus was as pacific and quietist as the Gospel tradition holds, and if he repudiated the Messianic role publicly, why did he arrange his entry into Jerusalem as a Messianic demonstration? Brandon rejects the theory that Jesus was the victim of a situation he could not control – that he was somehow swept along by popular forces he could not resist. But even for Brandon all this does not mean that Jesus was himself a Zealot.

That Jesus chose for one of his disciples a man who was known as 'the Zealot', and who was thus distinguished from the other disciples, suggests that Jesus himself was not a recognized Zealot leader, and that his movement was not an integral part of the Zealot resistance against Rome. Nevertheless, the presence of a Zealot among Jesus' disciples, Brandon believes, indicates that Zealot principles and aims were not incompatible with intimate participation in Jesus' mission. No explicit repudiation of Zealotism is attributed to Jesus, and the Gospels attest to the fact that Jesus' disciples were armed and that he himself was not above engaging in violence on at least one occasion. Where, then, did Jesus differ with the Zealots? To this question Brandon replies that Jesus' 'conviction about the imminence of God's kingdom, which would mean the end of Rome's sovereignty, caused him to be less concerned than the Zealots with the immediate prosecution of the resistance to Rome'.[11]

Much of Brandon's thesis, as we see, rests on the assumption that the author of Mark's Gospel portrayed Jesus in such a manner as to suit the sentiments and interests of his Gentile–Christian audience in Rome. Brandon maintains, however, that Josephus was similarly tendentious in his treatment of the Zealot movement. It is true that towards the end of his *Jewish War* (7:418–19) he pays tribute to the Zealots and *sicarii* who could not be forced to call Caesar lord. But for the most part he holds them responsible for precipitating the catastrophic war with the Romans and bringing disaster upon his people. He therefore calls the Zealots *lestai*, i.e., 'brigands', which is the same epithet the Romans used for the armed rebels who opposed their rule.

Josephus' writings contain a famous passage in which he says a few words about Jesus. This passage, referred to as the *Testimonium Flavianum* (*Antiq.* 18:63–4) is regarded with suspicion by scholars, since it appears to have been tampered with by a later hand. What Josephus has to say about Jesus is obviously of great interest, for depending on how Josephus' brief statement is interpreted, the image of Jesus will vary accordingly. Thus Brandon critically reconstructed the passage to suit his own thesis. First then, let us take a look at what Josephus has to say, and then consider Brandon's treatment of it.

Testimonium Flavianum (Josephus on Jesus)

It is virtually certain that Josephus did in fact write at least one paragraph about Jesus in his *Jewish Antiquities*, since it is in the same work, but a different context, in which he also discusses the circumstances which led to the stoning of James the brother of Jesus (*Antiq.* 20:200). The extant statement about Jesus reads in this manner:

> About this time there lived Jesus, a wise man, if indeed one ought to call him a man. For he was one who wrought surprising feats and was a teacher of such people as accept the truth gladly. He won over many Jews and many of the Greeks. He was the Messiah. When Pilate, upon hearing him accused by men of the highest standing amongst us, had condemned him to be crucified, those who had in the first place come to love him did not give up their affection for him. On the third day he appeared to them restored to life, for the prophets of God had prophesied these and countless other marvellous things about him. And the tribe of Christians, so-called after him, has still to this day not disappeared.

The suspicion emerged as early as the sixteenth century that this passage may not be authentic. The principal grounds for questioning its genuineness are:

1   Josephus describes himself as a loyal Pharisaic Jew, and as such he could not have written that Jesus was the Messiah.
2   Origen explicitly states (*c.* AD 280) that Josephus did not believe in Jesus as the Christ. In the seventeenth century Richard Montague, Bishop of Norwich, declared the phrase, 'he was the Messiah', a Christian insert, and ever since scholars have maintained that the passage was forged in whole or in part.
3   The passage appears abruptly, breaking the continuity of the narrative which deals with a series of riots.[12] Some Josephus scholars have suggested that in place of the phrase, 'he was the Messiah', one should read, 'the so-called Christ'; and following the phrase 'on the third day', one should read, 'according to their report', which had been removed by a Christian censor. Other scholars hold, however, that *lego menos* should

not be translated 'so-called' or 'alleged', but rather as 'said to be' or 'who is spoken of' or, simply, 'called', as in Matthew 1:16: 'Joseph the husband of Mary, of whom Jesus was born, who is called Christ'.

If we accept that the passage in its present form could not have been written by Josephus, is there any way to determine what he actually wrote? Emil Schürer, the brilliant nineteenth-century historian, proposed a way of approximating the actual statement. If we eliminate the phrases which are incompatible with Josephus' religious outlook, and leave intact only the non-Christian and neutral sentences, the result is the following text:

> at about this time lived Jesus, a wise man . . . He performed astonishing feats (and was a teacher of such people as are eager for novelties or the unusual). He attracted many Jews and many of the Greeks . . . upon an indictment brought by leading members of our society, Pilate sentenced him to the cross, but those who had loved him from the very first did not cease to be attracted to him . . . The brotherhood of the Christians, named after him, is still in existence.[13]

The brevity of the statement suggests that a later interpolator not only added certain words and phrases to the original wording, but also omitted parts of what he found in his copy. It is more than likely that Josephus wrote more than what we have before us. Material is missing from the text which has been replaced by a few unilluminating phases. As C.K. Barrett has proposed, 'Christian writers, adding material in praise of Jesus, may quite well have omitted what they thought derogatory to his person'.[14] And the editors of Schürer's work have observed:

> Although Josephus certainly did not call Jesus the Messiah, and did not assert that his resurrection on the third day had been announced by divine prophets, the impression gained from an intimate study of his report is that he was not on the whole unsympathetic towards Jesus. The words *eteron ti deinon ethorybei tous 'Ioudaious* ['another outrage threw the Jews into an uproar'], which introduces the paragraph following immediately on the Jesus passage, indicate that Josephus viewed the execution of Jesus as a 'dreadful event' and that the Jews were disturbed by the outcome of the case.[15]

It is also noteworthy that nothing in Josephus' statement lends any support to the thesis that Jesus had been involved in revolutionary activity or associated with the Zealot movement. This, as we shall see presently, is a problem Brandon tries to deal with in his commentary on the Josephus passage. As a rule Josephus speaks of the Zealots with scorn and contempt. While he describes the founder of the Zealot movement, Judas the Galilean and his grandson Menaham as *sophistai* ('sophists') (*War* 2:433), he refers to Jesus as a *sophos aner*, a 'wise man'. This strongly points to the likelihood that the

Pharisaic circles to which Josephus belonged had not at that time given Jesus a bad name. This is further supported by Josephus' account of the resentment among the 'fairminded' Jews of the stoning of Jesus' brother James at the order of a Sadducean high-priest.

How then does Brandon treat the Josephus passage concerning Jesus? He agrees that Josephus must have written something about Jesus because it is altogether unlikely that he would have regarded Jesus as less significant than the Messianic pretenders whom he mentions. The Jewish origin of Christianity was too well known in Rome to have allowed Josephus to ignore the subject. Besides, Brandon argues, mentioning Jesus would have served Josephus' apologetic purpose, since he could tell his Roman audience that the Jewish leaders delivered him for execution, just as they sought to prevent the Jewish revolt. Brandon therefore proposes that Josephus not only wrote about Jesus, but that what he had to say was of a condemnatory character. Brandon makes this assumption because the Josephus passage follows immediately after the description of Pilate's suppression of disturbances caused by the use of temple funds for the construction of an aqueduct. Brandon finds the concluding words of this account significant: 'Thus ended the uprising' (*Antiq.* 18:62). Then comes the passage about Jesus which, in turn, is followed by Josephus' recording of the troubles that befell the Jews of Rome at about the same time. These are the grounds for Brandon's conjecture that Josephus, far from having referred to Jesus as a 'wise man', described him as a *sophistes* and a *goes*, a 'sophist' and a 'charlatan'. In other words, in Brandon's reconstruction of the passage he has Josephus describe Jesus in the very same terms as he did the leaders of the Zealots.

For Brandon, such an evaluation of Jesus suits everything we know about Josephus and his apologetic aim: he would thereby have informed his Gentile readers that the Christian movement which they disliked, 'had indeed originated in Judea, but the Jewish authorities, realizing its pernicious nature, had dealt promptly with its founder, by providing the local Roman governor with the necessary evidence of his guilt to justify his execution'.[16] Finally, we should note that Brandon, like Robert Eisler before him, sets great store by the Slavonic Josephus. This work relates that an anonymous wonder-worker, bearing some resemblance to Jesus, was associated with a planned attack on the Romans in Jerusalem, which was anticipated and bloodily suppressed. We see, then, that Brandon's view of Jesus is a provocative one, deserving of serious critical examination.

Critical Assessments of the Reimarus–Eisler–Brandon Thesis

One of the more enlightening assessments of this thesis comes from Oscar Cullmann, who sees Jesus and his disciples fighting on two fronts: on the one hand, against the Sadducean aristocracy that assented to Roman domination, and, on the other, against the Zealotic wing of the Pharisees. For Cullmann,[17] scholars like Eisler and Brandon have gone too far in making of Jesus himself a Zealot or a para-Zealot. On the other hand, it is a gross error, he believes, to underestimate the impact made by the Zealotic movement on the teachings and life of earliest Christianity. Cullmann accepts as a fundamental fact that Jesus was condemned to death by the Romans as a rebel. This was a miscarriage of justice: although Jesus had within his innermost circle Zealots and former Zealots, he himself ultimately rejected their outlook. Yet from the standpoint of contemporary outsiders the difference between his outlook and theirs was not easily discerned. This seems evident from Acts 5:36–7, where Rabbi Gamaliel, counselling the Sanhedrin to caution in dealing with the apostles Peter and John, mentions Judas the Galilean and another rebel leader named Theudas. The passage is significant for two reasons: first because it shows that the Zealot question was very much alive; and secondly because it reveals that Gamaliel associated the Jesus movement with that of the Zealots. To outsiders, then, the two movements appeared to have something in common. Affinities between the two movements may have been perceived even after Jesus' death. In Acts 21:38 a Roman tribune (official) mistakes Paul for a well-known rebel leader: 'Are you not the Egyptian, then, who recently stirred up a revolt and led the four thousand men of the Assassins out into the Wilderness?' The insurrection of 'the Egyptian' is also recorded by Josephus (*War* 2:261ff).

It is quite likely that the 'Galileans' mentioned by Jesus in Luke 13:1 were members of the Zealot movement. There we read that some of those present told Jesus 'of the Galileans whose blood Pilate had mingled with their sacrifices. And he answered them, "Do you think that these Galileans were worse sinners than all the other Galileans because they suffered thus? I tell you, no" . . .' This, Cullmann believes, probably refers to a blood-bath launched by Pilate against all the Galileans within his reach, a reaction, no doubt, to a Zealot uprising. It is significant that this event was brought to the attention of Jesus precisely. It was assumed, evidently, that he took a special interest in such people.

Like Brandon, Cullmann draws attention to the fact that Jesus had Zealots in his inner circle. In Luke 6:15 and in Acts 1:13 Simon the Zealot is listed among Jesus' disciples. This is the same individual who is designated '*ho kananaios*' (= Zealot) in Mark (3:18) and Matthew (10:4), traditionally mistranslated, as I remarked earlier, as 'Simon the Canaanite'.

It has been suggested by several scholars that some of Jesus' other disciples may have been associated with the resistance movement. John 6:71, in the Codex Sinaiticus, renders Iscariot as *ish karioth*, literally a man from *karioth*; but no place by that name is known. It has therefore been proposed that Iscariot may be a Semitic transcription of the Latin word *sicarius* ('assassin') which is philologically plausible. And if Judas Iscariot was in fact an adherent of the Zealot movement as this would imply, his betrayal would become much more intelligible, for he would have had a Messianic ideal quite different from that of Jesus, and his entry into the circle of the disciples would have rested on a misapprehension of Jesus' mission. It is quite possible that Judas had perceived Jesus as a Messiah-King after the traditional model, who, with God's help, would bring down Roman rule by force and establish the Kingdom of Heaven on earth. If this was Judas' original perception of Jesus, his betrayal may have been motivated by disillusionment – rather than by 30 pieces of silver.

And what about Peter? We will recall that when Jesus in Caesarea Philippi taught his disciples that the 'son of man' must suffer, this shocked Peter, who rebuked Jesus and was rebuked in return: 'Get behind me, Satan! For you are not on the side of God, but of man' (Mark 8:27–33). For Jesus recognizes that the temptation confronting him here is that he should assume the leadership of the political-military movement. Following Eisler, Cullmann calls attention to a philological consideration which makes it possible that Peter was associated with the Zealots. In Matthew 16:17, Jesus says to him, 'Blessed are you, Simon Bar-Jona!'. Now despite the interpretation of this name given in the Fourth Gospel (John 1:42 and 21:15), scholars are doubtful that 'Bar-Jona' can be translated as 'son of John'. There is no documentary evidence anywhere else that Jona is an abbreviation of the Hebrew *Yohanan*, i.e., John. Furthermore, according to an old Hebrew lexicon cited by G. Dalman,[18] *barjona* is a word borrowed from Accadian, meaning 'terrorist', which appears to be the prototype of the Hebrew word *biryon*, which also denotes one who uses force against another. Finally, James and John, the sons of Zebedee, may also have been associated with the Zealot movement. In Mark 10:37 they make this request from Jesus: 'Grant us to sit, one at your right hand and one at your left, in your glory.' This is the kind of request one would expect from a Zealot. James and John were passionate by nature : they once wished to burn down a Samaritan village which had refused to receive Jesus, but he forbade them. He styled them 'sons of wrath' or 'sons of thunder' (Heb. *benei regesh* or *benei raash*) – which Cullmann takes as evidence of their Zealotic tendencies. So we have at least one disciple, 'Simon the Zealot', who unquestionably belonged to the resistance movement (unless one argues, as some scholars have, that he was a *former* Zealot); and there are four others who probably belonged to the movement – Judas Iscariot, Peter and the sons of Zebedee.

Jesus, however, was neither a Zealot nor a para-Zealot, but rather a charismatic figure who, despite himself, had an especially strong attraction for such individuals, and who therefore had to come to terms with the Zealot question almost daily. He was misunderstood by those closest to him, and therefore frequently subject to the temptation of yielding to their misapprehension. It was the Zealot ideal, 'the devil', that constituted the true temptation for Jesus. This was true, writes Cullmann,

> from the very beginning, when the devil offered him world dominion after his baptism, to the moment when he rebuked Peter as Satan, and finally to the decisive moment in Gethsemane, when the devil once again tempted him in the same way as in the beginning – as the Gospel of Luke accurately interprets (4:13): 'and when the devil had ended every temptation, he departed from him until an opportune time'. There in Gethsemane for the last time the question is posed, whether Jesus will yield to the pressure of his disciples and offer resistance to the Roman soldiers who have come to arrest him. At the end of the prayer Jesus is satisfied: he is unalterably determined to finish his course, fulfilling his messianic calling as the suffering son of man.[19]

Owing to his awareness of his ideological differences with Peter, Jesus has a presentiment of the latter's denial, which may have been due to human weakness, but is more likely to have been the result of disillusionment. The denial most probably occurred when he saw that Jesus would not defend himself.

Culmann proposes that Jesus appears to have had a strong antipathy towards the existing forms of the power-state. In Luke 13:31ff it is precisely the Pharisees, whose motives are so often impugned in the Gospels, who warn Jesus to get 'away from here, for Herod wants to kill you'. In Jesus' reply he called Herod a 'fox'. And in response to a dispute among the disciples as to which of them was to be regarded as the greatest, Jesus says, 'The kings of the Gentiles exercise lordship over them [their subjects]; and those in authority over them are called benefactors' (Luke 22:25). Thus if we may employ Machiavellian metaphors to describe Jesus' view, he believed that the state is based on force and deceit, and that the rulers are alternately 'lions' or 'foxes', in accordance with their interests. As agents of the state the tax-collectors are especially hated by the people for their collaboration with the heathen power. Jesus shares the people's contempt for the tax-collectors whom he names in the same breath with heathens and prostitutes (Matt. 18:17; 21:31). On the other hand – and this demonstrates the complexity of Jesus' outlook – Jesus received the tax-collectors and sinners because 'Those who are well have no need of a physician, but those who are sick' (Matt. 9:12). Indeed, we even find a tax-collector among his disciples (Matt. 10:3). One can hardly imagine greater enemies in the Jewish society of the time than Zealots and tax-collectors.

That Jesus attracted such opposing elements to himself suggests that he transcended the differences between them, although it is doubtful that they understood this. Some of Jesus' most difficult sayings, Cullmann believes, are best understood as criticisms and rejections of the Zealotic outlook: 'Do not resist one who is evil' (Matt. 5:38). Or '. . . the kingdom of heaven has suffered violence, and men of violence take it by force' (Matt. 11:12). Cullmann maintains that Jesus recognized that the followers of Judas the Galilean were genuinely committed to the Kingdom of heaven. He nevertheless repudiated their actions because the Kingdom, he believed, could not be brought into being by means of human power. That is why he withdrew from those who wanted to 'take him by force to make him king' (John 6:15). The saying in the Sermon on the Mount (Matt. 7:15) about the false prophets 'who come . . . in sheep's clothing but inwardly are ravenous wolves', may also be directed at some of the Zealots. In John 10:8 Jesus makes this statement: 'All who came before me are thieves and robbers', the same language which both the Romans and Josephus used for the Zealots. In verse 11, Jesus refers to himself as the good shepherd who 'lays down his life for the sheep'. And Cullmann comments: 'The false shepherds do not spare the life of the sheep. Are not the Zealot leaders in mind here, who led their followers to certain death at the hands of the Romans? It is impossible to think of the prophets or John the Baptist as among the thieves and robbers. It seems to me all but certain that the Zealot leaders, like Judas of Galilee, are in mind here . . .'[20]

If, however, we look at Jesus from the outside, as it were, we can see why his inner circle and the large crowds about him might have been mistaken for advocates of Zealotism. It is almost certain, as we have noted several times, that even those closest to him had failed to grasp his true intentions. The Zealots and Zealot-sympathizers among his followers failed to understand that for Jesus the Kingdom of Heaven was God's work alone and that the way it would come about was God's secret alone. For the Zealots it was armed resistance against the heathen power that would call forth God's help in realizing the Kingdom; for Jesus human actions were also essential in evoking God's aid – but these were peaceful actions guided by the highest ethical ideals of Judaism. This helps us to understand why Jesus displayed a rather consistent resistance to being called Messiah. As soon as anyone referred to him as such, he commanded him to remain silent. On almost every occasion, including the most decisive moments of his life, he intentionally avoided the title. That his conception of himself was not that of the traditional Jewish Messiah is strongly indicated by this pattern of conduct. At Caesarea Philippi when Peter answered 'you are the Messiah', Jesus' response was neither a confirmation nor a denial, but rather a command to tell no one. He then proceeds to teach them that the 'son of man' – most probably thus referring to himself (see p.123) – 'must suffer many things'. What seems, therefore, to be preserved in the Gospel is the recollection that Jesus never applied the title 'Messiah' to himself, precisely because it was too heavily weighted with Zealotic ideology.

But what about Jesus' statement concerning the 'sword', which both Eisler and Brandon consider so supportive of their theory? These are the words that Luke attributes to Jesus:

> 'When I sent you out with no purse or bag or sandals, did you lack anything?' They said, 'Nothing'. He said to them, 'But now, let him who has a purse take it, and likewise a bag. And let him who has no sword sell his mantle and buy one. For I tell you that this scripture must be fulfilled in me, "and he was reckoned with transgressors"; for what is written about me has its fulfilment.' And they said, 'Look, Lord, here are two swords'. And he said to them, 'It is enough'. (Luke 22:35–8)

This statement stands in the Passion narrative just before the account of the arrest in Gethsemane, where it is clear that at least one disciple wore and used a sword. Cullmann rejects all symbolic interpretations of 'sword' in this context, insisting that the word must be taken literally. 'For it is in fact grouped with such concrete things as purses, bags and clothing. Here, then, Jesus really commanded his disciples to take a sword with them . . . Jesus knew that the death that was about to befall him would mean persecution for his followers. And yet they are to proclaim the Gospel. It is for their defense that they are to be equipped with a sword at this time.'[21] Cullmann thus accepts the saying as authentic. But he rejects the Eisler-Brandon interpretation of this saying as evidence that Jesus had embraced Zealotism. For Cullmann the real meaning of the saying is Jesus' recognition that defensive sword-bearing may become necessary. In Gethsemane, when his disciples saw what was about to happen, they said, 'shall we strike with the sword?' 'And one of them struck the slave of the high-priest and cut off his right ear. But Jesus said, "No more of this!"' (Luke 22:49–51). Cullmann sees this event as characteristic of what he calls the 'tension' in the Jesus movement. Not everything in the Zealot resistance is condemned; they may defend themselves, but they may not wage war at their own initiative. Jesus defined the limits of their sword-bearing.[22]

'Is it lawful to pay taxes to Caesar or not?' (Mark 12:14). When Jesus replied to this question with 'Render to Caesar the things that are Caesar's, and to God the things that are God's', he placed himself in a precarious and compromising position. In Luke 23:2 Jesus' accusers say, 'We found this man . . . forbidding us to give tribute to Caesar'. They accused him, in other words, of being a Zealot leader. The fact that they could construe Jesus' reply this way, whether intentionally or not, shows that it was subtle and complex and open to misinterpretation. Cullmann has well conveyed Jesus' predicament:

If he answers yes, he will be shown up as a collaborationist and will disillusion the majority of the people; for it is precisely in this connection that these have rested such great hope in him. If he answers no, this is an avowal that he himself is a Zealot and indeed a leader of the Zealots; and we know what that meant to the Romans.[23]

Where Jesus appears to have differed fundamentally with the Zealots is with regard to the *means*, not the end. For Jesus the Kingdom could only be realized through the repentance of the whole people, including the worst sinners. But if this was in fact Jesus' outlook, why did he make a 'triumphant entry' into Jerusalem? Cullmann vehemently rejects the view that Jesus himself had intended his entry as a demonstration of political Messianism. That he entered riding a donkey and not a warhorse, 'could speak against a revolutionary intention'. We noted earlier, however, that in Zechariah 9:9 the Messianic King is triumphant and victorious even while he is humble and riding on a colt, the foal of an ass. And, indeed, Cullmann is forced to acknowledge

> that among the people and even among the disciples the entry itself was understood as a decisive act aimed at the establishment of the Kingdom of God within a national framework. W.R. Farmer ... rightly showed that the use of palm branches referred to the Maccabees' resistance movement, the remembrance of which certainly played an important role for the Zealots.[24] The keenest hopes of all Zealotists seemed at last to be on the way toward realization in Jesus. The entry into Jerusalem surely precipitated Jesus' arrest...[25]

Cullmann proposes that the words Jesus spoke at the Last Supper must have caused great disillusionment among his disciples, one of whom at least now understood the sense in which Jesus grasped his role. It was on that occasion, presumably, that Jesus informed his most intimate followers that he was not the triumphant Messiah-King. How otherwise says Cullmann, can we account for the disciples' behaviour in Gethsemane, where matters came to a head? Jesus realizes that they still hold out hope that he will relent and fulfil the role they so fervently desire him to fulfil. Informing them that his 'soul is very sorrowful, even to death', he falls on his face and prays: 'My Father, if it be possible, let this cup pass from me; nevertheless, not as I will, but as thou wilt' (Matt. 26:38). He is confronted with the same temptation, to construe his role in political military terms. But when the arresting party arrives, he refuses to allow his disciples to resist, and they all 'forsook him and fled' (Matt. 26:56). And Cullmann asks, if his most intimate friends had thus misunderstood him all along and to the very end, is it any wonder that the Roman state mistook him for a pretender to the royal throne and condemned him to death? The *titulus*, on Jesus' cross states a political crime: 'King of the Jews'.

In this regard everything is clearer in John's Gospel than in the Synoptics. The arrest in Gethsemane is made by the Roman cohort under the command of the captain (18:18). From the beginning the entire action proceeds from the Romans. In 11:48ff, the real motivation of the sacerdotal aristocracy becomes as clear as it can be: to preserve order and to prevent a provocation that would serve the Romans as a pretext for widespread, bloody reprisals. 'The Jewish authorities', writes Cullmann, 'had not the least intention of assuming responsibility for Jesus' death. For they feared the people, and knew Jesus was popular among them.'[26] On the way to his execution Jesus says, 'Daughters of Jerusalem . . . if they do this to green wood, what will they do to the dry?' (Luke 23:28–30). And Cullmann interprets: 'If the Romans execute *me* as a Zealot, who am no Zealot and who had always warned against Zealotism, what will they do then to the true Zealots! . . .'[27]

In his concluding statement, Cullmann observes that although the Eisler-Brandon thesis has been rightly rejected, their critics 'have thrown out the baby with the bath. They have not paid attention to the fact that Jesus' whole ministry was in continuous contact with Zealotism, that this formed the background, so to speak, of his activity, and that he was executed as a Zealot.' For Cullmann, Jesus was an 'eschatological radical', but 'not of this world' in the way the Zealots were.[28]

Martin Hengel,[29] a leading authority on the Zealot movement, has also addressed the key issues in a short monograph entitled, 'Was Jesus a Revolutionist?'. Hengel regards the crucifixion of Jesus by the Romans as a fundamental historical fact; the crime for which he was executed was sedition. The New Testament, as already noted, attests to this fact most directly in its quotation of the words in the inscription over Jesus' cross, preserved in Latin in John 19:19: *Iesus Nazarenus Rex Iudaeorum*: Jesus of Nazareth, the king of the Jews. The inscription is found in all four Gospels, though their respective wordings of it vary slightly. Because of these variations some distinguished scholars, for example, Rudolf Bultmann, have questioned its historicity. Others, like Paul Winter, accept its authenticity, but deny that Jesus ever claimed such a kingship or cooperated with the Zealots to overthrow the existing regime. So there are two questions here which need to be addressed separately, for the *titulus* may very well be historically authentic without necessarily reflecting how Jesus understood his role.

For Hengel, it is indisputable that Jesus was executed for political reasons, since the political nature of the charge against him pervades the entire account of his trial, from the first hearing before the Jewish authorities until the last before Pilate. Jesus was executed as a Messianic pretender, as someone who, together with his followers, appeared to be politically dangerous. The events that most lent credence to a Messianic claim on Jesus' part were his entry into Jerusalem and the so-called 'cleansing of the temple'. It is to consideration of those events that we now turn.

The 'Cleansing of the Temple'

The first point to be made is that the term 'cleansing' is misleading for it implies a prior profanation. Some scholars subscribe to the view that trade in and around the temple precincts was somehow tantamount to sacrilege. But the erroneousness of this view becomes quite evident if we bear in mind that the principal function of the temple was to serve as the place for the sacrificial cult, and that the cult required a supply of suitable animals. Thus buying and selling were necessary for the temple as an institution which served not only the inhabitants of Jerusalem and Palestine but many thousands of pilgrims as well. Jews from all parts of the Diaspora made pilgrimages to the holy city during the major holidays and festivals. Defined standards of perfection were required of the sacrificial animals and birds. This being the case, even a Galilean Jew would have found it more convenient to buy a dove, for example, in Jerusalem than to transport it from Galilee to the temple only to find on his arrival that it was unacceptable. As E.P. Sanders has observed, the presentation of 'an unblemished dove as a sacrifice for certain impurities or transgressions was a requirement . . . of God to Israel through Moses'.[30] Trade in the temple precincts was not necessarily offensive to the pious Jews of Jesus' time. Trade, writes Gunther Bornkamm, is 'in keeping with the activities which up to the present day attend all pilgrimages. Merchants and money-changers do their business, offer for sale beasts for sacrifice, and exchange the foreign money of the pilgrims into ancient Hebrew or Phoenician currency, which was prescribed for commerce and the temple dues. Care was taken, as we know, that the sacred parts of the temple were not touched by this.'[31]

Nevertheless, Jewish scholars have called attention to the strong possibility that Jesus, as a pious Jew, may in fact have found this scene offensive. Mark (11:16) states that after Jesus 'overturned the tables of the money-changers and the seats of those who sold pigeons, . . . he would not allow anyone to carry anything through the temple'. Citing the rabbinic literature pertaining to the temple, I. Abrahams points out that in this instance Jesus 'sided with those who ordained that the temple must not be made a public thoroughfare (TB Yebamoth 6b). Others went further and forbade frivolous behaviour outside the temple precincts and in the neighborhood of the Eastern gate (Berachot 54a). Similar rules were applied to the synagogues (Megillah 27–8) . . . That Jesus is applying an established rule and not innovating is confirmed by the fact that he cites old prophetic texts (Isa. 56:7; Jer. 7:11) in support of his attitude.'[32] Joseph Klausner, following G. Dalman, suggests that, given the fact that in Jesus' time it was the Sadducean aristocracy that controlled the temple, it is possible that the outer court was not regarded as too sacred 'to permit the sale of doves and pigeons or of money-changing for the purchase of seals for the various temple offerings . . .'[33] This provoked Jesus' indignation. He entered the outer court, most probably with his disciples, and, with the help of his followers and some of the people already present, he threw down the tables of the money-changers and the seats of those who sold doves, and allowed no man to carry any vessel through the temple. Then, basing himself on Isaiah 56:7 and Jeremiah 7:11, he taught, and said to them, 'Is it not written, "my house shall be called a house of prayer for all nations"? But you have made it a den of robbers' (Mark 11:17). Klausner believes that both the action and the sentiment gained the approval of many people present, but that the high-priests were enraged.

The outer courtyard of the Herodian temple, in which this event took place, may also have served as the *agora* or forum in Jerusalem. It measured over 450 meters in length by about 300 meters in width.[34] In the northwest corner was the fortress of Antonia, where a Roman cohort of some 500–600 soldiers was stationed. The fortress was connected to the temple courtyard by a wide staircase which made the temple precincts easily accessible to the Roman troops in times of social disturbances. The proximity of the fortress to the courtyard is also evident from the description of the events surrounding the arrest of Paul (Acts 21:27ff). And Josephus informs us that at the great festivals the Romans used to station additional guards on the western portico of the outer temple, in order to observe the goings-on in the large outer court (*Antiq.* 20:192). Any conspicuous disturbances would unavoidably have brought about the intervention of the garrison. Martin Hengel has therefore concluded that

> In the so-called temple-cleansing we have, apparently, a prophetic demonstration or, one could also say, provocation, in which it was not a matter of driving out all those who sold, and the money-changers – for such action would not have been possible without a large contingent of troops and a corresponding general riot, and would inevitably have led to intervention on the part of the temple guards and the Romans. We are dealing, rather, with a demonstrative condemnation of their trade, a condemnation which was directed at the same time against the ruling temple aristocracy, which derived profit from it . . . Such an episode did not call forth intervention on the part of the occupation forces, but it did make the hierarchy the deadly foes of Jesus.[35]

This speaks against the Eisler-Brandon interpretation of the 'cleansing' episode as an act of insurrection. Though it was no insurrection, it none the less became a source of anxiety to the governing priestly nobility. The latter may have been concerned over what appeared to be a Messianic challenge to its leadership; but they were more concerned over what the Roman reaction would be if this popular, charismatic, Galilean rabbi continued to draw large crowds to himself with his provocative words and deeds. For it was not only Jesus' deeds on this occasion, but also his words that caused concern. In response to a disciple's admiring remark about the 'wonderful stones' and 'wonderful buildings' of the temple, Jesus replied, 'Do you see these great buildings? There will not be left here one stone upon another, that will not be thrown down' (Mark 13:1–2). Some scholars take this to be a 'prediction' after the fact – i.e., a reflection of the actual destruction of the temple by the Romans in AD 70. If, however, Jesus actually uttered these words, their meaning was eschatological, identical to the meaning of the utterance he was accused of making by the witnesses: 'I will destroy this temple that is made with hands, and in three days I will build another, not made with hands' (Mark 14:58). If Jesus' action in the temple courtyard together with his words about the temple were understood eschatologically by the crowds, this surely would have heightened their enthusiasm for this charismatic figure and their expectations of a dramatic, God-ordained change soon to come. And such enthusiasm, in turn, would have increased the anxiety of the Jewish leadership, which was held responsible by the Romans for violations of law and order.

11

The Arrest, Trial and Execution

Jewish self-rule, prior to the war against Rome, applied to affairs of an internal character. The Jewish establishment in Judea was responsible for arbitrating all matters pertaining to the religious life of the nation. Josephus nowhere suggests that the Romans accepted jurisdiction over Jews in matters of religious significance; and all the cases he recounts in which Jews were executed at the order of the Roman governor involve political, not religious offences. From the book of Acts we learn that all the cases dealt with by the Sanhedrin entailed transgressions of a religious nature. When the Jews of Corinth accuse Paul of 'persuading men to worship God contrary to the law' [of Moses], the proconsul Gallio decides that this is a religious matter and refuses to try the case; he even pays no attention to the fact that the head of the synagogue is beaten in front of the tribunal (Acts 18:12–17). When, however, Paul and Silas are accused of a political offence in Philippi – disturbing the city and advocating practices 'which it is not lawful for us Romans [i.e., citizens] to accept or practice' – the magistrates take action (Acts 16:19ff). This is in keeping with what we know from other sources about the policy of Roman officialdom: they respected the religious autonomy of the areas under their control.

In John 18:12–27 we read that it was the Roman soldiers, accompanied by the officers of the temple, who arrested Jesus, brought him to the residence of the high-priest for interrogation, and from there to the praetorium for a hearing before Pilate. As Paul Winter has observed:

> There is nothing incredible in the account of John 18:12–13, 28 which states that a Roman military commander, having arrested Jesus, conducted him to the local Jewish official with the order to prepare the judicial proceedings for the governor's court and, this done, to hand him back to the imperial authority. A preliminary examination was required prior to the trial before Pilate. There was the need to question Jesus, interrogate witnesses, translate their depositions, and prepare the charge-sheet. Pilate apparently knew what the charge was ['are you King of the Jews?'] (Mark 15:2), though with the exception of

Luke 23:2 ['We found this man perverting our nation, and forbidding us to give tribute to Caesar ...], no evangelist specifies the charge or a charge-sheet.[1]

What was the motive of the Sadducean aristocracy in bringing this charge against Jesus? Mark (15:10) says that it was out of 'envy' that they did so. John, however, states that they were motivated by fear: 'If we let him go on thus, everyone will believe in him, and the Romans will come and destroy both our holy place and our nation' (11:48). According to John, then, the Jewish aristocracy feared the abolition of Jewish autonomy as a consequence of the Jesus movement – which makes more sense than Mark's notion that they acted out of envy.

There is a discrepancy between the Synoptics and John where the circumstances of Jesus' arrest are concerned. Matthew, Mark and Luke make no mention of Roman participation in the event. John, in contrast, states that Jesus was arrested by Roman military personnel. Whom are we to believe? Given the anti-Jewish animus of the Fourth Gospel, in which Jesus' specific adversaries are lumped into the general category of 'the Jews', it is noteworthy that John provides this significant detail concerning Jesus' arrest. That John seems more sympathetic to the Romans than to the Jews is evident in the words he places in Jesus' mouth in response to Pilate: 'he who delivered me to you has the greater sin' (19:11). It is therefore highly improbable that John, whose sympathies lay with the Romans, would have introduced this item of information without support of the tradition. So we have the Synoptic version of the arrest by a Jewish police force and the Johannine version by Roman soldiers.

We must remind ourselves that Mark most probably wrote his Gospel in Rome shortly after the war of AD 70, and that he had a special interest in stressing the apolitical character of the young Christian movement. In that light we can see why he might have been inclined to excise the particular item concerning Roman troops. It is thus easier to explain why Mark passed over the Roman participation in silence, than to explain why John would have related this item if it had not come from a reliable tradition.[2] John states that the Roman personnel were accompanied by the 'officers of the Jews', as does Luke (22:52); so it is quite likely that both Roman soldiers and temple police took part in the arrest.

Another important fact that emerges from these accounts is that Jesus was arrested at night: 'Have you come out as against a *rebel* [not 'robber'], with swords and clubs to capture me? Day after day I was with you in the temple teaching, and you did not seize me' (Mark 14:48–9). The emphasis here is on the public and open character of Jesus' activity; he is not the leader of a clandestine band who conducts his affairs at night. Jesus' words also strongly suggest that his popularity at the moment was such that the authorities could not have seized him during the day without causing considerable social tumult. As Paul Winter surmises, we have here a trace of an early tradition which implies that the arrest of Jesus was undertaken as a precaution against possible insurrectionist activities. That Jesus was perceived as a leader of a seditious or politically dangerous movement may also be inferred from this statement, 'And with him they crucified two *revolutionaries* [this, not 'robbers', is the meaning of the Greek word *lestes* in this context], one on his right and one on his left' (Mark 15:27; cf. Matt. 27:38; Luke 23:32; John 19:18). The Gospels have therefore preserved the fact that 'Jesus was arrested, accused, condemned and executed, on a charge of rebellion'.[3]

We learn from Josephus (*War* 2:169–77; *Antiq.* 18.55–64, 85–7) that Pilate was a no-nonsense, inflexible, harsh and obdurate official. Luke (13:1–2) conveys the same when he informs us that Pilate mingled the blood of the Galileans with their sacrifices. Yet in his interaction with the mob and the Jewish leadership, the Pilate of the Gospels is portrayed as a feeble and indecisive figure. Most instructive is a comparison of the passages in which the Evangelists refer to Pilate's final decision (Mark 15:15; Matt. 27:26; Luke 23:24; John 19:16). 'All are reluctant', writes Winter, '*to state plainly that the sentence of death was pronounced by the governor.* It is evident that Jesus could never have been put to death by the manner of crucifixion unless a verdict to this effect had been given by a Roman magistrate. If a capital sentence, passed by a Jewish court of law, required the governor's confirmation to be put into effect, such a sentence would not have resulted in the condemned person's crucifixion, but it would have been carried out in accordance with Jewish penal procedure.[4] The truth comes out, however, in the Fourth Gospel, which states that Pilate gave the orders for the inscription on the cross: 'Jesus of Nazareth, the King of the Jews' (19:19); and that it was the 'soldiers', i.e., Romans, who crucified Jesus (19:23). Finally, there is the account in all the Gospels of how Joseph of Arimathea, 'a respected member of the council, . . . took courage and went to Pilate, and asked for the body of Jesus' so that it could be properly buried (Mark 15:43–5; Matt. 27:58; Luke 23:50–2; John 19:38). It is evident, then, that the sentence and execution was the work of the Romans, for otherwise the governor's permission for burial would have been unnecessary.

This brings us to the question of whether the Jewish authorities had the right to impose capital punishment, and if so, what form it assumed. It is almost universally agreed among scholars that in the time of Jesus crucifixion was a typically Roman penalty. There was no provision in Jewish law for hanging a condemned individual alive on a stake or a cross. There was, however, an ancient provision that the corpse of an executed criminal be affixed to a stake, evidently as a deterrent example, but that it be taken down for burial before nightfall (Deut. 21:22–3). Inasmuch as it is still a matter of dispute among scholars whether capital crimes were punished by stoning in the first century, we need to say a word about this matter.

Stoning was a legal form of capital punishment among several ancient nations, for example, the Persians, Macedonians, Greeks and Iberians, but *not* among the Romans, Babylonians and Assyrians. According to the evidence of the Hebrew Scriptures (the Old Testament), stoning was in fact a customary mode of execution imposed for idolatry (Lev. 20:2; Deut. 13:10ff; 17:5), blasphemy (Lev. 24:14, 16;1 Kings 21:10, 13), profanation of the sabbath (Num. 15:32–6), divination or sorcery (Lev. 20:27), rebellion against parents (Deut. 21:18–21), adultery (Deut. 22:21–4) and the appropriation of objects placed under the ban (Josh. 7:25).[5] The apparent reason why this method of punishment figures prominently in the ancient law is that it lends itself to the greatest possible participation of the people. In the regulations for stoning the participation of the whole community is often explicitly called for (Lev. 24:14, 16; Num. 15:35ff, Deut. 13:10; 17:7; Josh. 7:25; 1 Kings 12:18; Lev. 24:23; Deut. 21:21; Lev. 20:2). Grave offences inflicted wounds on the whole community, so everyone was responsible to God for the punishment of the offenders. In order to reduce the likelihood of evidence being given lightly or falsely, the witnesses cast the first stones (Deut. 13:10; 17:7). According to Lev. 24:14 the witnesses laid their hands on the head of the condemned individual before the stoning, which was carried out outside the camp or the city gates. All those thus executed for capital crimes were hung on a stake until evening.

Definite evidence exists that stoning, as a method of capital punishment, was in force in the New Testament period. As noted earlier, Josephus (*Antiq.* 20:200) reports that Ananus, the high-priest, had James, the brother of Jesus, stoned for transgression of the Law. And the Fourth Gospel relates that the people wanted to stone Jesus (John 8:59; 10:31–3; 11:8). Finally, there is the stoning of Stephen in Acts 7:59ff. Thus it seems indisputable that stoning was *the* Jewish form of capital punishment for religious crimes against the community. If, therefore, Jesus had committed such a crime, he would have been executed by stoning.[6] Paul Winter, after a fastidious examination of the relevant Talmudic evidence, reaches the same conclusion: 'before the year 70 AD the Sanhedrin had full jurisdiction over Jews charged with offenses against Jewish religious law, and had the authority openly to pronounce and carry out sentences of death in accordance with the provisions of Jewish legislation. Only after the fall of Jerusalem was the Sanhedrin deprived of its right to execute persons whom it had tried and sentenced to death.'[7] In this light, then, the statement which John ascribes to the Jews in 18:31 should be interpreted thus: 'It is not lawful for us to put any man to death' [for the commission of political crimes] – in Jesus' case, for the *alleged* commission of such crimes.

The Gospels speak of a supposed custom of setting a prisoner free at the feast of Passover. In Mark and Matthew this is related as if it were the governor's prerogative. In John it becomes a Jewish custom – 'one, however, with which Pilate appears to have been better acquainted than the Jews themselves; [since] it needed his prompting to remind the people of its existence.'[8] The Evangelists state that the crowd was free to request from Pilate the pardoning of any prisoner; but they imply at the same time that the choice was restricted to two individuals, one of them being Barabbas, 'among the rebels in prison, who had committed murder in the insurrection' (Mark 15:7). Now, even if such a custom did exist, Winter convincingly observes,

> and the crowd's choice fell on Barabbas, nothing could have prevented the governor, if he had wished to do so, from releasing Jesus in addition to Barabbas. This would have been an easy thing for him to do if he had pronounced Jesus not guilty. Custom or no custom, the sentencing of Jesus did not depend on the acquittal of Barabbas. The writers of the Gospels are anxious to show that Pilate's good efforts were in vain. Thoughtful readers must come to the conclusion that all the efforts of the evangelists were no less futile.[9]

Winter also notes that in the Fourth Gospel the mockery of Jesus is the work of the Roman soldiers, not of the Sanhedrin as in Mark and Matthew, and not of the temple police as in Luke.

Winter proposes, therefore, that the following sequence of events can be affirmed with certainty:

> that Jesus was arrested by Roman military personnel (John 18:12) for political reasons (Mark 14:48) and then conducted to a local Jewish administrative offical (Mark 14:53a; Luke 22:54; John 18:13a) during the same night. The following morning, after a brief deliberation by the Jewish authorities (Mark 15:1a; Luke 22:66), he was handed back to the Romans for trial (Mark 15:1b; Luke 23:1; John 18:28a). The governor sentenced Jesus to death by crucifixion (Tacitus; Mark 15:15b, 26), the sentence being carried out in accordance with Roman penal procedure (Mark 15:15b, 24a, 27).[10]

But Winter acknowledges that a basic question remains to which no certain answers can be given: What was the immediate cause of this chain of events? What, precisely, did Jesus do to provoke such actions against him? Winter agrees that Jesus himself was no Zealot. Still, the 'triumphal entry' bore all the marks of a Messianic demonstration, both to the participants and to those who observed it from a distance. The gospel tradition interpreted Jesus' entry into the capital city of Judea as a symbolic seizure of power in which Jesus was hailed as the new King. The 'cleansing of the temple' was less significant in Winter's eyes, although the editors of Winter's book remark that 'Winter came to feel that he had underestimated the significance of the "cleansing" . . .'[11] As for the Jewish authorities, they took action against Jesus not out of self-interest, but in the hope of preventing the Romans from intervening with extreme punitive measures on the pretext of unrest. We have noted the swift and harsh Roman reactions to popular movements of the time; so there can be little doubt that so far as Pilate was concerned, 'he would have seen sufficient reason for ordering the crucifixion if he had come to feel that Jesus' itinerant preaching tended to excite the masses to expect the end of the existing order'.[12]

More on the Reimarus–Eisler–Brandon Thesis

This thesis is based on the fundamental fact that Jesus was executed for sedition. We have seen in chapter 10, however, that he may very well have been the victim of circumstances, executed as a rebel though he was not one. His execution for sedition proves not that he actually was a Zealot or para-Zealot, but only that he was perceived as a popular and politically dangerous charismatic figure. The fact that Jesus' disciples were not arrested together with him and went free, creates a big problem for Brandon's thesis that Jesus was associated with the Zealot movement, since it suggests that the Romans did not look upon them as members of a seditious organization. Or, as Peter Richardson has proposed, perhaps 'we tend to overstress the actual solidarity between Jesus and his disciples; maybe the sense of corporateness was not so strong as we generally assume'.[13]

It will help to clarify further the actual causes of Jesus' execution if we say a few more words about the revolutionary theory of Jesus, discussed at greater length in the previous chapter. Reviewing this theory from Reimarus to Brandon, Ernst Bammel notes that for Reimarus Jesus must have been well aware of the political implications of a Messianic demonstration; yet several of his actions in Jerusalem certainly had the appearance of such a demonstration. Wilhelm Weitling, a friend of Karl Marx, took a similar but more radical position in 1845, portraying Jesus as a proto-communist. Frederick Engels and Karl Kautsky followed suit. However, scholars with no socialist or Marxian proclivities, also discerned an element of truth in Reimarus' view. No less a figure than Julius Wellhausen, for example, remarked that '*bis zu einem gewissen Grade könnte Reimarus Recht haben*' [up to a certain point Reimarus could be right]. And Bammel comments: 'In this way he [Wellhausen] testifies to the fact that every concept that takes the Messianic terminology as constitutive and refrains from spiritualizing it is under a certain obligation to admit quasi-Zealot ingredients in the Gospel accounts.'[14] And somewhat later Bammel writes: 'what is truly revolutionary in Jesus is his *animus* against the law, his lack of compliance with what was, on the basis of the law, the established order of the day, his relationship to God and his regard for the individual . . . Jesus revolted against the Torah of his fathers . . .'[15]

This opinion is fairly typical of an influential school in contemporary New Testament studies. We have seen, however, that far from having exhibited any alleged animus against the Law, Jesus relied exclusively on the Torah, the prophets and the other writings of the Hebrew Scriptures, for his stand on the various religious issues of the time. Whether it was the question of what was permitted on the sabbath, or the questions of divorce, dietary laws or the washing of hands before eating, Jesus always cited prooftexts from the Torah to justify his stance. Doubtless, he differed with some of his Jewish contemporaries over these issues and others. He diverged from *some* of the Pharisees over certain teachings of the oral law. One can fully recognize the creative genius and originality of the Sermon on the Mount, for instance, without construing it as antithetical to the Law, as have many scholars. Given the remarkable heterogeneity of Judaism in the first century, including the diversity within the Pharisaic movement itself – at least two major schools and several minor ones – there is no good reason for viewing Jesus' teaching as having somehow gone outside the bounds of Judaism. One can also fully acknowledge that Jesus innovated in the greater stress he placed on the ethical dimension as applied to the 'lost sheep of Israel'; but again, there is nothing in his words or deeds that should give anyone licence to read him out of Judaism. The religio-intellectual exchanges which Jesus had with some of his learned contemporaries are best understood as an intramural debate; and as we know, differences within a community often generate more intensity than differences with outsiders. Jesus was a charismatic religious virtuoso who challenged specific traditions of the elders; but to construe this as 'animus' against the Law is no less than preposterous.

One must also take exception to Bammel's demand that the Gospels be 'spiritualized'. For no matter how much we 'spiritualize' the Messianic terminology, a fundamental question remains: why did Jesus enter Jerusalem in such a manner as to create the impression that his entry was a Messianic demonstration? One might object that Jesus had never intended it as a 'triumphal entry'. Then why do the Gospels describe it as such, drawing on the symbolism of Zechariah 9.9, in which the 'King' is triumphant – though humble at the same time? If we reject all Zealotic and quasi-Zealotic elements in Jesus' conception of Messianic deliverance, we still need to address the question of what meaning the entry into Jerusalem had for Jesus himself. What was his self-understanding as he rode into the holy city on a colt, greeted by cries of 'Hosanna! Blessed be he who comes in the name of the Lord!'? The evidence reviewed so far suggests that Jesus' understanding of his role was quite different from that of the disciples and the crowds. They appear to have perceived him in the political-military terms of the traditional Jewish Messiah. This tradition, however, was neither worldly nor spiritual. It was neither of these exclusively because it was both, at one and the same time. Even the Zealots, after all, never supposed for one moment that they would liberate the Holy Land by their own efforts alone. Their armed resistance was carried out in the expectation of divine intervention and cooperation.

What meaning, then, did the entry to Jerusalem have in Jesus' own mind? The answer that best fits the evidence is that he may in fact have seen himself in some kind of Messianic role. The special relationship he believed he had with God the Father whom he addressed as '*Abba*', prompted him to test God's will by committing himself to a course of action that might call forth a gracious and merciful response. Even as he is arrested and instructs a disciple to put his sword back into its place, he is able to say, 'Do you think that I cannot appeal to *my* Father, and he will at once send me more than twelve legions of angels?' (Matt. 26:53). Jesus thus went up to Jerusalem in the hope (and expectation?) that his *Abba* would send down legions of angels to put an end to the heathen domination of the Holy Land, and to usher in the new era. That is the reason why it is wrong to suppose that by 'spiritualizing' the Messianic terminology of the Gospels, we eliminate its political implications. For as Christopher Rowland has aptly observed: 'It must be said that Jesus' teaching *did* have implicit political consequences, insofar as it was through and through eschatological. Even if we must reject the assertion that Jesus was himself a Zealot, there can be little doubt that his message was understood in this way by some of his followers . . . Thus even if Jesus renounced the methods of the Zealots, his goal of a new age was deeply disturbing to those who preferred the compromises of the present age to the uncertainties of the new.'[16] And Rowland continues:

> At the very least we must say that Jesus' claim to be the agent of the coming kingdom of God placed him on the same level as the Messiah of Jewish hope whose task it was to be the agent of God's reign of righteousness. We may suspect, however, that the reluctance of Jesus to accept the title 'son of David,' or to use the title Messiah of himself may lie with the bellicose connotations of that title and its related concepts in current usage . . . Like A. Harvey, I would want to look for Jesus' messianic consciousness in that group of passages which speak of Jesus as the one anointed with the Spirit, whose mission heralded the kingdom (Luke 4:16ff; Matt. 11:2ff; cf. Isa. 35:5ff; 61:1ff). It is . . . in this sense that Jesus saw himself as the anointed one.[17]

We must agree, then, that insofar as the Brandon thesis depicts Jesus as a Zealot or para-Zealot, it is misleading and wrong. For Jesus appears to have urged a total reliance on God. This total reliance, however, as 'spiritual' as it may have been, was essentially eschatological and, therefore, unavoidably political in its consequences. Bammel tacitly recogizes this when he states that the redemption of Israel was the dominant function of the Messianic King in *all* branches of Jewish eschatology. It was the widespread expectation of a redemption soon to come that expressed itself in the events surrounding the Feeding, when the crowds wanted to take Jesus by force and make him king. It may also have been the proclamation of John the Baptist that prompted the crowds to view Jesus in this light, and perhaps even to test him.

Brandon had proposed that the entry into Jerusalem together with the episode in the temple courtyard was a rather largescale affair in which Jesus and his followers attempted to seize control of the temple and its treasury. The force accompanying Jesus was presumably too strong to be captured. But David R. Catchpole has convincingly countered that this proposition 'defies all probability. Had this been so, the silence of Josephus, who includes in his accounts many more trivial events than that would have been, is inexplicable.'[18] Catchpole cites the several instances recounted in Josephus in which the Romans swiftly put an end to disturbances of the political order; he then makes the important observation 'that Jesus was not arrested straightaway or *in situ*, while the disciples were not arrested at all. The action in the temple must therefore have been trivial in size and, moreover, as Mark himself indicates, an action by Jesus alone.'[19] Catchpole observes that there is no evidence in the texts of 'unjustifiable exploitation, for example, undue profit-making or financial irregularity . . . Jesus' intervention does not protect the [allegedly] exploited buyers by expelling the exploiting sellers, but instead both buyers and sellers are ejected'. The consequence and apparent aim of Jesus' action become evident in the fact that trade in the temple courtyard is interrupted, at least temporarily. Following Cecil Roth, Catchpole therefore sees Jesus' action as having been inspired by an ancient prophecy: 'there shall no longer be a trader in the house of the Lord of hosts on that day' (Zech. 14:21). The 'cleansing', then, was no abortive *coup d'état*, but a religiously inspired action.[20]

This has a direct bearing on the nature of Jesus' activities in Jerusalem and how they were perceived. Everyone concerned, the disciples, the less intimate followers and the crowds, understood the coming of the Messiah in the traditional Jewish terms – at once worldly and transcendental. This was the expectation that gave rise to the false prophets and 'deceivers' described by Josephus (*Antiq.* 20:97ff; 20:167); and this was the expectation that moved the disciples to 'test' Jesus. All the textual evidence strongly indicates that Peter, James and John the sons of Zebedee, and Judas Iscariot were simply unwilling to view Jesus as anything other than what they intensely wished him to be: the victorious Messianic King. Scholars have even suggested that Judas' real motive was to force Jesus into a confrontation in which he could only prove victorious.

Jesus thus faced a dilemma: he felt himself called to save Israel and yet could not adopt the only policy that the disciples and the people would understand and accept. We can pinpoint the event in Jerusalem that led to a drop in Jesus' popularity. The question designed 'to entrap him in his talk', succeeded in eliciting from Jesus a reply that disappointed many of those present. As soon as he said, 'Render to Caesar the things that are Caesar's' (Mark 12:17), the crowds began to doubt that he was the one destined to free them from the Roman-Edomite yoke and to restore the kingdom to Israel. Does this mean, however, that the people of Jerusalem, disappointed by Jesus' answer, chose to save the notorious prisoner Barabbas instead?

'Not this man, but Barabbas'

Luke makes no mention of an annual custom to release one prisoner; but he does say of Barabbas that he was 'a man who had been thrown into prison for an insurrection started in the city, and for murder' (23:19). In John it is Pilate who brings up the subject of the custom, referring to it as a Jewish practice. There is no reference to this so-called custom either in Josephus or in the rabbinic literature. In several ancient manuscripts of Matthew's Gospel, Barabbas is called 'Jesus Barabbas'. The name 'Jesus' (Heb. *Yeshua*), having been quite common in first-century Judea, it is entirely possible that Barabbas bore it. William Riley Wilson has therefore convincingly suggested that 'since the name Jesus was especially sacred to the early church it would have been most natural for the early Christians to dissociate it from the murderer Barabbas. This would have been accomplished by gradually omitting Barabbas' given name from the oral and written records of the trial. If this suggestion is correct, the few manuscripts which give the name Jesus Barabbas are the only surviving evidence of the insurrectionist's full name.' Just prior to the Passover season this 'Jesus Barabbas' had been involved in an uprising against the Roman government. This is Wilson's reconstruction of the events that took place before Pilate, in front of the praetorium:

> In the eyes of many Jews gathered for the Passover Barabbas was a national
> hero, and as the day arrived for the execution of some of those involved in the
> revolt a crowd of Jews swarmed about the praetorium. Stirred by intense

nationalistic feelings, they demanded the release of the patriot, Jesus Barabbas.

At that moment Jesus of Nazareth was on trial before the governor. Hearing the crowd chant Barabbas' name, Pilate stopped to ask whether this Jesus was the man whose release they sought. Barabbas' supporters then expressed their indifference to Jesus of Nazareth, perhaps even saying, 'Let him be crucified, but release Barabbas'. To the followers of Jesus, who presumably were also outside the praetorium, this cry seemed perverse and inhuman. Jesus was innocent of any political crimes, yet the crowd sought only the release of the murderer [insurrectionist] who deserved to die [under Roman law]. Subsequently, the indifference of Barabbas' supporters to Jesus was gradually reinterpreted as the bitter and open hostility of the people as a whole. Needless to say, such popular hostility is unhistorical. The Jews gathered for the Passover would never have begged a Roman procurator to kill a fellow countryman simply because they did not agree with all his teachings or doubted that he was the Messiah . . . Some commentators have supposed that the mob sought Jesus' death because they were disappointed that he had not taken a firm stand against Rome; they hated him because he had frustrated their hopes. Such idle speculation is necessary only if we accept the Gospel description of the mob scene. Nothing in the historical situation justifies such a view. Jesus did not die because certain Jews stood outside the trial chambers asking that he be killed or that an insurrectionist be freed. Pilate executed Jesus because he thought him guilty [of a political Messianic claim]. The vast majority of Jews in Jerusalem must have mourned many others who died in this manner under the procurators.

Regrettably, many modern readers of the New Testament find no difficulty in accepting this bitter calumny against the Jewish people of Jesus' day. This is evidence of how effectively the Gospels have laid the blame for Jesus' death at the feet of his own people.[22]

12

The Resurrection Appearance

It was under Persian and Hellenistic influence that the idea of the immortality of the soul first emerged in Judaism. This idea is absent from the Hebrew Scriptures, where one finds neither the fear of natural death nor the expectation of an afterlife. In pre-Maccabean times there are only vague hints of a belief in the immortality of the soul. Indeed, Joshua ben Sirah (*c.* 200–180 BC) held the view that eventually became the Sadducean position with regard to the dead: 'Remember him not for he hath no hope . . .' And 'when the dead is at rest let his memory rest' (38:21, 23). Somewhat later, however, as we have noted, the book of Daniel (12:2) voiced for the first time the belief that those who sleep in the dust of the earth shall awake to everlasting life – a belief that became the cornerstone of the faith and lore of the Pharisaic movement. Following Daniel, the apocalyptic visionaries began to depict graphically the delights of the new life granted in the 'end of days' to the righteous and the humble. The Ethiopic Enoch, one of the earliest of such visionaries, wrote that 'Then shall they rejoice with joy and be glad, and unto the holy place shall they enter; and its fragrance shall be in their bones, and they shall live a long life on earth, such as thy fathers lived. And in their days shall no sorrow or plague or torment or calamity touch them' (25:6). In Daniel the resurrected saints will shine as the brightness of the firmament, and in Enoch (108:12) they are attired in raiments of light.

Such claims were never taken seriously by the rationalistic Sadducees who found no grounds for such yearnings in the Scriptures. Nevertheless, the belief in another world (Heb. *ha-olam haba*) gained strength continually. It helped to solve the age-old theodicy problem of why the righteous suffer while the evil prosper in the world. The book of Job had left too many questions unanswered. Furthermore, the idea of a renewed existence was implied in the eschatology of the great Hebrew prophets. 'What the Jew craved for himself', wrote G.F. Moore, 'was to have a part in the future golden age of the nation, as the prophets depicted it . . . It was only so, not in some blissful lot for his individual self apart, that he could conceive of perfect happiness.'[1] Or in the words of the Jewish historian S.W. Baron, 'at the end of days – this became the growing conviction – not only the national body then in existence, but Israel of all history, of the generations past as well as of those yet unborn, would participate in the universal reign of God'.[2] The Jewish idea of renewed life and a new world were bound up together; it was a synthesis of personal resurrection and prophetic eschatology. By the time of the first century the schools both of Hillel and Shammai believed in the resurrection of the material form.[3]

Personal resurrection, before or independently of the dawning of the 'world to come', was unthinkable. Little wonder that the apostles were sceptical when told that Jesus had risen. The women who had seen how Jesus' body was laid, returned after the sabbath to find an empty tomb; and when they related to the apostles that Jesus had risen, 'these words seemed to them an idle tale, and they did not believe them' (Luke 24:11). Even after the disciples saw Jesus in a vision, 'some doubted' (Matt. 28:17).

The pioneer Jewish historian Heinrich Graetz observed that Jesus 'is the only mortal of whom one can say without exaggeration that his death was more effective than his life. Golgotha, the place of skulls [sic], became to the civilized world a new Sinai.'[4] It is a most interesting fact that Christianity first emerged not so much from the teachings of Jesus as from the faith in his resurrection. The conduct of James, Peter and Paul, not to mention the other disciples, confirms this proposition; for they all had a change of heart. James did not at first believe in his brother; Peter denied and abandoned Jesus; and Paul persecuted the early community. Paul relates that Jesus was raised on the third day 'and that he appeared to Cephas [Peter] then to the twelve. Then he appeared to more than 500 brethren at one time . . . Then he appeared to James, then to all the apostles. Last of all, . . . he appeared also to me. For I am the least of the apostles, unfit to be called an apostle, because I persecuted the church of God' (1 Cor. 15:4–9). Paul firmly believed that Jesus 'has been raised from the dead, the first fruits of those who have fallen asleep' (1 Cor. 15:20). Evidently this faith was not invented by Paul, but was already held by the Jerusalem, Jewish-Christian community prior to Paul's conversion. Jesus, the preacher of the Kingdom of Heaven, had become the object of Christian preaching.

In the Judaism of the time there was a commonly accepted faith in the 'revival of the dead' (Heb. *tehiat hametim*), which was to take place at some distant time. The disciples, however, believed that they had personally witnessed the beginning of the actual Resurrection. It was this belief that in the minds of the disciples transformed the crucified Jesus into the Messiah, who would soon triumphantly return. The belief in Jesus' resurrection became, in the words of Jacob Jocz, 'the cornerstone upon which the faith in the Messiahship of Jesus was built. Paul's whole theology centers round this fact. It is not the cross but the Resurrection which is the starting-point of Pauline thought. It was also the Resurrection which became the *kerigma* of the primitive church. That Christ was risen from the dead was their *evangelion*.'[5]

The rational stimulus for the belief in Jesus' resurrection appears to have been the fact that the women who set out with spices and ointments to pay their last respects, 'did not find the body' (Luke 24:3). It is of interest that in the earliest debates over the veracity of the Christian claim of Jesus' resurrection, neither the Jews nor the Christians denied that the tomb was soon empty. But the theory that the empty tomb was somehow a 'signal of transcendence', a first stimulus for the conviction that Jesus had been raised, is not without its problems:

1   The empty tomb implies *bodily* resurrection, which played no part of any significance in the preaching of Jesus.
2   The apostles themselves did not believe the women's story that Jesus had risen.
3   Paul makes no mention of an empty tomb.

From 1 Corinthians 15 and other letters we gain the distinct impression that Paul thought of the resurrection not as a resuscitation of flesh and blood, but as the ascent of the spirit or soul into a new realm of being: 'So it is with the resurrection of the dead. What is sown is perishable, what is raised is imperishable . . . It is sown a physical body, it is raised a spiritual body' (1 Cor. 15:42–4). And in Philippians we read: 'we await a Saviour, who will change our lowly body to be like his glorious body . . .' (3:21). What Paul and the other apostles saw, evidently, in the resurrection appearance was a vision of Jesus' glorified spirit; and even though he is said in Luke to have taken the bread, blessed and broken it, he does not himself partake of the bread and soon vanishes 'out of their sight' (Luke 24:30–1). So it would seem that soon after Jesus' death, those who had known him personally and even those who perhaps had not (e.g., Paul), affirmed that Jesus had risen and appeared to them, in the spirit, not in the flesh.

The intriguing question, of course, is how to account for the conduct of Peter and the other disciples who had deserted Jesus and then came back to make such an affirmation. If they deserted him out of fear, which is likely, then we can agree that as they reflected on the traumatic events of the very recent past, they experienced intense feelings of remorse and guilt for having failed to act with honour and courage. The vision was a manifestation of their desire to repent and atone; they did so by means of a renewed and invigorated resolve to propagate the new Christian message. The same logic would apply to James the brother of Jesus; for although he had never deserted Jesus, he apparently did not believe in him during his lifetime. And Paul undoubtedly experienced pangs of conscience. As for the other disciples, their sense of solidarity with Jesus – for reasons which are now clear to us – had certainly not been sufficient to hold them together at the point of crisis. This strongly suggests 'the importance of the resurrection of Jesus for re-establishing the group of disciples and giving to them a mission to Israel and beyond. It is the resurrection, sealing the Passion, that impresses upon the group its character as a distinctive entity within Israel.'[6]

How did the resurrection-idea accomplish this end? When the disciples had recovered somewhat from the panic that seized them with the arrest and execution of Jesus, they most surely came together again to mourn their beloved master. The reassembled experienced not only remorse and guilt, but extreme perplexity. If Jesus was the Messiah, why did he endure such a terrible death? How could the Messiah be subject to pain? There was no *tradition* in Judaism of a suffering Messiah; but there was a passage in Isaiah 53 that appeared to prophesy the recent tragic circumstances:

> Surely he has borne our griefs and carried our sorrows; yet we esteemed him stricken, smitten by God, and afflicted. But he was wounded for our transgressions, he was bruised for our iniquities; upon him was the chastisement that made us whole, and with his stripes we are healed. All we like sheep have gone astray; we have turned every one to his own way; and the Lord has laid on him the iniquity of us all. He was oppressed, and he was afflicted, yet he opened not his mouth; like a lamb that is led to the slaughter, . . . so he opened not his mouth . . .

It is the people of Israel who are described in these words; but in the vexatious circumstances in which the disciples found themselves, it did not seem far-fetched that this prophecy applied to Jesus. Thus by interpreting Scripture, a time-honoured Jewish custom, these Jewish-Christians provided a solution to the central question: why had Jesus suffered and died? With the help of Holy Writ everything that happened to Jesus was shown to have been providentially determined. The disciples declared that they had heard Jesus say he would be persecuted unto death. A new messianic significance was thus imputed to Jesus' life and death.

But if the Messiah has suffered and died, what about the Kingdom of Heaven? When and how will it come about? Their deep and intense yearnings and hopes provided the answer: he shall return soon with legions of angels. This generation will not pass away, they believed, before they see 'the son of man coming on the clouds of heaven with power and great glory; and he will send out his angels with a loud trumpet call, and they will gather his elect from the four winds, from one end of heaven to the other' (Matt.

24:30–1). Jesus' followers were hourly expecting his return, differing from the other devout Jews only in their belief that the Messiah had already appeared and that his resurrection was the beginning of the new era.

In the meantime, while waiting for the Parousia, the belief in Jesus' death and resurrection provided these earliest Christians with a powerful idea, powerful because it spoke to a fundamental human need. To be sure, the majority of the Jews had already taken for granted the Pharisaic axiom that the righteous will receive everlasting life in the world to come. In the pagan world, however, when Paul spoke of the 'resurrection of the dead, some mocked; but others said, "We will hear you again about this"' (Acts 17:32). Paul fought hard against those who mocked or who were sceptical: 'how can some of you say that there is no resurrection of the dead? But if there is no resurrection of the dead, then Christ has not been raised; if Christ has not been raised, then our preaching is in vain and your faith is in vain . . . For if the dead are not raised, then Christ has not been raised. If Christ has not been raised, your faith is futile and you are still in your sins. Then those who have fallen asleep in Christ have perished . . . But in fact Christ has been raised from the dead, *the first fruits of those who have fallen asleep*' (1 Cor. 15:12–20). It is therefore with good reason, as Wayne A. Meeks has remarked, that 'many modern historians have suggested that this promise of individuals' resurrection was a major factor in the emotional appeal of Christianity in the pagan world'.[7] The great American psychologist William James has written about this fundamental human need:

> The fact that we *can* die, that we *can* be ill at all, is what perplexes us; the fact that we now for a moment live and are well is irrelevant to that perplexity. We need a life not correlated with death, a health not liable to illness, a kind of good that will not perish, a good in fact that flies beyond the Goods of nature.[8]

This good which 'flies beyond the Goods of nature', was the Jewish-Christian promise to the pagan world of everlasting life after death. In this respect Paul remained a Pharisee to the end, assuaging anxiety and offering consolation with the declaration 'that we who are alive, who are left until the coming of the Lord, shall not precede those who have fallen asleep . . . the dead in Christ will rise first; then we who are alive, who are left, shall be caught up together with them in the clouds to meet the Lord . . .; and so we shall always be with the Lord. *Therefore comfort one another with these words*' (I Thess. 4:13–18).

13

The First Christians

Paul's letters and the Acts of the Apostles are our earliest sources of information about the emergence of the Jewish-Christian community in Jerusalem. The book of Acts tells the story of how a small band of disciples transformed itself into a social movement. The importance of Acts may be seen in the fact that without it we would know virtually nothing about the period between the execution of Jesus and the time when Paul came into prominence.

Not too long after the tragedy of the crucifixion the disciples reassembled. In their condition of terrible grief and guilt they envisioned Jesus in their midst and asked him: 'Lord, will you at this time restore the kingdom of Israel?' (Acts 1:6). If the author of Acts – most scholars believe it was Luke – opens his story with this question, it can only mean that the restoration of the independent kingdom of Israel was a central preoccupation of the disciples from the very first moment that they reconvened. They were in a state of spiritual crisis, for the tragic and unexpected death of their master had traumatically frustrated their hopes for redemption. The answer they received to their question was this: 'It is not for you to know times or seasons which the Father has fixed by his own authority' (Acts 1:7). This was the time when the disciples gradually began to apply Isaiah 53 to Jesus as the Messiah: 'He was despised and rejected . . . wounded for our transgressions . . . He was oppressed, and he was afflicted, yet he opened not his mouth; like a lamb that is led to the slaughter . . .' The crucified Messiah was not a victorious and conquering King, but a sacrificial lamb. Yet the kingdom of Israel would, of course, be restored by him – but unexpectedly 'like a thief in the night' (I Thess. 5:2; Matt. 24:37–9, 42–4; Luke 17:24). This fundamental change in outlook on the part of the disciples means that they refused to believe that Jesus was a false Messiah. Indeed, even those who had not believed in him during his lifetime – his mother and brothers, for example – changed their attitude after the crucifixion. This surely attests to the powerful influence of Jesus' personality and to the profound impression he made on all those close to him by his religious virtuosity. By applying Isaiah 53 to Jesus, the small band of followers could end their disillusionment and renew their hopes for redemption.

In the first years of its growth, Simon Peter stood at the head of the group, which numbered about 120 persons (Acts 1:15). Later, Peter's place was taken by James the brother of Jesus. Simon, James and John the son of Zebedee, brother of the slain James, were referred to as the 'pillars' of the group (Gal. 2:9). Calling themselves 'Nazarenes', after Jesus of Nazareth, the members of this new congregation prayed and held their meetings in a synagogue. The only article of faith distinguishing the Nazarenes from other devout Jews was their belief in the suffering Messiah who would soon reappear on the Day of Judgment at the right hand of Power to establish the Kingdom of Heaven, which naturally included the restoration of the independent kingdom of Israel.

In Acts 3 we are told that when Simon Peter and John went up to the temple in the hour of prayer, Peter healed in the name of 'Jesus Christ of Nazareth'. This angered the Sadducean priests and the temple police who held that it is forbidden to heal the sick in the name of anyone but God (Acts 4:1). (Pharisees are not mentioned at all.) From the standpoint of the Sadducean priests, Peter and John represented a sect that believed in a false Messiah, whose teaching was held to be more important than the Torah's commandments. Thus began the persecution of the Nazarene leaders at the hands of the temple authorities. Peter and John were arrested and detained overnight. When their case was heard they defended themselves by arguing that their doctrine was no different from that of the Pharisees who also believed in the resurrection of the dead, and that it was on the basis of this article of faith that they taught that Jesus had risen. To the high-priests this doctrine was that of 'unlearned and ignorant men' (Acts 4:13), so they were set free with the warning never again to mention the name of Jesus. However, Peter and John continued to preach and heal in Jesus' name and soon they were arrested once again (Acts 5:17–18). Although friends had helped them escape, they were apprehended and brought before the Sanhedrin for judgment. When the apostles reaffirmed their faith that God had raised Jesus as the King-Messiah, the Sadducean members wished to impose the death penalty and turn them over to the Romans for execution, as they had done with Jesus. It was at this point that the leading Pharisee named Gamaliel, viewing the followers of Jesus as Zealots, counselled caution:

Men of Israel, take care what you do with these men. For before these days Theudas arose, giving himself out to be somebody, and a number of men, about four hundred, joined him; but he was slain and all who followed him were dispersed and came to nothing. After him Judas the Galilean arose in the days of the census and drew away some of the people after him; he also perished, and all who followed him were scattered. So in the present case I tell you, keep away from these men and leave them alone; for if this plan or undertaking is of men, it will fail; but if it is of God, you will not be able to overthrow them. You might even be found opposing God! (Acts 5:34–9)

Heeding this advice, the council released the apostles after a beating and a warning not to speak any more in the name of Jesus. There is in fact a historical error in this passage from Acts. Theudas actually appeared after these events, while Judas the Galilean, who emerged in the time of Quirinius' census, lived long before Theudas. Nevertheless, there is no reason to doubt the essence of the account, namely, that a highly esteemed Pharisee interceded on behalf of Peter and John.

Acts next informs us that a conflict developed between the 'Hebrew' and 'Hellenistic' Christians – i.e., between the Palestinian Jewish-Christians and the Greek-speaking Jewish-Christians from the Diaspora (6:2). The issues seem to have been leadership and preaching and the two sides reached a compromise: The 'twelve', being Palestinian Jews, would preach to their Aramaic-speaking compatriots while the seven Greek-speaking 'ministers' would supervise the common fund and preach the gospel to the Hellenistic Jews.

Among the seven there was one named Stephanos (Stephen), who debated with those who belonged to the Jerusalem synagogues of the Cyrenians, Alexandrians and Cilicians (Acts 6:8, 9). It is possible that Saul of Tarsus, a Hellenistic Jew from Cilicia, participated in the debates. He was still an enthusiastic Pharisee at this time who opposed with all his might the opinions of Stephen concerning the 'crucified Messiah'. During these debates some of those present claimed they heard Stephen say, 'Jesus of Nazareth will destroy this place [i.e., the temple], and will change the customs that Moses delivered to us' (6:14). In response to his accusers Stephen delivered a long sermon (7:1–53) containing harsh words, though no actual blasphemy.[1] The impression we get from the texts is that Stephen's speech was delivered out of doors before a crowd near the meeting place of the Sanhedrin; and that it was the crowd that took him out of the city and stoned him – evidently with Saul's consent if not his actual participation (8:1). Stephen's provocative statement appears to have stirred up a general persecution of the Nazarenes in Jerusalem, the Hellenistic disciples bearing the brunt of it and deciding, finally, to disperse themselves throughout Judea and Samaria. The 'twelve', however, who were all Palestinian Jews and fully observant of the Law, were unaffected by the persecution. With Peter at their head they remained in Jerusalem carrying on the affairs of the new congregation undisturbed (8:2).

There seem to have been significant doctrinal differences between the Hellenists and the Hebrews. Philip, one of the seven and therefore a Hellenistic Jew, fled to Samaria where he attempted to proclaim the gospel of the crucified Messiah. There he met Simon the magician and prevailed upon him to confess faith in Jesus. When Philip's activity in Samaria became known to James the brother of Jesus, he questioned its legitimacy in the light of the disciple's awareness that they were not to go to the Samaritans (Matt. 10:5). He therefore sent Peter and John the son of Zebedee to counteract Philip. We may infer from the meeting in which Simon the magician tried to bribe Peter, that he was aware of Jesus' opposition to preaching among the Samaritans (Acts 8:14–24). Leaving Samaria, Philip turned south and on the road to Gaza he met the Ethiopian eunuch of Candace, queen of Ethiopia. The eunuch, a 'God-fearer' who had yet to be baptized as a proselyte, was reading aloud from Isaiah 53 (doubtless from the Septuagint) and expressing his perplexity concerning the passage, 'as a lamb led to the slaughter': 'About whom, pray, does the prophet say this, about himself or about someone else?' (Acts 8:34). Philip's reply that it referred to Jesus commended itself to the eunuch who, when they came to a stream, requested and received baptism in the name of Jesus. Although the Ethiopian had been a 'God-fearer' i.e., a Jew by conviction, his conversion was the first of a non-Jew to the Nazarene congregation of Judaism.

Enter Saul (Paul) of Tarsus

But Saul, still breathing threats and murder against the disciples of the Lord, went to the high priest and asked him for letters to the synagogues at Damascus, so that if he found any belonging to the Way, men or women, he might bring them bound to Jerusalem. (Acts 9:1–2)

There is good reason to suppose that it was Saul who, out of a fanatical opposition to the faith in a crucified Messiah, played a key role in the death of Stephen (Acts 8:1; 7:58; 22:20; 26:10). Yet it was this Saul who became the founder of Christianity as a new religion. Saul was born in the city of Tarsus in Cilicia in *c.* 5–10 AD. Scholars assume that his forebears had fled from Judea when it was conquered by the Romans in the time of Pompey. Tarsus was a large, cosmopolitan, commercial 'metropolis', a border city on the trade route between East and West. Having grown up in such surroundings, Paul quite naturally spoke Greek and acquired a knowledge of Greek culture. His father must have been well-to-do, for he had acquired Roman citizenship, a privilege bestowed outside Rome proper on only the wealthy and influential. Thus Paul was born into Roman citizenship (Acts

22:28), which was to become indispensable to his mission. In accordance with Jewish tradition he learned a trade, tentmaking, which served him well after he became an apostle; his possession of a marketable skill meant that, unlike some of the other disciples, he did not have to depend upon the communities he visited for support (1 Cor. 9:6–15).

When Saul was a young man his father sent him to Jerusalem to study the Torah in the twofold sense – the Scriptures and the learning and lore of the Pharisaic movement. Paul says of himself, 'I am a Jew born in Tarsus of Cilicia, but brought up in this city [Jerusalem] and educated at the feet of Gamaliel according to the strict manner of the law of our fathers' (Acts 22:3). Again and again Paul emphasizes that he is a 'Pharisee, a son of Pharisees' and that 'according to the strictest party of our religion I have lived as a Pharisee' (Acts 23:6 and 26:5). In one polemical context he argued that 'if any other man thinks he has reason for confidence in the flesh, I have more: circumcised on the eighth day, of the people of Israel, of the tribe of Benjamin, a Hebrew born of Hebrews; as to the law a Pharisee . . .' (Phil. 3:4–5). We have no way of knowing whether Paul knew Jesus personally. We may assume that Paul had at least laid eyes on Jesus, since otherwise it would be hard to understand how he could have pictured him on the road to Damascus. He may even have witnessed the fearsome spectacle of the crucifixion, which together with the stoning of Stephen haunted his conscience and led to the vision. When some of those who had been persecuted in Jerusalem fled to Damascus, Saul the zealous Pharisee could not rest: Jesus' disciples would corrupt the Jews of Damascus as well. So he obtained from the high-priest letters authorizing him to arrest and bring back the fleeing Nazarenes to Jerusalem. On the road to Damascus Paul saw flashes of light from heaven and, falling to the ground, he heard a voice saying, ' "Saul, Saul, why do you persecute me?" And he said, "Who are you, Lord?" And he said, "I am Jesus, whom you are persecuting; but rise and enter the city, and you will be told what you are to do"' (Acts 9:3–6). It was this experience that won Paul over to the followers of Jesus.

Paul began to preach the new faith to the Damascus Jews, but the disciples there were suspicious of him, finding it hard to believe that a man with his past could be converted so suddenly. The Jews among whom he preached were also confounded and angry that so zealous a persecutor of the Nazarene sect had now become its ardent advocate. Finally, by preaching to the circumcised Arab proselytes to Judaism he aroused the anger of the governor who ordered his arrest and confinement. Paul's opponents guarded the gates of Damascus in an effort to prevent his escape, but the followers of Jesus in that city 'took him by night and let him down over the wall, lowering him in a basket' (Acts 9:22–5; 2 Cor. 11:32). Paul travelled to Arabia and then came back to Damascus (Gal. 1:17), fearing to return to Jerusalem where he was bitterly hated by the followers of Jesus. Only 'after three years' (Gal. 1:18) did he decide to 'visit Cephas' – i.e., to become acquainted with Simon Peter and to learn from him details about Jesus and his teaching. Remaining with Cephas 15 days, he saw no other apostle except James the brother of Jesus. The others feared Paul, suspecting that he was a spy and provocateur (Acts 9:26).

Even Peter and James treated Paul with reserve, accepting him fully only after the recommendation of Joseph Barnabas, a Levite from Cyprus who is described as 'a good man, full of the Holy Spirit and of faith' (11:24), who 'sold a field which belonged to him, and brought the money and laid it at the apostles' feet' (Acts 4:37).

On the authority of Peter and James, Paul began to work among the Greek-speaking Jews; but his opinions soon proved so offensive that they conspired to kill him. When this became known to some of his friends, they urged him to flee to half-pagan Caesarea, where the influence of the Jews was weak, and from there, a principal seaport, Paul returned to his native Tarsus.

The book of the Acts of the Apostles then shifts our attention to Peter (9:32–11:18; cf. 1 Cor. 9:5), of whom it is said that he 'went here and there' carrying the gospel, healing the sick (Aeneas) and reviving the deathly ill (Tabitha). He also travelled to Caesarea where he met Cornelius, 'a centurion of what was known as the Italian Cohort' (Acts 10:1ff), and dined with him. He then baptized Cornelius and his family and friends in the name of Jesus (Acts 10:45–8). Peter thus dined with and baptized a Gentile who had not been circumcised, actions which greatly disturbed James the brother of Jesus and the other devout Nazarenes. In his defence Peter related that he had received a special revelation from Jesus saying that 'What God has cleansed, you must not call common' (Acts 10:9–11:18).

At first the Hellenistic Jewish-Christians, who had fled to Antioch following the death of Stephen, proclaimed the gospel to Jews only (Acts 11:19). Later, however, the 'men of Cyprus and Cyrene' began to preach to the Greeks. The names of these teachers have been preserved: 'Barnabas, Symeon who was called Niger [the Black], Lucius of Cyrene, Manaen, a member of the court of Herod [Antipas] the tetrarch, and *Saul*' (Acts 13:1). All five of these Jewish-Christian teachers had spent time in Jerusalem, and they knew that the Pharisees had long preached Judaism to the Gentiles making 'God-fearers' and proselytes of them. Why should the disciples of Jesus not do likewise? In Palestine the followers of Jesus were called 'Nazarenes'; but to the Antioch Gentiles the concept 'Jesus of Nazareth' was not particularly meaningful. Hence, a new name for the new faith emerged. Inasmuch as the Gentile, Greek-speaking converts were primarily interested in the Messiahship of Jesus, his role as a 'saviour', they began for the first time to call the believers in Jesus 'Christians', i.e., 'Messianists' (Acts 11:26). But neither Barnabas nor any of the other unknown teachers in Antioch had any success in converting Jews or pagans in large numbers.

This task was left for Paul to accomplish. After fleeing from Jerusalem he returned to Tarsus where, over a period of several years, his conception of the new faith matured. He was also active in those years as an organizer (Gal. 1:21–3). Evidently he was so successful that Barnabus travelled to Tarsus for the express purpose of bringing Paul back to Antioch to assist him in his missionary work (Acts 11:25–6). So fruitful were their joint efforts that the mixed 'Messianic' congregation of Antioch sent them on a mission to nearby areas.

In Palestine, meanwhile, in response to complaints lodged against the Nazarenes for transgressing the law, King Agrippa I had James the son of Zebedee executed, and Peter imprisoned. Peter managed to escape, however, most likely with the aid of sympathetic Pharisees. Appearing briefly to his fellow Nazarenes assembled in the house of Mary the mother of John Mark, he informed them that he was free and that he must leave Jerusalem: 'Tell this to James and to the brethren' (Acts 12:2–19). It was at this time that James the brother of Jesus took Peter's place at the head of the congregation; and it was under James' leadership that the Nazarene congregation punctiliously observed the twofold law and honoured the temple. Hence they remained undisturbed by the Sadducean authorities for about 20 years until c. AD 62, when the high-priest Ananus convened the Sanhedrin on his own authority and sentenced James to be stoned. From Josephus we learn that this Sadducean sentence greatly offended the Pharisees who

> secretly sent to King Agrippa (II) urging him, for Ananus had not even been correct in his first step, to order him to desist from any further such actions. Certain of them even went to meet Albinus, who was on his way from Alexandria, and informed him that Ananus had no authority to convene the Sanhedrin without his consent. Convinced of these words, Albinus angrily wrote to Ananus threatening to take vengeance upon him. King Agrippa, because of Ananus' action, deposed him from the high priesthood which he had held for three months . . . (*Antiq.* 20: 200–3)

Here we see that the main opposition to the followers of Jesus came from the Sadducean high priesthood. The Pharisees, in contrast, viewed the Nazarenes as just another Jewish congregation – indeed, one with which they had much in common: a belief in the coming of the Messiah, the resurrection of the dead and the observance of the twofold Law. Up to the time of the destruction of the temple in AD 70, there were three instances of extreme actions taken against the first Christians in Judea: the stoning of Stephen, the execution of James the son of Zebedee, and the stoning of James the brother of Jesus. The first was the work of an angry crowd; the second a response to Sadducean pressure; and the third an unlawful act perpetrated by a high-priest against the will of the Pharisees. It appears that apart from these tragic but isolated instances, the Jewish-Christian community in Jerusalem remained unmolested during the 40 years from the crucifixion of Jesus to the destruction of the temple (from *c.* AD 30 to 70).

The Apostolic Council

The Christian church of Antioch, like most of the churches outside Palestine, now consisted of both Jewish and non-Jewish Christians. Owing to Paul's success, the Christians of pagan origin were either a substantial minority or even a majority. As meals were taken in common, it was difficult to observe the Jewish dietary laws. At first Peter 'ate with the Gentiles' (Gal. 2:12); but when this became known to James the brother of Jesus, he sent emissaries to Antioch demanding that the Gentile Christians should be circumcised and that they should fully observe the twofold Law, including the dietary regulations. And if the Gentile Christians failed to accept James' ruling, the Jewish-Christians were to separate themselves. Peter then 'drew back and separated himself' and even Barnabas did the same (Gal. 2:12–13). Paul, however, criticized their behaviour, arguing that baptism and faith in the Messiah (Christ) were sufficient and that circumcision should not be required of the Gentile converts. His opinion met with strong opposition.

At about this time there was a terrible drought and famine in Judea, and Paul and Barnabas were selected to carry donations of food and money from Antioch to Jerusalem. Thus the opportunity presented itself for a small conference to address the questions at issue (Acts 15:1–29; Gal. 2:1–10). After much debate Peter was the first to call for a compromise. Then James spoke, and the conference adopted his proposal: ' . . . that we should not trouble those of the Gentiles who turn to God, but should write them to abstain from the pollution of idols and from unchastity and from what is strangled and from blood' (Acts 15:19–21). Despite the explicitness of these terms, Paul continued to teach not only the Gentiles but the Diaspora Jews as well that they need not 'circumcise their children or observe the customs' (Acts 21:21).

14

Paul's Reinterpretation of Jesus' Teaching

There was a time in the history of New Testament criticism when scholars maintained that Paul, having been born and educated in a Hellenistic culture and having spent all but a few of his mature years in heathen environments, must have absorbed their religious and philosophical conceptions. Jewish and non-Jewish scholars alike viewed Paul's Hellenistic background as the key to his distinctive reinterpretation of Jesus' teaching. In some treatments of Paul, the Palestinian and Diaspora Judaism of his time were dichotomized as if they were two water tight compartments. From this angle it was not difficult to point to the apparently non-Jewish character of the antitheses so prevalent in Paul's letters, such as spirit and flesh, works and faith, and others. In recent decades, however, it has been increasingly recognized that Paul, like Jesus, never intended to separate from Judaism; and that even the concepts Paul uses, though similar to those of the pagan mystery cults, have quite another meaning for Paul.

Both the book of Acts and Paul's letters attest to his solid Jewish background and his adherence to the Pharisaic method of scriptural exegesis. His erudition is evident in the scriptural quotations and allusions found throughout the letters. And he himself states that he studied in Jerusalem at the feet of Rabbi Gamaliel (I), a highly respected Pharisee who, as we saw earlier, counselled that the followers of Jesus be left in peace. Inasmuch as Paul was a persecutor of Jesus' earliest followers, he must have been more of a rigourist than his teacher – which once again points to the wide range of views that was possible in the Pharisaic movement. That Paul later made an about-face suggests that despite his rigourism he was quite impressed with Jesus. In keeping with the rabbinic methods of his time, Paul reinterprets certain facets of Judaism and creates new applications for scriptural passages. In time he comes to believe that through the Law alone there could be no salvation, and the circumcision of the heart was more important than circumcision of the flesh. Hundreds of years earlier, however, Jeremiah had already said that the Lord would make a new covenant with Israel and put his law in 'their inward parts, and in their heart' (31:31).

Even the most meticulous adherence to the twofold Law, Paul believed, could not bring salvation; but this does not mean that he rejected the Law or sought to abrogate the Torah. Throughout his letters he upholds the ethical principles of the Torah: God is the God of Jew and Gentile alike, he says, 'and he will justify the circumcised on the ground of their faith and the uncircumcised because of their faith. *Do we then overthrow the law by this faith? By no means/ On the contrary, we uphold the law*' (Rom. 3:29–31). Like Jesus, Paul also justifies his stance with prooftexts. For example

> For what does the Scripture say? 'Abraham believed God, and it was reckoned to him as righteousness' . . . How then was it reckoned to him? Was it before or after he had been circumcised? It was not after, but before he was circumcised. He received circumcision as a sign or seal of the righteousness which he had by faith while he was still uncircumcised. The purpose was to make him the father of all who believe without being circumcised and who thus have righteousness reckoned to them, and likewise the father of the circumcised who are not merely circumcised but also follow the example of the faith which our father Abraham had before he was circumcised. (Rom. 4:1–12)

This is a fairly typical example of the Pharisaic-Rabbinic method of citing Scripture to defend a given opinion or ruling. As for the commandments, it goes without saying that Paul teaches, 'You shall not commit adultery, You shall not kill, You shall not steal, You shall not covet, and any other commandment, are summed up in this sentence: You shall love your neighbour as yourself' (Rom. 13:8ff). Even the dietary regulations are not dismissed out of hand, but rather subordinated to the love commandment. Paul was persuaded that nothing is unclean in itself; 'but it is unclean for anyone who thinks it unclean. If your brother is being injured by what you eat, you are no longer walking in love' (Rom. 14:14–15). The same applies to circumcision and other ordinances, which are also subordinated to what counts: 'Keeping the commandments of God' (I Cor. 7:19).

Paul's conception of Jesus as the sacrificial lamb whose death was expiatory is also distinctively Jewish: the Messiah was crucified and died of his own free will in order to atone by his blood for the sins of this world. If you obey the commandments and maintain steadfast faith in his return, then he will shortly appear at the right hand of God to bestow upon you eternal life and the Kingdom of Heaven. In the Israelite sacrificial cult, the blood of the expiatory victim symbolizes life – a life offered to God as a substitute for another. Paul looks upon Jesus as the Passover offering: 'For Christ, our paschal lamb, has been sacrificed' (1 Cor. 5:7). Jesus was the new Passover. 'His crucifixion', writes Phillip Sigal, 'was the bondage. His resurrection was the Exodus . . . The shedding of the blood was expiatory and therefore redemptive, as was the original Passover lamb . . .'[1]

In all these respects, then, Paul had always remained firmly rooted in Judaism. As for his protest against the burdensome yoke of the numerous ordinances regulating daily life, he was not un-Jewish in this regard either. In the time of Jesus and Paul the more rigourist school of Shammai was dominant in the Pharisaic movement. In these terms Jesus and Paul may have had more in common with the more lenient school of Hillel. As B.H. Branscomb has observed, 'during the lifetime of Jesus the party of Hillel was not yet in control. The significance of this is obvious. It means that an active and rapidly growing party within the ranks of the scholars was at the time in vigorous protest against the currently accepted interpretation of the Torah . . .'[2] The rejection of circumcision and certain other ordinances therefore remained for Paul a legitimately Jewish position – albeit an extreme one as he no doubt realized. It 'would be erroneous', writes W.D. Davies, 'to think that Paul regarded Christianity as the antithesis of Judaism as has so often been claimed. On the contrary, it appears that for the apostle the Christian faith was the full flowering of Judaism, the outcome of the latter and its fulfilment, . . . The Gospel for Paul was not the annulling of Judaism but its completion, and as such it took up into itself the essential genius of Judaism.'[3] And in the same vein Adolph Deissmann writes: 'The most genuine characteristics of the Jewish nature were preserved by Paul when he became a Christian . . . In opposition to mechanical divisions of the Jewish and Christian elements in him, we need not hesitate to call him the great Jewish-Christian of the earliest age.'[4]

Once Paul became a follower of Jesus, however, it is doubtful that he continued meticulously to observe the traditional practices of the twofold Law. In Acts 'he cut his hair for he had a vow' (18:18) and he 'purified himself . . . and went into the temple' (21:26). The first action appears to have been voluntary and the second under the urging of James the brother of Jesus, to dispel the rumours that Paul did not live 'in observance of the law' (21:24). There is reason to suspect, however, that where the law was concerned, Paul behaved opportunistically. To Jew and Gentile alike he made whatever concessions were necessary to win them over to the new faith: 'To the Jews I became as a Jew, in order to win Jews; to those under the law I became as one under the law – *though not being myself under the law* – that I might win those under the law. To those outside the law I became as one outside the law – not being without law toward God but under the law of Christ – that I might win those outside the law' (1 Cor. 9:20–1), italics added). It appears to be true, then, as Roger Mohrlang has remarked, that 'There is nothing in his [Paul's] writings to suggest that his ordinary daily life and conduct are governed by legal regulations *halachic* – style, nor is such a perspective reflected in his ethical teaching'.[5] But Mohrlang agrees that 'Paul's negation of the soteriological and regulatory aspects of the law in no way denies the validity of its moral demands in his thinking.'[6] Indeed, even a cursory reading of his letters will show that Paul not only continues to make moral demands, but that those demands are based on the ethical principles of the Decalogue and other Mosaic legislation.

And yet one cannot simply shrug off the argument that Paul was also influenced by the religious movements of the Hellenistic world of his day. W.D. Davies was among the first to argue effectively that Palestinian Judaism was no watertight compartment sealed against all Hellenistic influences, since 'there was a Graeco-Jewish "atmosphere" at Jerusalem itself'.[7] And if there were Hellenistic influences in Jerusalem itself, then how much stronger were those influences in Tarsus, where Paul grew up, and in all the other cities in which he spent his adult life! Paul did not sit down and mechanistically put together a doctrine consisting of Jewish and Hellenistic elements. It was rather an 'unconscious interpenetration' of such elements. In the words of Robin Scroggs, 'what is striking is that the integration (or eclecticism) of the cultures is so deep in the Apostle's mentality that he was probably unaware, most of the time, in what respect he was "Jewish" and in what respect "Greek" . . .' What is remarkable is 'the complete, unconscious interpenetration'.[8] Scroggs then goes on to document the integration of both elements. In Romans, for example, Paul's citations from the Torah roughly follow the sequence of the Torah books themselves, Genesis, Exodus, Leviticus, etc. Paul refers to all three divisions of Scripture: Torah (Pentateuch), *Neviim* (Prophets) and *Ketuvim* (Writings). On the other hand, Scroggs also finds in Romans (5–8) a definite Hellenistic influence:

> small structures and stylistic characteristics which are found in Hellenistic literature (including Hellenistic Judaism). The *diatribe* style is at least as lively in this homily as in the other. There are two examples of the chain or 'mystic ladder', a device common to Hellenistic literature . . . The evidence all points to the conclusion that in these chapters Paul has produced for the Romans a self-enclosed and complete homily which could be called a sermon in diatribe style.[9]

But one can go further and discern in Paul's letters more than Hellenistic literary influences. In 1 Cor. 11:1, Paul wrote: 'Be imitators of me, as I am of Christ'. 'With these words', writes Geza Vermes, 'Paul, deviating from the Jewish imitation of God, introduced intermediaries between the imitator and his ultimate divine model. Thus originated the trend, still conspicuous in the more ancient forms of Christianity, to multiply mediators and intercessors

Son of god: Honorific title?

between the faithful and God: Jesus, Paul, Mary the mother of Jesus, the Martyrs, the saints. With increasing vehemence,' Vermes continues,

> . . . the religiosity of primitive Christianity became trained on the Mediator in place of God. Prayers continued to be addressed to the father, but more and more frequently to 'the Father of our Lord Jesus Christ' (Rom. 15:6; 2 Cor. 1:3; 11:31, etc.). Little by little the Christ of Pauline theology and his Gentile church took over from the holy man of Galilee. Subject to God, but already enthroned at his side (1 Cor. 15:28; Rom. 8:34; Eph. 1:20; Col. 3:1, etc.), he then – no doubt in response to the needs and hopes of non-Jewish Christianity – imperceptibly grew to be the 'image of God' (2 Cor. 4:4), the 'effulgence of God's glory and the stamp of his nature' (Heb. 1:3), and finally, the equal of God. 'I bid you', writes Ignatius bishop of Antioch to Polycarp bishop of Smyrna, in the first decade of the second century, 'I bid you farewell always in our God Jesus Christ' (*Epistle to Polycarp*, ch. 8) – and all this despite Jesus' own protest against being called 'good': 'No one is good but God alone' (Mark 10:18), and his reaffirmation of the first commandment: that 'the Lord our God, the Lord is one' (Mark 12:29–30).[10]

H.J. Schoeps agrees that for all of his Jewishness, Paul departs from the Jewish world-view. What Schoeps has to say on the subject is so important that we need to present his analysis at length. Paul teaches that the 'Messiah has died and has risen again, – an event which in Jewish eschatology is not provided for or foreseen'.[11] In 1 Corinthians 10:16–17 we read: 'The cup of blessing which we bless, is it not a participation in the blood of Christ? The bread which we break, is it not a participation in the body of Christ?' (cf. 11:23–6). This whole conception, writes Schoeps, 'has ceased to be Jewish and reminds one rather of the Hellenistic mysteries. With Paul, the Eucharist becomes part of the "class of mystery cults"' (119). From a Christological standpoint, it was a disappointment and an embarrassment 'that world history after the resurrection of Christ has proceeded just as before' (122); '. . . the fact that an atonement of humanity through the death of the incarnate Son of God appears impossible from a Jewish point of view springs from this, namely, that the idea of the Son of God in its Pauline form takes us outside Judaism' (127).

Although the *separate* elements of Paul's doctrine can be found in Judaism, his synthesis is foreign to it. The elements which Paul combined were:

1 the idea of a vicarious, atoning sacrifice;
2 a suffering servant of God (Isa. 53);
3 the 'binding of Isaac'.

But Paul synthesized these elements in such a manner as to violate the fundamental principle of monotheism. In Schoeps' words, the fact that Paul

combined these conceptions with the messianically understood *Aquedath Yitzhak* ['binding of Isaac'] in such a way as to transfer the story from Abraham and Isaac to the eternal God himself and His incarnate Son, and thus exalted the Messiah beyond all human proportions to the status of real divinity – this is the radically un-Jewish element in the thought of the apostle. For this there is no possibility of derivation from Jewish sources, but – if indeed it is a question of derivation – it is impossible to refute the idea of a link with heathen mythological conceptions filtered through the Hellenistic syncretism of the time. (149)

Jesus had called God '*Abba*', so the Evangelists referred to Jesus as 'son of God' (Matt. 11:27). On Jesus' lips '*Abba*' signified the uniquely intimate relationship he felt he had with God the Father. Among the disciples 'God's son' implied only the elevated rank of a Messianic King. Paul, however, took this honorific title and transformed it into a mythological-ontological category of thought. For Paul, Jesus Christ 'is from heaven' (1 Cor. 15:47). 'All things were created through him and for him. He is before all things, and in him all things hold together' (Col. 1:17–18); he is 'seated at the right hand of God' (Col. 3:1; Rom. 8:34); at his Parousia all human beings will 'appear before the judgment seat of Christ' (2 Cor. 5:10). For Paul, then, Jesus is nothing less than a supernatural being like the gnostic heavenly entities that descend to earth. Jesus thus became the rock from which all drank during the desert wanderings of the Israelites: 'they drank from the supernatural rock which followed them, and the Rock was Christ' (1 Cor. 10:4). 'The equation of the *Christos*', writes Schoeps, 'with God Himself, which cancels the line of demarcation between the God of the Old Testament and the Messiah, leads logically to the fact that Paul transfers all the Old Testament statements about God to the exalted *Christos Iésous*' (153). Thus Paul has, in effect, deified Jesus and gone outside the ideas current in the Jerusalem Jewish-Christian congregation. Pauline

Christology and soteriology is a dogmatic impossibility from the standpoint of strict Jewish transcendent monotheism. Judaism of every tendency, both before and contemporary with Paul, . . . rejected any compromise. Thus in the last analysis, the Christian doctrine of the incarnation must be utterly repudiated on the ground of the Jewish experience of God: that God as the formless cannot be embodied in any kind of form, that he as the Infinite, prior to all forms, was the creator of every form. (167)

As for the question of Paul's attitude towards the Law, here, too, Schoeps demonstrates that though Paul begins with some Jewish premises, he draws un-Jewish inferences from them. Paul asserts that no man can be righteous before God by means of the Law (Gal. 3:10–13, citing Deut. 27:26). His underlying assumption is that no human being is capable of fulfilling the *whole* law, i.e., the numerous ('613') injunctions and proscriptions. Paul 'solves' this problem by means of a one-sided emphasis on faith: the crucifixion of the Messiah was in truth his elevation, as was promised in Isaiah 52:13, and it took place in order to do away with the 'curse' of the Law by transforming the curse into a blessing. Schoeps' comment on this conception of things is that 'The problematic character of a *complete* fulfilment of the law was well enough realized, but the Jews have never despaired about the "fulfilability" of the law, and have never allowed its sacred character to be violated' (193). The 'unfulfilability' of the law for Paul led to his assertion that its manifest purpose was to increase sins. But 'Every child of the Jews,' writes Schoeps, 'whether the Diaspora or the Judaism of Palestine is in question, knows that the law had no other purpose than that of being given by God in order to be kept and not transgressed, in order to increase resistance to sin and not augment sin . . . The Holy One created the evil impulse, but he also created the Torah as a remedy against it' (195).

Paul's fundamental misapprehension lies in his failure to remember the inseparable connection between the covenant and the Law. The covenant made at Sinai was a sacral, legal act of *reciprocity*: God commanded the children of Israel to obey his statutes and ordinances with all their heart and with all their soul, and if they do so obey him, then they shall be a people holy to the Lord their God (Deut. 26:17–18). This expresses quite succinctly what was understood by the election of Israel. God's blessing and curse are contingent upon the attitude and conduct of the people. Schoeps therefore concludes that

> Because Paul had lost all understanding of the character of the Hebraic *berith* [covenant] as a partnership involving mutual obligations, he failed to grasp the inner meaning of the Mosaic law, namely, that it is an instrument by which the covenant is realized. Hence the Pauline theology of law and justification begins with the fateful misunderstanding in consequence of which he tears asunder covenant and law, and then represents Christ as the end of the law. (218)

Paul taught that the Law is annulled with the coming of Jesus, but his Jewish contemporaries looked out of the window, so to speak, and saw that the world had not changed. If they understood Paul to mean that the covenant was also annulled, then it is little to be wondered at that they forcefully rejected his doctrine.

A Fence Around the Law

We need to recall that one of the major aims of the Pharisaic revolution in the time of the Maccabees was to find a means of ensuring the preservation of Judaism and preventing a recurrence of the type of crisis that had led to the Maccabean uprising. It was with this aim in view that the scholars and teachers sought, in the words of the Mishnah, to 'make a fence around the Law' (Mish. Aboth 1.5). It was precisely this fence that Paul's doctrine threatened to destroy. He rejected the validity of the values and norms of the twofold Law governing the everyday life of the Jewish people. Inasmuch as the adherence to these values and norms accounted for the distinctive religio-ethnic character of the Jewish people, an acceptance of Paul's doctrine would have been fateful in its effect: either the fence would have been torn down, or it would have rotted away. Intuitively if not consciously this danger was recognized not only by Paul's non-Christian Jewish contemporaries, but also by James the brother of Jesus and the other 'pillar apostles'. That is why they sought to establish an ethical minimum of the Law which would be valid and binding for the Gentile converts to the Jewish-Christian movement; and that is why they were so disturbed to learn that Paul was telling not only the Gentiles but the Jews as well that they need not circumcise their children or observe the customs and ordinances of Moses. Doubtless it was the 'pillar apostles' who were in harmony with Jesus' own understanding of the Law; and it was Paul who unwittingly laid the doctrinal foundation for the separation of Christianity from the Jewish people.

Notes

Preface

1 H.H. Gerth and C.W. Mills (eds), *From Max Weber: Essays in Sociology* (London, Routledge & Kegan Paul, 1948), pp. 246–7.
2 Ibid., p. 248.
3 Ibid., 296.

1 The Unifying Principles

1 Josephus, *The Life*, tr. H. St J. Thackeray, the Loeb Classical Library, vol. I (Cambridge, Mass., Harvard University Press, 1976), p. 2. Hereafter all references to this work will be cited as *Life*, in parentheses immediately following the quoted passage. All references to Josephus' other writings, also in the Loeb Classical Library series, vols I–IX, will be cited in the same manner: *Against Apion (Ag. Ap.)*; *The Jewish War (War)*; *Jewish Antiquities (Antiq.)*.
2 H. St John Thackeray, *Josephus: The Man and the Historian* (New York, Jewish Institute of Religion Press, 1929), p. 19.
3 Ibid., p. 27.
4 Ibid., p. 49.
5 R.J.H. Shutt, *Studies in Josephus* (London, Society for Promoting Christian Knowledge (SPCK), 1961), p. 122.
6 Thackeray, *Josephus: The Man*, p. 76.
7 F.J. Foakes Jackson, *Josephus and the Jews* (London, SPCK, 1930), p. 63.
8 Literally 'teaching' in Hebrew, it is a digest of rabbinic discussions of the religious ordinances governing everyday life. The Hebrew word for these ordinances is *halakhah*, 'religious practice', plural *halakhoth*. The Mishnah, the first part of the Talmud, meaning 'study' or 'learning', is a codification of the Oral Law, arranged according to subjects and divided into sixty-three tractates.
9 This is a term apparently coined by Josephus.
10 Josephus' statement that the Law was read weekly coincides with the Rabbinical tradition (Jerusalem Talmud, Megilla, IV:1), which ascribes to Moses the introduction of public reading of the Law on sabbaths and festivals.

2   Varieties of Jewish Religious Experience

1   S.W. Baron, *A Social and Religious History of the Jews* II (New York, Columbia University Press, 1952), p. 35.
2   All references to the New Testament are cited from the Revised Standard Version.
3   Emil Schürer, *The History of the Jewish People in the Age of Jesus Christ* II, ed. by Geza Vermes and Fergus Millar (Edinburgh, T. & T. Clark, 1973), p. 392.
4   Ellis Rivkin, *A Hidden Revolution* (Nashville, Abingdon, 1978), p. 217.
5   Ibid., pp. 220–1.
6   Jesus, as we shall see, applied this prooftexting method with great skill.
7   Rivkin, *Hidden Revolution*, pp. 245–6.
8   The Great Synagogue was 'a body of 120 elders, including many prophets, who came up from exile with Ezra; they saw that prophecy had come to an end and that restraint was lacking; therefore they made many new rules and restrictions for the better observances of the Law'. See *The Mishnah*, translated from the Hebrew by Herbert Danby (London, Oxford University Press, 1933), p. 446, n. 5.
9   Rivkin, *Hidden Revolution*, p. 249
10   Ibid., p. 250
11   See Schürer, *History of the Jewish People*, pp. 555ff.
12   *Hypothetica*, 11:4, 11:10, and 11:12; cited in Schürer, ibid., p. 566.
13   *Quod omnis probus* 12 (86–7); cited in Schürer ibid., p. 567.
14   Schürer, ibid., pp. 584–5.
15   IQS I:1–2; 5:1–6; cited in Schürer, ibid., p. 590.
16   The group described by Philo as the Therapeutae bears considerable resemblance to the Essene/Qumran community. Most scholars favour the hypothesis that the Therapeutae were an Egyptian branch of the Palestinian Essene movement.
17   Y. Yadin, *Masada: Herod's Fortress and the Zealots' Last Stand* (New York, Random House, 1966), pp. 97–8; 108–9; 168–71.
18   Martin Hengel, *Die Zeloten* (Leiden/Köln, E.J. Brill, 1961), p. 64.
19   Ibid., p. 111.
20   Ibid., p. 148.
21   Ibid., p. 254.
22   Ibid., p. 272.
23   G.F. Moore, *Judaism* I (Cambridge, Mass., Harvard University Press, 1927–30), p. 81.
24   Hengel, *Die Zeloten*, pp. 340–1.

3   The Messianic Idea in Israel

1   See Emil Schürer, *The History of the Jewish People in the Age of Jesus Christ*, ed. by Geza Vermes and Fergus Millar (Edinburgh, T & T. Clark, 1973), pp. 488ff.
2   See R.H. Charles (ed.), The Apocrypha and Pseudepigrapha, 2 vols (Oxford,

Clarendon Press, 1983; first published in 1913).

3 Schürer, *History of the Jewish People*, II, p. 522.

4 Josephus says 'about 30,000' while according to the book of Acts it was 4,000. See Acts 21:38 where Paul is mistaken for the Egyptian 'who recently stirred up a revolt and led the 4,000 men of the assassins out into the wilderness'.

5 See A.C. Headlam, 'Theudas', *Hasting's Dictionary of the Bible* IV (1903), p. 750.

4 Jesus the Pious Palestinian Jew

1 H.H. Gerth and C.W. Mills (eds), *From Max Weber: Essays in Sociology* (London, Routledge and Kegan Paul, 1970), p.287.

2 Hebrew *Yehoshua* ('yahweh saves!') shortened to *Yeshua* or even to *Yeshu*, which is how he was popularly known.

3 Rudolf Bultmann, *Theology of the New Testament*, tr. Kendrick Grobel, vol. I (New York, Charles Scribner's Sons, 1951), p. 34.

4 ' . . . every spirit which confesses that Jesus Christ has come in the flesh is of God, and every spirit which does not confess Jesus is not of God. This is the spirit of antichrist, of which you heard that it was coming, and now it is in the world already' (I John 4:2ff). 'Docetism' is the term used to describe the heresy that Jesus merely appeared to be human but actually was not. This heresy continues to thrive in some popular forms of contemporary Christianity.

5 Herbert Braun, *Jesus of Nazareth* tr. Everett R. Kalin (Philadelphia, Fortress Press, 1979), p. 1.

6 Bultmann, *Theology of the NT*, p. 35.

7 There are well over 80 quotations by Jesus from the Hebrew Scriptures. They cover all five books of the Torah, plus the Psalms and the Prophets, notably Isaiah, Job and Daniel.

8 His parents found Jesus ' . . . in the Temple, sitting among the teachers, listening to them and asking them questions; and all who heard him were amazed at his understanding and his answers' (Luke 2:46).

9 'Jesus, when he began his ministry, was about thirty years of age . . .' (Luke 3:23).

10 T.W. Manson, *The Teaching of Jesus* (Cambridge, Cambridge University Press, 1963), pp. 48–9.

11 T.W. Manson, *Only to the House of Israel: Jesus and the Non-Jews*, (Philadelphia, Fortress Press, 1955), p. 2.

12 Ibid., p. 24.

13 Manson, *The Teaching of Jesus*, p. 304, italics added.

14 Ibid., p. 304, n. 2, italics added.

15 Ibid., p. 305.

16 'Think not that I have come to abolish the law and the prophets; I have come not to abolish them but to fulfil them.'

17 Manson, *The Teaching of Jesus*, p. 304, n. 2.

18 See W.R. Farmer's Introduction to Pierson Parker's *The Gospel Before Mark* (Chicago, Ill., University of Chicago Press, 1953), p. xxxv.

19 Hans-Herbert Stoldt, *History and Criticism of the Marcan Hypothesis*, tr. and ed. by Donald L. Niewyk (Macon, Mercer University Press, 1980), p. 249. Originally published in 1977 as *Geschichte und Kritik der Markushypothese* (Göttingen, Vandenhoeck und Ruprecht).

20 Ibid., p. 260.

21 John Rist, *On the Independence of Matthew and Mark* (Cambridge, Cambridge University Press, 1978), p. 107.

22 Ibid., p. 108.

23 Ibid.

24 David R. Catchpole, *The Trial of Jesus* (Leiden, E.J. Brill, 1971), pp. 107–8.

25 Rudolph Bultmann, *Theology of the New Testament*, tr. Kendrick Grobel, vol. I (New York, Charles Scribner's Sons, 1951), p. 54.

5 Jesus' Distinctive Religious Virtuosity

1 Edward Schillebeeckx, *Jesus: An Experiment in Christology*, tr. Hubert Hoskins (New York, Vintage Books, 1981), p. 261.

2 Morton Smith, *Jesus the Magician* (New York, Harper and Row, 1978), p. 143.

3 Hebrew, from the verb *darash*, 'to inquire'; an interpretation of Scripture aiming to extract its fullest meaning.

4 James A. Sanders, 'From Isaiah 61 to Luke 4, in Jacob Neusner (ed.), *Christianity, Judaism and other Greco-Roman Cults*, I (Leiden, E.J. Brill, 1975), p. 93.

5 Ibid., p. 97.

6 *Saint John and the Synoptic Gospels* (1938), cited in R.H. Lightfoot, *St John's Gospel* (Oxford, Clarendon, 1956), p. 29.

7 Lightfoot, Ibid., pp. 4–5 and 30.

8 Ibid., p. 42.

9 Geza Vermes, *Jesus the Jew* (New York, Macmillan, 1973), pp. 79–80.

10 Ibid., pp. 80–1.

11 Ibid., p. 87.

12 Eighteen centuries later, a similar tension would give rise to the Hasidic movement founded by the Baal Shem-Tov.

13 Max Weber, *Economy and Society*, vol. II, ed. by Guenther Roth and Claus Wittich (New York, Bedminster Press, 1968), pp. 631–2.

14 In due course we shall consider the possibility that Jesus was *not* born in Bethlehem and that the fact was known among his contemporaries.

15 Jacob Jocz, *The Jewish People and Jesus Christ*, 3rd edn (Grand Rapids, Michigan, Baker Book House, 1949), p. 148.

6 Jesus and the Torah (the Law)

1 Max Weber, *Economy and Society*, vol. II, ed. by Guenther Roth and Claus Wittich (New York, Bedminster Press, 1968), p. 617.

2 TB is the standard abbreviation employed by scholars in referring to the Babylonian Talmud.
3 I. Abrahams, *Studies in Pharisaism and the Gospels* (Cambridge, Cambridge University Press, 1917), p. 135.
4 Phillip Sigal, *The Emergence of Contemporary Judaism*, vol. 1 (Pittsburgh, Penn., Pickwick Press, 1980), p. 412.
5 Phillip Sigal, 'Aspects of Mark pointing to Matthean priority', in William R. Farmer (ed.), *New Synoptic Studies: The Cambridge Gospel Conference and Beyond* (Macon, Ga; Mercer University Press, 1983), p. 198.
6 Ibid., p. 199.
7 Christopher Rowland, *Christian Origins* (London, SPCK, 1985), p. 159.
8 See David R. Catchpole, *The Trial of Jesus* (Leiden, E.J. Brill, 1971), p. 109.
9 Rowland, Christian Origins, p. 158.
10 Herbert Braun, *Jesus of Nazareth*, tr. Everett R. Kalin (Philadelphia, Fortress Press, 1979), p. 70.
11 Ibid., p. 73.
12 Ibid., p. 75.
13 Ibid., p. 78.
14 Ibid., p. 79.
15 E.P. Sanders, *Jesus and Judaism* (Philadelphia, Fortress Press, 1985), p. 256.
16 Ibid., p. 257.

7 Who was the First Evangelist?

1 In the present discussion I rely on Hans-Herbert Stoldt's *History and Criticism of the Marcan Hypothesis* (see ch. 4, n. 19). This is a masterful account of how the theory of Marcan priority emerged, and an equally masterful analysis of the theory's basic weaknesses.
2 This quote is from p. 402 of Griesbach's Latin text, cited in Stoldt, ibid., p. 9. Hereafter all quotations from Stoldt's book will be cited by the page number in parentheses immediately following the quoted passage.
3 The twelve exceptions are: Mark 3:20–30; 4:26–34; 6:17–29; 6:45–8:25; 9:11–13; 9:41–10:12; 10:35–45; 11:11; 11:12–15a, 19–27; 12:28–34; 14–3–9; 15–1.
4 There is a third option which we have already touched upon, that Matthew and Mark wrote independently of each other, basing themselves on oral traditions. See John Rist's work, ch. 4, n. 21 above.
5 Martin Dibelius, *Formgeschichte des Evangeliums* (1919), p. 219.
6 Rudolf Bultmann, *Geschichte der synoptischen Tradition* (1921), p. 362.
7 See C.H. Talbert and E.V. McKnight, 'Can the Griesbach hypothesis be falsified?', *Journal of Biblical Literature*, 91 (1972), pp. 338–68; and the rejoinder in the same journal by George W. Buchanan, 'Has the Griesbach hypothesis been falsified?', 93 (1974), pp. 550–72.
8 Phillip Sigal, 'Aspects of Mark pointing to Matthean priority', in W.R. Farmer (ed.), *New Synoptic Studies* (Macon, Ga, Mercer University Press, 1983), pp. 206–7.

9   Ibid., pp. 207–8.
10 Pierson Parker, 'The posteriority of Mark', in W.R. Farmer, ibid., p. 68ff.
11 Ibid., p. 142.
12 Martin Hengel, *Studies in the Gospel of Mark*, tr. John Bowden (London, SCM Press, 1985), p. 12.
13 Ibid., p. 13.
14 Ibid., p. 29.
15 Ibid., p. 46.
16 W.R. Farmer, *The Synoptic Problem* (New York, Macmillan, 1964), pp. 227–8, italics added.
17 Ibid., p. 283.

8 Jesus' Originality and Creative Genius

1   W.D. Davies, *The Setting of the Sermon on the Mount* (Cambridge, Cambridge University Press, 1964), p. 2. In the present discussion I rely on Davies' highly cogent defence of the view that the SM must be understood in terms of Jesus' own setting, and not merely that of the early church. Hereafter, page reference to Davies' work will be cited in parentheses immediately following the quoted passage.
2   C.G. Montefiore, *The Synoptic Gospels*, 2nd edn, vol. I (London, Macmillan, 1927), p. 656.
3   'Rashi' is an acronym for Rav Shlomo Yitzhaki, one of the greatest of the medieval Jewish commentators on the Talmud and the Scriptures.
4   Montefiore, *The Synoptic Gospels*, p. 659.
5   Floyd V. Filson, *A Commentary on the Gospel According to St. Matthew* (London, Adam and Charles Black, 1960), p. 3.
6   Ibid., p. 30.
7   Friedrich Nietzsche, *On the Genealogy of Morals*, tr. Walter Kaufmann and R.J. Hollingdale (New York, Vintage Books, 1969), p. 25–6.
8   Ibid., pp. 33–4.
9   Ibid., p. 35.
10 For an application of this thesis see Irving M. Zeitlin, *Ancient Judaism: Biblical Criticism from Max Weber to the Present* (Cambridge, Polity Press, 1984).
11 A.E. Harvey, *Jesus and the Constraints of History*, The Bampton Lectures, 1980 (London, Duckworth, 1982), p. 53.
12 Ibid., pp. 55–6.
13 Roger Mohrlang, *Matthew and Paul* (Cambridge, Cambridge University Press, 1984), pp. 19–20.
14 George W. Buchanan, 'Matthean Beatitudes and traditional promises', in W.R. Farmer (ed.), *New Synoptic Studies: The Cambridge Gospel* Conference and Beyond (Macon, Ga, Mercer University Press, 1983), p. 180.
15 See Joseph Klausner, *Jesus of Nazareth*, tr. Herbert Danby (New York, Macmillan, 1943), p. 387.
16 *Tanna* (pl. *Tannaim*; adj. *Tannaitic*): The rabbinic authorities of the first two

centuries, from Hillel and Shammai to Rav Yehuda ha-nasi. It is their opinions and traditions which we find in the *Mishnah*.

17 Klausner, *Jesus of Nazareth*, p. 387, nn. 60, 62, 63.

18 Ibid., pp. 387–8.

19 Ibid., p. 389, italics added.

20 Joachim Jeremias, *The Parables of Jesus*, rev. edn, tr. H.S. Hooke (London, SCM Press, 1963), p. 23.

21 Martin Hengel, *Studies in the Gospel of Mark*, tr. John Bowden (London, SCM Press, 1985), p. 96.

9 The Kingdom of Heaven and the Role of the Messiah

1 See the fuller discussion of this literature in part I, Chapter 3, 'The Messianic Idea in Israel.'

2 Cullen Murphy, 'Who do men say that I am?', *The Atlantic*, December 1986, pp. 37–8.

3 C.H. Dodd, *The Parables of the Kingdom* (London, Nisbet, 1935), pp. 105–6.

4 C.H. Dodd, *The Founder of Christianity* (London, Macmillan, 1970), p. 90.

5 Amos N. Wilder, *Eschatology and Ethics in the Teaching of Jesus*, rev. edn. (New York, Harper and Brothers, 1950), pp. 54–5.

6 T.W. Manson, *The Teaching of Jesus* (Cambridge, Cambridge University Press, 1963), p. 132.

7 *Mekhilta*, ed. by Friedmann, p. 66b, quoted in Manson, ibid., p. 132.

8 Hans Conzelmann, *Jesus*, tr. J. Raymond Lord (Philadelphia, Fortress Press, 1973), p. 70.

9 Geza Vermes, *Jesus and the World of Judaism* (Philadelphia, Fortress Press, 1984), p. 90.

10 Ibid., p. 107.

11 C.F.D., Moule, *Essays in New Testament Interpretation* (Cambridge, Cambridge University Press, 1982), pp. 76–7.

12 Ibid., p. 78.

13 Ibid., p. 165.

14 Gunther Bornkamm, *Jesus of Nazareth*, tr. Irene and Fraser McLuskey with James M. Robinson (New York, Harper and Row, 1960), p. 178.

15 Thomas Sheehan, *The First Coming* (New York, Random House, 1986), p. 177.

16 Rowland, *Christian Origins* (London, SPCK, 1985), p. 136.

17 Eusebius, *Historia Ecclesiastica* II, 23; cited in Joseph Klausner, *Jesus of Nazareth*, tr. Herbert Danby (New York, Macmillan, 1943), p. 41.

18 Emil Schürer, *The History of the Jewish People in the Age of Jesus Christ*, vol. I, rev. and ed. by Geza Vermes and Fergus Millar (Edinburgh, T. & T. Clark, 1973), p. 407.

19 Ibid., p. 411.

20 Ibid., p. 420.

10 Jesus the Revolutionary?

1   The name of the spot at which Jesus was crucified (Matt. 27:33; Mark 15:22; John 19:17) is from the Hebrew for skull *gulgolet,* of which Calvary is the Greek and Latin equivalent. The place takes its name either from the shape of the hill or from the skulls there at the place of execution.

2   Robert Eisler, *The Messiah Jesus and John the Baptist* (New York, Dial Press, 1931).

3   See S.G.F. Brandon, *Jesus and the Zealots* (Manchester, Manchester University Press, 1967) and *The Trial of Jesus of Nazareth* (New York, Stein and Day, 1968).

4   This Aramaic word, when transliterated in English language Bibles, is often rendered as 'Cananaean' and translated as 'Canaanite', which are, respectively, meaningless and erroneous.

5   Brandon, *The Trial of Jesus,* p. 67.

6   Ibid., p. 71.

7   Ibid., p. 76.

8   Brandon, *Jesus and the Zealots,* p. 327.

9   Ibid., p. 334.

10 'Revolt in the desert?', *New Testament Studies* (Cambridge), 8 (1961–2), pp. 135–41.

11 Brandon, *Jesus and the Zealots,* p. 356.

12 See the editor's comments, *Jewish Antiquities* 18:63, vol. 9, p. 49.

13 Emil Schürer, *The History of the Jewish People in the Age of Jesus Christ,* vol. I, rev. and ed. by Geza Vermes and Fergus Millar (Edinburgh, T. & T. Clark, 1973), p. 437.

14 C.K. Barrett, *The New Testament Background: Selected Documents* (London, SPCK, 1956), p. 198.

15 Schürer, *History of the Jewish People,* vol. I, pp. 440–1.

16 Brandon, *Jesus and the Zealots,* p. 364.

17 See Oscar Cullmann, *The State in the New Testament,* (New York, Charles Scribner's Sons, 1956).

18 *Aramäisch-neuhebräisches Wörterbuch,* 2nd ed. 1922.

19 Cullmann, *The State in the NT,* p. 18.

20 Ibid., p. 22.

21 Ibid., p. 32.

22 If we follow Cullmann in this respect, it implies that Jesus recognized that his disciples would be unable or unwilling to turn the other cheek. It is noteworthy that the Essenes carried arms for protection against brigands (*War* 2:124–5).

23 Cullmann, *The State in the NT,* p. 35.

24 W.R. Farmer, 'The palm branches in John 12:13', *Journal of Theological Studies,* 1952, pp. 62ff.

25 Cullmann, *The State in the NT,* p. 38 But Cullmann leaves unexplained why Jesus permitted himself to enter Jerusalem in a manner that could be thus misinterpreted. We shall address this question in due course.

26 Ibid., p. 45.

27 Ibid., p. 48.

28 Ibid., p. 49.
29 See Martin Hengel, *Was Jesus a Revolutionist?*, tr. William Klassen (Philadelphia, Fortress Press, 1971).
30 E.P. Sanders, *Jesus and Judaism* (Philadelphia, Fortress Press, 1985), p. 65.
31 Gunther Bornkamm, *Jesus of Nazareth*, tr. Irene and Fraser McLuskey with James M. Robinson (New York, Harper and Row, 1960), p. 158.
32 I. Abrahams, *Studies in Pharisaism and the Gospels* (Cambridge, Cambridge University Press, 1917), p. 85.
33 Joseph Klausner, *Jesus of Nazareth*, tr. Herbert Danby (New York, Macmillan C 1943), p. 314.
34 André Parrot, *The Temple of Jerusalem* (Studies in Biblical Archaeology, 5), tr. B.E. Hooke (London, SCM, 1957), pp. 76–100.
35 Hengel, *Was Jesus a Revolutionist?*, pp. 17–18.

11   The Arrest, Trial and Execution

1 Paul Winter, *On the Trial of Jesus*, 2nd edn, rev. and ed. by T.A. Burkill and Geza Vermes (Berlin and New York, Walter De Gruyter, 1974), p. 43.
2 Ibid., p. 64.
3 Ibid., p. 69.
4 Ibid., p. 79.
5 Josef Blinzler, 'The Jewish punishment of stoning in the New Testament period', in Ernst Bammel (ed.), *The Trial of Jesus* (London, SCM Press, 1970), p. 147ff.
6 Ibid., p. 161.
7 Winter, *On the Trial*, p. 109.
8 Ibid., p. 133.
9 Ibid., p. 142.
10 Ibid., p. 192.
11 Ibid., p. 201, n. 17.
12 Ibid., p. 207.
13 Peter Richardson, 'The Israel-idea in the Passion narratives', in Bammel (ed.), *Trial of Jesus*, pp. 8–9.
14 E. Bammel, 'The revolution theory from Reimarus to Brandon', in E. Bammel and C.F.D. Moule (eds), *Jesus and the Politics of his Day* (Cambridge, Cambridge University Press, 1984), p. 28.
15 Ibid., pp. 55–6, italics added.
16 Christopher Rowland, *Christian Origins* (London, SPCK, 1985), p. 174.
17 Ibid., p. 182.
18 D.R. Catchpole, 'The "Triumphal Entry"', in Bammel and Moule (eds), *Jesus and Politics*, p. 332.
19 Ibid., p. 333.
20 Catchpole, 'Triumphal Entry'.
21 This may be inferred from the following statement by Luke: 'and all the multitudes who assembled to see the sight, when they saw what had taken place,

returned home beating their breasts' (23:48).

22   William Riley Wilson, *The Execution of Jesus* (New York, Charles Scribner's Sons, 1970), pp. 142–3.

12   The Resurrection Appearance

1   G.F. Moore, *Judaism* II (Cambridge, Mass., Harvard University Press, 1927–30), p. 312.

2   S.W. Baron, *A Social and Religious History of the Jews*, vol. II (New York, Columbia University Press, 1952), p. 40.

3   I. Abrahams, *Studies Pharisaism and the Gospels* (Cambridge, Cambridge University Press, 1917), p. 168.

4   Heinrich Graetz, *History of the Jews*, vol. II (Philadelphia, Jewish Publication Society of America, 1956), pp. 165–6.

5   Jacob Jocz, *The Jewish People and Jesus Christ*, 3rd edn. (Grand Rapids, Mich., Baker Book House, first published 1949), p. 152.

6   Peter Richardson, 'The Israel-idea in the Passion narratives', in E. Bammel (ed.), *The Trial of Jesus* (London, SCM Press, 1970), p. 10.

7   Wayne A. Meeks, *The First Urban Christians: The Social World of the Apostle Paul* (New Haven, Conn., Yale University Press, 1983), p. 181.

8   William James, *The Varieties of Religious Experience* (New York, Collier Books, 1961), p. 123.

13   The First Christians

1   According to the old Talmudic rule, a blasphemer was one who pronounced the name of God itself (Mish. Sanh. 7:5).

14   Paul's Reinterpretation of Jesus' Teaching

1   Phillip Sigal, *The Emergence of Contemporary Judaism*, vol. 1 (Pittsburgh, Penn.: The Pickwick Press, 1980), p. 417.

2   B.H. Branscomb, *Jesus and the Law of Moses* (London, Hodder, 1930), p. 54.

3   W.D. Davies, *Paul and Rabbinic Judaism*, 2nd edn (London, SPCK, 1955), p. 323.

4   English translation, p. 98, cited in Davies, ibid., p. 322.

5   Roger Mohrlang, *Matthew and Paul: A Comparison of Ethical Pespectives* (Cambridge, Cambridge University Press, 1984), p. 40.

6   Ibid., p. 41.

7   Davies, *Paul and Rabbinic Judaism*, p. 8.

8   Robin Scroggs, 'Paul as rhetorician: Two homilies in Romans 1–11', in Robert Hamerton-Kelly and Robin Scroggs (eds), *Jews, Greeks and Christians* (Leiden, E.J. Brill, 1976), p. 271.

9   Ibid., p. 285.
10 Geza Vermes, *Jesus and the World of Judaism* (Philadelphia, Fortress Press, 1984), p. 56.
11 H.J. Schoeps, *Paul: The Theology of the Apostle in the Light of Jewish Religious History* (London, Lutterworth Press, 1961), p. 106. Page references to this work are hereafter cited in parentheses immediately following the quoted passage.

Bibliography

Abrahams, I., *Studies in Pharisaism and the Gospels*, Cambridge, Cambridge University Press, 1917.

Allegro, John Marco, *The People of the Dead Sea Scrolls*, Garden City, NY, Doubleday, 1958.

Argyle, A.W., *The Gospel According to Matthew*, Cambridge, Cambridge University Press, 1963.

Baeck, Leo, *The Pharisees and Other Essays*, New York, Schocken Books, 1947.

Bammel, Ernst, ed., *The Trial of Jesus*, Cambridge Studies in Honour of C.F.D. Moule, London, SCM Press, 1970.

Bammel, Ernst and Moule, C.F.D., eds, *Jesus and the Politics of His Day*, Cambridge, Cambridge University Press, 1984.

Banks, Robert, *Jesus and the Law in the Synoptic Tradition*, Cambridge, Cambridge University Press, 1975.

Baron, S.W., *A Social and Religious History of the Jews*, vol. II, New York, Columbia University Press, 1952.

Barrett, C.K., *The New Testament Background: Selected Documents*, London, SPCK, 1956.

Benko, Stephen, *Pagan Rome and the Early Christians*, Bloomington, Ill., Indiana University Press, 1984.

Bickerman, Elias, *Four Strange Books of the Bible: Jonah, Daniel, Koheleth, Esther*, New York, Schocken Books, 1967.

Bickerman, Elias, *The God of the Maccabees*, tr. Horst R. Moehring, Leiden, E.J. Brill, 1979.

Black, Matthew, *The Scrolls and Christian Origins*, New York, Charles Scribner's Sons, 1961.

Bonsirven, Joseph, S.J., *Palestinian Judaism in the Time of Jesus Christ*, tr. William Wolf, New York, Holt, Rinehart and Winston, 1964.

Bornkamm, Günther, *Jesus of Nazareth*, tr. Irene and Fraser McLuskey with James M. Robinson, New York, Harper and Row, 1960.

Brandon, S.G.F., *Jesus and the Zealots: A Study of the Political Factor in Primitive Christianity*, Manchester, Manchester University Press, 1967.
—— *The Trial of Jesus of Nazareth*, New York, Stein and Day, 1968.
Branscomb, B.H., *Jesus and the Law of Moses*, London, Hodder, 1930.
Braun, Herbert, *Jesus of Nazareth*, tr. Everett R. Kalin, Philadelphia, Fortress Press, 1979.
Buchanan, George W., 'Has the Griesbach hypothesis been falsified?', *Journal of Biblical Literature*, 93, 1974.
Bultmann, Rudolf, *Form Criticism*, tr. by Frederick C. Grant, New York, Willett, Clark, 1934.
—— *Theology of the New Testament*, tr. Kendrick Grobel, vol. I, New York, Charles Scribner's Sons, 1951.
Campenhausen, Hans von, and Chadwick, Henry, *Jerusalem and Rome: The Problem of Authority in the Early Church*, Philadelphia, Fortress Press, 1966.
Catchpole, David R., *The Trial of Jesus: A Study in the Gospels and Jewish Historiography from 1770 to the Present Day*, Leiden, E.J. Brill, 1971.
Charles, R.H., ed., *The Apocrypha and Pseudepigrapha*, 2 vols, Oxford, Clarendon Press, 1983 (first published in 1913).
Charlesworth, James H., ed., *John and Qumran*, London, Geoffrey Chapman, 1972.
Conzelmann, Hans, *Jesus*, tr. J. Raymond Lord, Philadelphia, Fortress Press, 1973.
Cullmann, Oscar, *The State in the New Testament*, New York, Charles Scribner's Sons, 1956.
—— *Jesus and the Revolutionaries*, tr. Gareth Putnam, New York, Harper and Row, 1970.
Davies, W.D., *Paul and Rabbinic Judaism*, 2nd edn, London, SPCK, 1955.
Christian Origins and Judaism, Philadelphia, The Westminster Press. 1962.
—— *The Setting of the Sermon on the Mount*, Cambridge, Cambridge University Press, 1964.
—— *Introduction to Pharisaism*, Philadelphia, Fortress Press, 1967.
—— *Jewish and Pauline Studies*, Philadelphia, Fortress Press, 1984.
Davies, W.D., and Finkelstein, Louis, eds, *The Cambridge History of Judaism*, vol. 1, Cambridge, Cambridge University Press, 1984.
Deissmann, Adolf, *The Religion of Jesus and the Faith of Paul*, tr. W.E. Wilson, London, Hodder and Stoughton, 1923.
—— *The New Testament in the Light of Modern Research*, London, Hodder and Stoughton, 1929.
Dibelius, Martin, *Gospel Criticism and Christology*, London, Ivor Nicholson and Watson, 1935.
Dodd, C.H., *The Parables of the Kingdom*, London, Nisbet, 1935.

—— *History and the Gospel*, New York, Charles Scribner's Sons, 1938.

—— *The Founder of Christianity*, London, Macmillan, 1970.

Dungan, David L., *The Sayings of Jesus in the Churches of Paul*, Philadelphia, Fortress Press and Basil Blackwell, 1971.

Dunn, James D.G., *Unity and Diversity in the New Testament*, Philadelphia, The Westminster Press, 1977.

Eisenberg, Azriel, *The Synagogue Through the Ages*, New York, Bloch Publishing Co., 1974.

Eisler, Robert, *The Messiah Jesus and John the Baptist*, New York, Dial Press, 1931.

Farmer, William R. *The Synoptic Problem*, New York, Macmillan, 1964.

—— *New Synoptic Studies*, Macon, Ga, Mercer University Press, 1983.

Filson, Floyd N., *A Commentary on the Gospel According to St. Matthew*, London, Adam and Charles Black, 1960.

Foakes, Jackson, F.J., *Josephus and the Jews*, London, SPCK, 1930.

Gager, John G., *Kingdom and Community*, Englewood Cliffs, NJ, Prentice-Hall, 1975.

Gerth, H.H., and Mills, C.W., eds, *From Max Weber: Essays in Sociology*, London, Routledge and Kegan Paul, 1948.

Glatzer, Nahum N., ed., *Jerusalem and Rome: The Writings of Josephus*, New York, Meridian Books, 1960.

Graetz, Heinrich, *History of the Jews*, II, Philadelphia, Jewish Publication Society of America, 1956.

Grant, Michael, *The Jews in the Roman World*, New York, Charles Scribner's Sons, 1973.

Grant, Robert M., *The Formation of the New Testament*, New York, Harper and Row, 1965.

—— *Early Christianity and Society*, San Fransisco, Harper and Row, 1977.

Gutmann, Joseph, *Ancient Synagogues: The State of Research*, Chico. Ca, Scholars Press, 1981.

Hagner, Donald A., *The Jewish Reclamation of Jesus*, Grand Rapids, Mich., Academie Books, Zondervan Publishing House, 1984.

Hamerton-Kelly, Robert and Scroggs, Robin, eds, *Jews, Greeks and Christians*, Leiden, E.J. Brill, 1976.

Harvey, A.E., *Jesus and the Constraints of History*, The Bampton Lectures, 1980, London, Duckworth, 1982.

—— *Alternative Approaches to New Testament Study*, London, SPCK, 1985.

Hengel, Martin, *Die Zeloten*, Leiden/Köln, E.J. Brill, 1961.

—— *Was Jesus a Revolutionist?* tr. William Klassen, Philadelphia, Fortress Press, 1971.

—— *Property and Riches in the Early Church*, tr. John Bowden, London, SCM Press, 1974.

—— *Between Jesus and Paul: Studies in the Earliest History of Christianity*, tr. John Bowden, London, Fortress Press, 1983.

—— *Studies in the Gospel of Mark*, tr. John Bowden, London, SCM Press, 1985.

Holmberg, Bengt, *Paul and Power*, Sweden, CWK Gleerup, 1978.

Hultgren, Arlund J., *Jesus and His Adversaries*, Minneapolis, Augsburg Publishing House, 1979.

James, William, *The Varieties of Religious Experience*, New York, Collier, 1961.

Jeremias, Joachim, *The Parables of Jesus*, rev. edn. tr. H.S. Hooke, London, SCM Press, 1963.

Jocz, Jacob, *The Jewish People and Jesus Christ*, 3rd edn. Grand Rapids, Mich.: Baker Book House, 1981 (first published 1949).

Josephus, Loeb Classical Library, 10 vols. Cambridge, Mass., Harvard University Press, 1926–81.

Kissinger, Warren, *The Sermon on the Mount*, Metuchen, NJ., Scarecrow Press and American Theological Library Association, 1975.

Klausner, Joseph, *From Jesus to Paul*, tr. William F. Stinespring, New York, Macmillan, 1943.

—— *Jesus of Nazareth*, tr. Herbert Danby, New York, Macmillan, 1943.

Knox, John, *The Death of Christ*, New York, Abingdon Press, 1958.

Kung, Hans and Moltmann, Jürgen, eds, *Conflicting Ways of Interpreting the Bible*, New York, Seabury Press, 1980.

Lightfoot, R.H. *St. John's Gospel*, Oxford, Clarendon Press, 1956.

Manson, T.W., *Only to the House of Israel? Jesus and the Non-Jews*, Philadelphia, Fortress Press, 1955, 1964.

—— *The Teaching of Jesus*, Cambridge, Cambridge University Press, 1963.

Mantel, Hugo, *Studies in the History of the Sanhedrin*, Cambridge, Mass., Harvard University Press, 1961.

Meeks, Wayne A., *The First Urban Christians*, New Haven, Conn., Yale University Press, 1983.

Meier, John P., 'Jesus among the historians', *New York Times Book Review*, 21 December 1986.

Mohrlang, Roger, *Matthew and Paul: A Comparison of Ethical Perspectives*, Cambridge, Cambridge University Press, 1984.

Montefiore, C.G., *The Synoptic Gospels*, 2nd edn, vol. 1, London, Macmillan, 1927.

—— *Rabbinic Literature and Gospel Teachings*, London, Macmillan, 1930.

Moore, G.F., *Judaism*, Cambridge, Mass., Harvard University Press, 1927–30.

Moule, C.F.D., *Essays in New Testament Interpretation*, Cambridge, Cambridge University Press, 1982.

Murphy, Cullen, 'Who do men say that I am?' *The Atlantic*, December 1986.

Murphy-O'Connor, Jerome, O.P., ed., *Paul and Qumran*, London, Geoffrey Chapman, 1968.

Neusner, Jacob, *The Rabbinic Traditions about the Pharisees Before 70*, Part III, Conclusions, Leiden, E.J. Brill, 1971.

—— *From Politics to Piety: The Emergence of Pharisaic Judaism*, Englewood Cliffs, NJ, Prentice-Hall, 1973.

—— ed., *Christianity, Judaism and Other Greco-Roman Cults*, Part I, Leiden, E.J. Brill, 1975.

Nietzsche, Friedrich, *On the Genealogy of Morals*, tr. Walter Kaufmann and E.J. Hollingdale, New York, Vintage Books, 1969.

Orchard, Bernard and Longstaff, R.W., eds, *J.J. Griesbach: Synoptic and Text-Critical Studies, 1776–1976*, Cambridge, Cambridge University Press, 1978.

Parker, Pierson, *The Gospel Before Mark*, Chicago, Ill., University of Chicago Press, 1953.

Parkes, James, *The Conflict of the Church and the Synagogue*, London, The Sancino Press, 1934.

—— *Jesus, Paul and the Jews*, London, SCM Press, 1936.

Parrot, André, *The Temple of Jerusalem* (Studies in Biblical Archeology, 5,) tr. B.E. Hooke, London, SCM Press, 1957.

Rabin, Chaim, *Qumran Studies*, Oxford, Oxford University Press, 1957.

Richardson, Peter, *Israel in the Apostolic Church*, Cambridge, Cambridge University Press, 1969.

Rist, John M., *On the Independence of Matthew and Mark*, Cambridge, Cambridge University Press, 1978.

Rivkin, Ellis, *A Hidden Revolution*, Nashville, Abingdon, 1978.

Robinson, T.H., *St. Mark's Life of Jesus*, London, SCM Press, 1922.

Rowland, Christopher, *Christian Origins*, London, SPCK, 1985.

Sanders, E.P., *Paul and Palestinian Judaism*, Philadelphia, Fortress Press, 1977.

—— *Jesus and Judaism*, Philadelphia, Fortress Press, 1985.

Sandmel, Samuel, *The Genius of Paul*, New York, Farrar, Straus and Cudahy, 1958.

—— *Anti-Semitism in the New Testament*, Philadelphia, Fortress Press, 1978.

Schiffman, Lawrence H., *Sectarian Law in the Dead Sea Scrolls*, Chico. Ca, Scholars Press, 1983.

Schillebeeckx, Edward, *Jesus: An Experiment in Christology*, tr. Hubert Hoskins, New York, Vintage Books, 1981.

Schoeps, H.J., *Paul: The Theology of the Apostle in the Light of Jewish Religious History*, London, Lutterworth Press, 1961.

—— *Jewish Christianity*, tr. Douglas R.A. Hare, Philadelphia, Fortress Press, 1969.

Schürer, Emil, *The History of the Jewish People in the Age of Jesus Christ*, 3 vols. rev. and ed. by Geza Vermes and Fergus Millar, Edinburgh, T. & T. Clark, 1973.

Scott, Ernest F., *The Varieties of New Testament Religion*, New York, Charles Scribner's Sons, 1943.

Segal, Alan F., *Rebecca's Children: Judaism and Christianity in the Roman World*, Cambridge, Mass., Harvard University Press, 1986.

Sheehan, Thomas, *The First Coming*, New York, Random House, 1986.

Shutt, R.J.H., *Studies in Josephus*, London, SPCK, 1961.

Sigal, Phillip, *The Emergence of Contemporary Judaism*, vol. 1, Pittsburgh, Penn., Pickwick Press, 1980.

Smith, Morton, *Jesus the Magician*, New York, Harper and Row, 1978.

Stoldt, Hans-Herbert, *History and Criticism of the Marcan Hypothesis*, tr. and ed. by Donald L. Niewyk, introduction by W.R. Farmer, Macon, Ga, Mercer University Press, 1980.

Stonehouse, Ned B., *Origins of the Synoptic Gospels*, Grand Rapids, Mich., Eerdmans, 1963.

Talbert, C.H., and McKnight, E.V., 'Can the Griesbach hypothesis be falsified?', *Journal of Biblical Literature*, 91, 1972.

Tasker, R.V.G., *The Gospel According to St. Matthew: An Introduction and Commentary*, Grand Rapids, Mich., Eerdmans, 1961.

Taylor, Vincent, *The Formation of the Gospel Tradition*, London, Macmillan, 1935.

Tcherikover, Victor, *Hellenistic Civilization and the Jews*, tr. S. Applebaum, Philadelphia, Jewish Publication Society of America, 1961.

Thackeray, H. St John, *Josephus: The Man and the Historian*, New York, Jewish Institute of Religion Press, 1929.

Theissen, Gerd, *The First Followers of Jesus*, tr. John Bowden, London, SCM Press, 1978.

Tidball, Derek, *The Social Context of the NT: A Sociological Analysis*, Grand Rapids, Mich., Academie Books, 1984.

Tuckett, C.M., *The Revival of the Griesbach Hypothesis*, Cambridge, Cambridge University Press, 1983.

Vermes, Geza, *Jesus the Jew*, New York, Macmillan, 1973.

—— *Jesus and the World of Judaism*, Philadelphia, Fortress Press, 1984.

Weber, Max, *Economy and Society*, 3 vols. ed. by Guenther Roth and Claus Wittich, New York, Bedminster Press, 1968.

Whittaker, Molly, *Jews and Christians: Graeco-Roman Views*, Cambridge, Cambridge University Press, 1984.

Wilder, Amos N., *Eschatology and Ethics in the Teaching of Jesus*, New York, Harper & Brothers, rev. edn, 1950.

Wilson, Stephen G., ed., *Anti-Judaism in Early Christianity*, vol. 2, *Separation and Polemic*, Waterloo, Iowa, Wilfrid Laurier University Press, 1986.

Wilson, William Riley, *The Execution of Jesus*, New York, Charles Scribner's Sons, 1970.

Winter, Paul, *On the Trial of Jesus*, 2nd edn, rev. and ed. by T.A. Burkill and Geza Vermes, Berlin and New York, Walter de Gryter, 1974.

Yadin, Y., *Masada: Herod's Fortress and the Zealots' Last Stand*, New York, Random House, 1966.

Zeitlin, Irving M., *Ancient Judaism: Biblical Criticism from Max Weber to the Present*, Cambridge, Polity Press, 1984.

Index